BEYOND THE BOUNDARIES

BOUNDARIES

Leading and re-creating
the successful enterprise

SECOND EDITION

CW00409072

BEYOND THE BOUNDARIES

Leading and re-creating the successful enterprise

SECOND EDITION

Doug Stace
Dexter Dunphy

The McGraw-Hill Companies, Inc.

Sydney New York San Francisco Auckland
Bangkok Bogotá Caracas Hong Kong
Kuala Lumpur Lisbon London Madrid
Mexico City Milan New Delhi San Juan
Seoul Singapore Taipei Toronto

McGraw·Hill Australia

A Division of The **McGraw·Hill** Companies

Hardcover edition 1994
Paperback edition 1996
Reprinted 1996, 1997, 1998, 1999
Second edition 2001
Reprinted 2004, 2005

National Library of Australia Cataloguing-in-Publication data:

Stace, D.
Beyond the boundaries: leading and re-creating the successful enterprise.
2nd ed.
Includes index.

ISBN 0 074 70841 4.

1. Corporate reorganizations — Australia. 2. Organizational change — Australian.
I. Dunphy, Dexter C. (Dexter Colboyd), 1934– . II. Title.

658.16

Published in Australia by
McGraw-Hill Australia
Level 2, 82 Waterloo Road, North Ryde, NSW 2113
Publishing Manager: Meiling Voon
Production Editor: Sybil Kesteven
Editor: Sarah Baker
Designed and typeset in 12/14 pt Bembo by Jan Schmoeger, Designpoint
Illustrator: Alan Laver, Shelly Communications
Indexer: Shirley Johnston
Printed on 80 gsm woodfree by Best Tri Colour Printing & Packaging Co. Ltd, Hong Kong.

Contents

Preface

This book is about managing organisational change successfully, and is designed to provide readers with a practical theory of change and framework for action. Now that the pace of change has sped up to Internet time, it is necessary to understand that change has become the steady state. The key issue for managers and change agents is how to lead change so that, rather than change being destructive and demoralising, it becomes an energising force.

Beyond the Boundaries is the result of over fifteen years of fruitful collaboration between the authors. It was first published in 1994 and has become a leading reference on change. After multiple printings, our publishers approached us in late 1999 to develop a new second edition—with new case studies, and new material on the implications for change management of the turbo-charged twenty-first century economy.

This seemed a good idea at the time! However, what began as a revision has become, twelve months later, a substantially new book. The central models of change are the same, but their business context, and the way in which we illustrate the models, is recast. Starting the revision was like pulling a thread from one part of a woollen jumper—the thread ran a long way further than we imagined. The end result is a renewed book, built around a theory of change management which we have been developing and validating in systematic research for over a decade. We also draw extensively from our observations of practice from our consulting experience in scores of global, national and regional organisations.

The ideas for this new edition were being generated and tested as we moved across the watershed of two centuries, and two millennia. There is a symbolism in that, for *Beyond the Boundaries* is a book about challenging assumptions and charting new paths ahead. We hope that you enjoy reading it, and that it will assist you in leading change which will help create the new economic and social wealth, industries and organisations of the twenty-first century.

Doug Stace and Dexter Dunphy

Acknowledgments

The research for this book took place predominantly under the aegis of the Centre for Corporate Change (CCC) in the Australian Graduate School of Management, a school of both the University of New South Wales and the University of Sydney. Towards the end of the preparation of this second edition we both made personal transitions: Doug to take up a senior research role as Visiting Professor with Cass Business School, City University, London, in addition to his continuing role as Adjunct Professor at the Australian Graduate School of Management; Dexter to a new senior role as Distinguished Professor at the University of Technology, Sydney. Our collaboration on change research and teaching continues. We are deeply indebted to the AGSM for its support of our research over many years.

We express particular gratitude to all those in the organisations we studied—some for the second or third time—who contributed their time and thought over a process of intensive systematic interviews, and extensive reviews of in-company material. We hope that we have given a fair and balanced view of their corporations.

We believe that this second edition maintains the standards of relevance, research rigour and theoretical excellence established in the first edition of the book and in our earlier bestseller, *Under New Management*. Our aim has been to link applied research with practical models and frameworks. We are also indebted to countless executive program attendees, other students of management and consulting clients who have helped us to strengthen our understanding of change through their comments, observations and experiences.

Production of the manuscript has had more of a high-tech feel this time around—with virtual chapters flying around in cyberspace. We are deeply indebted to Fran Prior for her fastidious and creative work in preparing the text and the many images we employ to illustrate the book. Sybil Kesteven, Meiling Voon and Sarah Baker of McGraw-Hill have also been most helpful in editing and keeping us to schedule, and we thank them for their work.

We are also deeply indebted to our partners Nitia Stace and Francine Bartlett for their superb support for the often lonely task of authors—working into the small hours to meet deadlines, and to finesse concepts. Their support has enhanced this book inestimably.

We complete this second edition at a time of simultaneous re-naissance, and deconstruction, in our societies, our organisations and our work lives. We hope that this book, with its new design, continues to stimulate an energy of ideas and action in the leadership, formation and re-creation of the successful enterprises of the twenty-first century.

About the authors

DOUG STACE is one of Australia's leading strategists, management authors and facilitators of strategic change. He is an Adjunct Professor of the Australian Graduate School of Management, and he also spends two months each year in research as a Visiting Professor of Cass Business School, City University, London. His strategy and change consultancy spans global, national and regional companies, public sector organisations and professional bodies—working with change leaders, managers, executive teams and boards.

He has published extensively in the area of strategic change and organisational transformation, with his current research focusing on the effective introduction of e-Change to corporations and on the leadership of global growth strategies and international competitiveness. He has also had extensive experience as a senior executive—giving his consultancies and teaching a refreshing blend of practical experience linked with leading edge research.

Doug holds the degrees of Bachelor of Arts, Master of Letters and Master of Educational Administration from the University of New England, and a Doctor of Philosophy from the Australian Graduate School of Management. He is a member of the international Strategic Management Society.

D EXTER DUNPHY is Distinguished Professor, University of Technology, Sydney—a position he took up in January 2000 after seventeen years as Professor of Management at the Australian Graduate School of Management. Dexter has been a leading change theorist, researcher and consultant for thirty years. His research is published in about sixty articles and sixteen books; he has consulted to numerous private sector organisations in Australia and overseas, advising on major organisational transformations, the design of human resource strategies and systems, troubleshooting and conflict resolution. He has also worked extensively with senior executives, managers and other professionals in enhancing their skills through executive workshops, mentoring and counselling. Dexter was Foundation Director of The Centre for Corporate Change at the AGSM from 1990–97.

Dexter has held visiting professorships at Harvard University (USA), Keio University (Japan), Shanghai First Medical College (PRC), The National University of Singapore and the Helsinki School of Economics and Business Administration (Finland). He has been a recipient of a Fulbright Senior Scholar Award, the University of NSW Vice-Chancellor's Award for Teaching Excellence, the Australian Human Resources Institute's Mike Pontifex Award for Outstanding Contribution to the Human Resources Profession, and the Australia and New Zealand Academy of Management's Distinguished Member Award for contributions to management research, scholarship, education and leadership.

Dexter holds the degrees of Bachelor of Arts (Hons), Master of Education (Hons) and Diploma of Education from Sydney University and a Doctor of Philosophy in Sociology from Harvard University.

Chapter 1
The dilemmas of change

An organisational metaphor

In 1845 Sir John Franklin set out on an expedition to find the fabled Northwest Passage linking the Atlantic and Pacific oceans through the Arctic Circle. It was a vitally important expedition because, if the Northwest Passage existed, it could have provided a link between Britain and her far-flung Empire. Sir John and his company of 138 officers and men sailed in two three-masted barques with auxiliary steam engines. He expected the voyage to last two to three years.

The conditions in the Arctic were, of course, dramatically different from those of England. However, the ships were equipped as replicas of English Royal Navy officers' clubs. Each ship had a 1200 volume library; there were copious china place settings, cutglass wine goblets and sterling silver tableware and cutlery. Each officer had his own set of cutlery, engraved with his initials and family crest. Unfortunately, items such as these took up so much space that room could be found for only twelve days' supply of coal for the auxiliary steam engines. They took no special clothing for the Arctic conditions, just the rather splendid naval uniforms, and equipment was standard: there were, for instance, no sleds.

It took twenty years to find the remnants of the expedition: the ships had been destroyed by the pack ice, but frozen bodies were found in groups, many kilometres from where their ships disappeared.

These were remnants of the scattered parties who had desperately sought survival in such unforgiving conditions. Some members of these parties were still dressed in their fine blue uniforms, edged with silk braid and gold buttons. Surprisingly, in the improvised sleds and the ship's boats they had dragged for tortuous kilometres were large quantities of ornate table silver!

A metaphor for our times? At the watershed of two centuries our organisations now face a business environment that is far removed from the world of regulated domestic economies so characteristic of much of the century just past. The new environment is as different as Franklin's icy Arctic wastes were to England's green and pleasant land. Many have crossed the watershed of the twentieth and twenty-first centuries ill equipped for the new environment of, for example, e-commerce, global business and changed generational values. They persist in doggedly dragging with them the cultural and business baggage of the past, despite all the evidence that it may well be a dangerous encumbrance.

The Northwest Passage was later explored successfully by the Norwegian Roald Amundsen. He adopted the methods used by the Eskimo, who understood the environment. Accompanied by two Eskimos and dogsleds, Amundsen became the first European to traverse the Northwest Passage. The environments faced by contemporary organisations are constantly reformulating so speed, dexterity and flexibility are vital for our organisations if they are to move forward progressively to become the new wealth creators. But how much do they need to change to thrive in a fast-changing business environment, and what are the dilemmas of change in this new world?

Dilemmas in change

In late 1992 and early 1993, an unusual drama unfolded in the boardroom of one of Australia's largest banks, Westpac Banking Corporation. Kerry Packer's private company, Consolidated Press Holdings, had seized 10% of Westpac in late 1992. Packer and his right-hand man, 'Chainsaw' Al Dunlap, developed a plan to radically slash costs and staff in an effort to turn around the Bank's disastrous

1992 losses of $1.5 billion. An informal meeting of directors with Packer and Dunlap on 17 December 1992 led to the resignation of the Managing Director, Frank Conroy, reportedly because the change program he proposed was not considered far-reaching or rapid enough for the board. Conroy's proposal involved downsizing the 45 000 person workforce by 25% over eighteen months.

The first official board meeting attended by Packer and Dunlap was on 15 January 1993, exactly one week after their official appointment as directors. It was widely assumed that their much more radical proposal would be accepted at this meeting. Instead, Packer and Dunlap themselves resigned after what was widely reported in the press as a fiery and acrimonious discussion.

Following this meeting, Westpac's Chairman and then Acting Chief Executive, John Uhrig, was reported as saying that Packer and Dunlap 'had been at odds with the rest of the bank's directors over the pace of change required'. The AMP Society's Managing Director at the time, Ian Salmon, also commented that 'our concern when Packer and Dunlap came on the scene was whether the bank could take a faster rate of change without doing damage to it. An unduly fast rate of change could do untold damage to the bank'.[1]

As the Westpac incident shows, the issues of change are complex and fraught with value judgments, and decisions involving clashes between powerful stakeholders can radically change careers and potentially sink organisations with proud histories of past success.

How rapidly to change? What to change? Which way to change? These are the central questions facing executives, managers and change agents today as they struggle to guide strategic organisational change in a dynamically changing business environment.

As it turned out, the more limited changes chosen by the Westpac board were sufficient for Westpac to turn its performance around under its next CEO, Robert Joss, and return to profitable performance. (In the first six months of 1993 alone its share price rose by over 25%, and by over 300% up to 2000.) So were Packer and Al Dunlap wrong?

After this incident, Al Dunlap left his collaboration with Packer and, in 1994, was appointed Chairman and CEO of Scott Paper in the United States. Scott Paper was the largest producer of consumer tissue products in the world, employing over 30 000 people, but in

1993 it had reported a net loss of US$277 million. Dunlap was appointed because he was known as a tough-minded turnaround specialist, hence his nickname 'Chainsaw' Al. Dunlap successfully turned the company around in two years, using the kinds of radical policies he and Packer had suggested for Westpac.[2] However, when he subsequently tried the same approach at Sunbeam Corporation in the late 1990s, Dunlap bankrupted the company, and he now enjoys less than star status.

What this series of incidents indicates is that there is no one right approach to change, effective in all circumstances. Yet the majority of corporate change gurus, particularly in the United States, advance such universal prescriptions for change that managers, acting on such simplistic approaches, can create corporate disasters. It would be comforting if a single, simple and universal prescription for change existed but the fact is, managers must exercise intelligent choices about change.

A place of no return

The problem is that the rate of competitive repositioning needed for our organisations to adapt to new environments is faster than most of us have ever experienced. Global markets have become more dynamic and volatile at the same time as we are experiencing quantum changes in technologies and global communications. The challenge is to gain the collective experience needed to successfully manage the change associated with the repositioning. In organisations large and small, commercial and not-for-profit, the boundaries of our knowledge are being stretched to breaking point. Most successful managers realise that they have to experiment, take risks and move beyond the boundaries if they are to create a sustainable future for their organisations.

Inside the organisation, hierarchies have been removed, predictable career paths have gone, new networks of suppliers, subcontractors and consultants have confounded the once simple concept of 'employee', and e-commerce is challenging our core notions of what an organisation is.

This is not just an economic revolution, it is a social revolution as well. Democratisation spawns individual choice. We can never return to the highly regulated world of work we once knew. The only way is ahead into the unknown, beyond the boundaries. The viable solutions will be <u>novel creations adapted to future conditions</u>, not relics of a previous era. <u>Organisational survival and growth depend on it.</u> Change—often massive change—confronts or beckons us on a daily basis. Initiating change, responding to change, planning change and implementing change have become a way of life in successful organisations. In both personal and organisational terms, <u>this means stepping out into</u> more change, and <u>more uncharted territory.</u>

Learning to live with dilemmas

The need to quickly implement far-reaching and often complex strategic change has led many managers and change agents to search for simple solutions and the one right way. This is reflected in the current spate of buzzwords referring to change methodologies, each approach acclaimed by fervent disciples as the only and universally applicable change methodology. Economic Value-Added, Balanced Scorecard, TQM, Benchmarking, Horizontal Organization and Re-engineering are a few of the buzz techniques commonly applied as panaceas. The appealing aspect of the promises held out for these types of change technologies is that they can absolve the manager from the onerous task of critically reviewing the full range of other competing approaches or devising a custom-made change program. They cut through complexity. However, the offer is often illusory, for particular change approaches usually apply to particular situations, and simple solutions sometimes ignore the complexity of real life.

There are five dilemmas that have to be managed in the modern organisation, and we will be dealing with them in this book. These dilemmas are often subject to oversimplification because they appear to represent contradictory opposites, and it is tempting to create a fad which strongly supports one end of the dilemmas they pose. We will be arguing, in contrast, that approaches that try to resolve these dilemmas by simplistically rejecting one of the choices may be immediately appealing but are, in fact, ineffective.

We will present and discuss these dilemmas:

1. Adaptive or rational strategy development?
2. Cultural change or structural change?
3. Continuous improvement or radical transformation?
4. Empowerment or leadership and command?
5. Economic or social goals?

Each dilemma is briefly summarised below, and is covered more substantially in other chapters.

Adaptive or rational strategy development?

This book is about how to manage strategic change successfully. It is appropriate therefore that our first dilemma deals with the nature of strategy development—an issue regularly confronting executives and business unit managers.

The concept of corporate strategy emerged during the 1960s and was primarily given initial shape by three writers: Kenneth Andrews, Alfred Chandler and Igor Ansoff. For these writers, strategy arose out of a deliberate and purposeful planning process. This process assessed and redefined the firm's activities in its business and societal environments. They viewed strategy as a rational, mindful, planned process based upon systematic analysis of the firm's changing environment. As a result of such a strategic decision-making process, the firm could make a logical and relatively small departure from its traditional strategy (incremental change) or a significant departure (discontinuous change).[3] The conditions for making such strategic changes were carefully researched and elaborated over time by these and other writers.

These notions were enthusiastically adopted by most large corporations in the 1970s. New corporate-planning departments sprang into existence; new consulting companies, such as McKinseys and BCG, were formed around the new ideas and rose to international prominence through their activities in popularising and adapting the new approaches; thousands of senior executives attended high-level seminars to learn the burgeoning range of new techniques. However, over time, doubts began to emerge about the value of such a deliberate, rational front-end approach to strategic design.

In the 1980s one of us was attending the annual corporate-planning workshop of a large multinational oil corporation. The meeting began with what was intended to be the regular presentation from the company's corporate planner on the current projections for key industry indicators, including world oil prices. He showed current projections as expected but, in a remarkable act of candour and personal courage, also proceeded to put up past annual projections and actual oil prices. The projections had been far removed from what actually happened. There ensued a serious discussion of the value of the rational planning approach to strategic decision making.

Presumably it was such experiences of growing disenchantment with formal intentional strategic planning procedures that prompted Henry Mintzberg to lead an attack on prevailing prescriptive concepts for strategy formulation and to argue that such approaches should be relegated to the garbage heap of history. To replace these approaches, Mintzberg argued for adaptive strategies—that is, post hoc patterns of the firm's behaviour that often emerge by trial and error, in unplanned ways. He argued that the development of strategy is not a process of conceptual analysis but of trial and error. He even went so far as to argue that strategy should not only be developed experientially but also that it should not even be made explicit, for 'explicit strategies…are blinders designed to focus direction and so to block out peripheral vision'.[4]

Out of this dilemma has come the realisation that the apparent contradiction between these two divergent approaches cannot simply be resolved by dismissing one side or the other as Mintzberg wanted to do. Ansoff, for example, has presented evidence indicating that Mintzberg's emergent approach to strategy works well in some circumstances while a range of other strategic approaches, including rational planning, work well in others.[5] Out of such discussions has also emerged the notion of 'strategic intent', originally introduced by Prahalad and Hamel.[6]

These authors contrast the traditional strategic orientation, with its heavy planning orientation and emphasis on achieving strategic fit, with strategic intent, which is a more flexible approach to competition based on leveraging a company's core competencies and resources. They point out:[7]

> For the past twenty years in the West, 'advances' in strategy have taken the form of ever more typologies, heuristics, and laundry lists, often with dubious empirical bases. Moreover, even reasonable concepts like the product life cycle, experience curve, product portfolios, and generic strategies often have toxic side effects. They reduce the number of options management is willing to consider. They create a preference for selling businesses rather than defending them. They yield predictable strategies that rivals easily decode.

Prahalad and Hamel argue against inflexibly applied top-down planning but nevertheless advocate a clearly articulated company vision or intent, expressed in exacting short-term goals which are flexible enough to allow for adaptation within the much broader vision or ambition for the company as new opportunities arise. Other writers such as Gratton[8] stress that for corporate strategy to live and work, people have to understand strategy, and strategy makers have to understand people. Strategy in the end is a process of engagement. These viewpoints provide a clear expression of the need to accept both sides of the dilemma we have discussed in order to find the optimum position at a particular point in time. In Chapter 3 we will further examine concepts and practical examples of strategy development, and introduce the concept of 'insta-strategy', an increasing phenomenon in many enterprises.

Cultural change or structural change?

Our second dilemma assumes that the corporation has a viable strategy but it poses issues about the most important 'levers' to pull for the implementation of strategic change. There are two streams in management thinking about the critical variables to address in making large-scale organisational change.

One group of theorists stresses a set of elusive 'soft' variables of skills, values and 'people' issues which can generally be clustered together under the concept of organisational culture. Organisational culture is the 'invisible force' in the organisation, particularly the values and norms shared by the dominant coalitions which shape decisions. Culture also centres on the creation and continuity of meaning which becomes embedded in assumptions, and the way organisational members go about their work. Within the organisation, people are as unaware of these unexamined assumptions as fish are of the water in which they swim. It is the organisational 'world taken for granted', often more apparent to the visitor than to the inmates.

For some theorists of change, the most powerful way to create significant organisational change is to confront, develop or remould the core cultural values of an organisation so that people experience a profound change in their understanding and purpose, and act differently as a result.

In contrast, there are other change advocates who view all this as too ethereal and imprecise. They advocate what they see as a more tough-minded approach which concentrates on more concrete and clearly definable variables such as formal structures, socio-technical systems and the 'sizing' of business units. These are the structuralists who are often working from an economic rationalist philosophy; their world is primarily one of calculated cost benefits: 'If you can't clearly define it, measure it, or count it, you might as well forget it; if you can't manipulate it to make a difference to the bottom line, it is of no significance' is the prevailing attitude. In fact, the lack of methodological rigour in many of the studies carried out by 'culturalists' has given 'structuralists' wonderful opportunities to discount the importance of cultural variables. For example, Carroll's critique of Peters and Waterman's 1980s bestseller, *In Search of Excellence*, showed that many of the companies that supposedly had 'cultures of excellence' failed to perform well over time.[9]

Unfortunately for the structuralists' arguments, however, rather better researched studies which do document strong relationships between cultural variables and organisational performance have begun to appear. Kotter and Heskett, for example, have shown dramatic relationships between cultural variables and bottom-line performance.[10] Denison also documents such a relationship and builds a detailed model showing how the relationship between culture and performance operates.[11] However, none of this negates the importance of paying attention to the 'harder' factors stressed by the structuralists. In fact later in this book we will present evidence that effective structuring is a critical variable in producing effective organisational performance. A realistic approach to making organisational change therefore needs to take account of both structural and cultural variables. Once again, simplicity may be appealing but it is illusory. We further examine concepts of structure in Chapter 3, and concepts of culture in Chapter 5.

Continuous improvement or radical transformation?

Our next dilemma brings us back to the crisis facing Westpac in the earlier part of this chapter. The choice faced by the Westpac directors was really about the speed with which to conduct a change which would be, in any event, transformational in character. The incident illustrates the importance of a debate that faces all organisations in the modern world: whether to make change gradually by a process of continuous improvement or whether to try to crash rapidly through, 'Dunlap-style', in an immediate transformation of strategy, structure and staffing levels.

The proponents of gradualism often pointed in the late 1980s to successful Japanese organisations and argued for introducing their techniques of continuous organisational improvement. Such programs of continuous improvement, they argued, could transform organisations over time as effectively as a more dramatic intervention which ran the risk of creating chaos and reducing staff commitment. The best known of the continuous improvement approaches has been Total Quality Management (TQM). While originating in the United States, it was taken up and developed in Japan and spread widely and rapidly throughout the world. By the mid-1990s large numbers of medium and large organisations in advanced economies had installed variants of TQM as a component of their search for global competitiveness.

In contrast to the continuous improvement advocated by proponents of TQM and similar approaches, such as traditional Organizational Development (OD), other change agents have argued for rapid radical transformation of organisations. These are the 'revolutionary change theories'[12] or Organizational Transformation

(OT) theories.[13] OT was referred to as 'second-generation OD'[14] because it departed from OD's traditional gradualism and acceptance of basic organisational assumptions in favour of challenging such assumptions in order to promote paradigmatic change and organisational repositioning. Beer,[15] Nadler and Tushman[16] and Bartunek and Moch[17] all developed models of the transformational process. Their models, however, tended to emphasise the 'positive' aspects of such change processes—for example, visionary or magical leadership and empowerment of employees, rather than dictatorial domination by executives acquiring power through takeovers, the firing of large numbers of employees, or the many other sweeping measures often associated with organisational transformation.

However, as Mirvis pointed out, almost half the top 800 US companies underwent massive restructurings in the 1980s. In the same decade there were 25 000 recombinations of publicly traded firms in the 'merger mania' or 'feeding frenzy' that swept Wall Street.[18] Similar events occurred in Australia and New Zealand in that era, and are continuing apace in the early years of the twenty-first century. Not all this change has been accomplished by charismatic leaders enthusiastically endorsed by their admiring and empowered employees!

This is a major dilemma: whether to change incrementally or by radical transformation. In the same organisation, at different times or in different units, both evolutionary and revolutionary approaches may be pursued with positive benefits. We must learn to live with a certain level of complexity, resolve the tension by accepting and understanding those circumstances in which revolutionary change is appropriate and those when continuous improvement is indicated. This 'situational' approach is central to the arguments we present in Chapter 4.

Empowerment or leadership and command?

Our next dilemma often excites highly emotional arguments because of the powerfully held values about the issues involved. These are two compelling imperatives of the contemporary organisation. On the one hand, the rate of change demands that those who operate closest to the action, including employees who daily relate to customers' rapidly shifting demands, be empowered to take decisions that allow a quick and effective organisational response. An example was given to us recently by an executive attending a conference in a small hotel in Florida. The executive wanted to organise an international video conference at virtually a moment's notice. She went to the assistant on the front desk, explained her need, and asked to see the hotel manager to see if arrangements could be made. The assistant explained that he could handle it himself, asked a few questions about what was needed, and in ten minutes the executive was being conducted to a private room where everything had been organised, including coffee and refreshments that she hadn't even requested. Clearly this hotel was an organisation where employees were empowered—that is, they had the authority to act on their own initiative and the knowledge and skills needed to use that authority effectively.

On the other hand, the rate of change also demands swift and decisive leadership action from the top of the organisation to turn around or exit from unprofitable businesses, invest in new ventures, enter into strategic alliances and to make many other such strategic redirections. Some of these major shifts have the capacity to disempower people by eliminating well defined roles, closing off business initiatives and systems to which they are committed, significantly altering their responsibilities and so on. In one organisation we studied, the incompatibility of the two approaches was starkly evident when, after a major and successful program of team building and employee empowerment, unit managers were all put on six months' notice that numbers of them would be 'excessed' unless profitability in their unit improved dramatically over that period. It is difficult to feel empowered, even when there has been substantial devolution of power, if someone is holding a gun to your head.

Once again, however, while it may be tempting to reject one or other of the horns of this dilemma, we will be arguing for a less simplistic approach. There are times and situations where twenty-first century organisations need decisive command structures, powerful enough to overrule the protests of special interest groups. There are also situations where employee empowerment is the essential ingredient for building the organisational capabilities needed for adaptation and success. The day of 'hired hands', who did what they were told and left their minds at home when they came to work, is finished. Future competitive advantage will be built primarily on human capabilities interacting with a firm's technological capabilities. Ouchi argues, for example, that <u>firms that consistently</u> achieve 'supernormal returns' systematically build *organisational capabilities* into their culture. <u>These capabilities are primarily systems which empower employees to act in ways that realise their fullest potential through teamwork.</u>[19] The dilemma for managers, however, <u>is how to combine command and empowerment without creating cynicism and loss of commitment.</u> These are some of the key issues which arise in Chapter 4, but which we cover in greater detail in Chapters 5 and 6. A spirited discussion of this dilemma is to be found in M. Beer and N. Nohria (eds), *Breaking the Code of Change.*[20]

Economic or social goals?

We have come through a period where economic neo-liberalism (or 'economic rationalism' as it is called in Australia) has been the dominant philosophy affecting decision makers in the Western world. Economic rationalism gives priority to economic goals, advocates a free market economy and relegates social goals to a position of lesser importance. According to this view, the firm should concentrate on maximising value for its shareholders and not be deflected into pursuing a broader range of objectives.[21]

However, a different and competing view, which represents a challenge to the dominant view that the business is there only to serve the interests of shareholders, is emerging.[22]

In this view 'in practice managers find they need to develop good relationships with more stakeholders than simply investors if their business is to succeed. Relationships with customers, suppliers, employees, lenders and the wider community are critical for the viability of most enterprises'.[23] This view sees the corporation not simply as a key unit in the economy, but also as a social actor with important social responsibilities beyond turning in a profit.

The dilemma here for managers is how to balance the demands of shareholders and other stakeholders so that the corporation contributes to wealth creation and also supports the viability of the community and the biosphere. Many business practices of the past are now unsustainable, or will be unsustainable in the future, impacting in destructive ways on community life and on the natural world on which we all ultimately depend. This is an issue we will take up in more detail in Chapter 8.

Embracing the dilemmas: Towards workable complexity

If we look at these five dilemmas together, two contrasting views of how to manage change emerge. We might label them, as in Table 1.1, the 'soft' and 'hard' approaches to managing change.

Table 1.1 Approaches to managing change

Soft	Hard
Adaptive strategy	Rational strategy
Cultural change	Structural change
Continuous improvement	Radical transformation
Empowerment	Leadership and command
Social goals	Economic goals

In the past most managers have tended to choose a soft or hard approach to change, and particular organisations have developed change cultures, persisting over time, favouring one approach or the other. However, as organisational needs change, boards have often replaced chief executives to ensure a change in leadership style and a significant change in the organisational mindset. For example, there is often a general shift from 'soft' to 'hard' management as boom times give way to recessionary times, and vice versa.

We argue in this book that we need more managers with the behavioural flexibility to shift the mix of soft and hard approaches in their leadership style to meet changing conditions. Managers need to develop a varied behavioural repertoire rather than remain fixed in a particular approach to change.

The five dilemmas that preoccupy practising managers are not simply theoretical issues but are also areas of significant choice with profound implications for the effectiveness of management action. Long ago the Taoist sage Lao-Tzu pointed out that all opposites coexist, the presence of each demands the other! For example, convex cannot exist without concave or, as in the Chinese symbol, yin without yang. If we are to manage these dilemmas successfully, we need to embrace them fully and resolve them by seeking flexible and emergent balanced actions that reflect the needs of particular situations.

We might ask: 'Even if simple solutions to these dilemmas are not available, why aren't there well tried and tested answers we can adopt to what are, after all, persisting issues in corporate change management?' The answer, which we will explore further in the next chapter, is that we have indeed gone beyond the old boundaries. Our situation today in this area is analogous to the intellectual upheaval that occurred in the field of physics between 1905 and 1925 when the classical approaches to physics collapsed. At the beginning of that period scientists had a clear view of reality based on a set of well tested Newtonian laws which they had assumed were immutable and would ultimately explain everything. As they began to explore the subatomic world of protons, neutrons and electrons, the emerging field of quantum physics acted like a black hole, sucking in the old Newtonian concepts and exploding them. As a result, the quantum physicists are still reinventing the forms of the universe.[24] Similarly, traditional management theory and practice did have workable solutions to key issues in the old familiar world that is disappearing. But today we need new solutions to current issues and consequently we are reinventing, or recreating, our corporations and enterprises.

After the transformation, what?

This book is about managing organisational change successfully: about facing the complexities and perplexities of modern management to create and lead the corporation of the future. There is no more compelling need in our modern economies than to create and build more dynamic and innovative corporations which can compete successfully in global terms. The competition from northern hemisphere economies, in particular, is unrelenting. While many of our leading organisations have passed through a period of major organisational transformation and renewal needed to successfully reposition themselves for survival and growth in tougher, more internationally competitive markets, the challenge is for constant reinvention. Many others have still to make such a transformation, or are currently making it.

We will discuss ways to achieve these difficult transformations and transitions. But we will also turn our attention to the growing need to answer, in specific, actionable terms, the question: 'After the initial transformation, what?'

More and more managers and change agents are searching for programs of action that will guide continuous improvement that is revolutionary in its scope. The critical requirement for longer term viability and success in the corporation of the future is the ongoing development of what are increasingly being referred to as *organisational capabilities* or *corporate competencies*. These are capabilities for the flexible initiation of new strategies and environmental responsiveness that reside in the corporation itself rather than only in the capabilities and skills of its individual members. Corporate competencies for change management constitute the critical capacity that is needed to create a learning organisation which is flexible, dynamic and adaptable in a rapidly changing and volatile environment.[25]

No single organisation has resolved all the issues of effective change implementation. However, from the research we have undertaken, we have created a model and theory of strategic change that indicates the key choices available and the change technologies that represent a best fit with each strategic choice. This is a powerful guide for managerial action which is designed to make strategic change happen. We invite you, the reader, to join us and the innovative managers in these leading-edge organisations, in going beyond the old boundaries to participate actively in redesigning and leading the corporations and enterprises of the twenty-first century.

References

1. S. Ellis & A. Lampe, 'Westpac too slow for Packer', *Sydney Morning Herald*, 15 January 1993, p. 21.

2. See 'Scott Paper Company', Harvard Business School Case 9-296-048, Harvard Business School, Boston, Mass., 1996.

3. H. Igor Ansoff, *Corporate Strategy*, rev. edn, McGraw-Hill, New York, 1987.

4. H. Mintzberg, 'The Design School: Reconsidering the basic premises of strategic management', *Strategic Management Journal*, 11, 3, 1990, pp. 171–95. See also H. Mintzberg & J. A. Waters, 'Of strategies, deliberate and emergent', *Strategic Management Journal*, 6, 1985, pp. 257–72.

5. H. Igor Ansoff, 'Critique of Henry Mintzberg's The Design School: Reconsidering the basic premises of strategic management', *Strategic Management Journal*, 12, 6, 1991, pp. 449–61.

6. C. K. Prahalad & G. Hamel, 'Strategic intent', *Harvard Business Review*, May–June 1989, pp. 63–76.

7. ibid., p. 72.

8. L. Gratton, *Living Strategy: Putting People at the Heart of Corporate Purpose*, Prentice-Hall, London, 2000.

9. D. T. Carroll, 'A disappointing search for excellence', *Harvard Business Review*, 61, 6, 1983, pp. 78–88. Also, 'Who's excellent now?', *Business Week*, 6 November 1984, pp. 76–8.

10. J. P. Kotter & J. L. Heskett, *Corporate Culture and Performance*, Free Press, New York, 1992.

11. D. R. Denison, *Corporate Culture and Organizational Effectiveness*, Wiley, New York, 1990.

12. C. J. G. Gersick, 'Revolutionary change theories: A multilevel exploration of the punctuated equilibrium paradigm', *Academy of Management Review*, 16, 1, 1991, pp. 10–36.

13. J. I. Porras & R. C. Silvers, 'Organization Development and Transformation', *Annual Review of Psychology*, 42, 1991, pp. 51–78.

14. ibid., p. 52.

15. M. Beer, 'Revitalizing organizations: Change process and emergent model', *Academy of Management Executive*, 1, 1987, pp. 51–5.

16. D. A. Nadler & M. L. Tushman, 'Organizational frame bending: Principles for managing reorientation', *Academy of Management Executive*, 3, 1989, pp. 194–204.

17. J. M. Bartunek & M. K. Moch, 'First-order, second-order and third-order change and organization development interventions: A cognitive approach', *Journal of Applied Behavioural Science*, 23, 1987, pp. 483–500.

18. P. H. Mirvis, 'Organization Development: Part II—A revolutionary perspective', *Research in Organizational Change and Development*, 4, 1990, pp. 1–66.

19. W. G. Ouchi, 'The economics of organization', in P. Evans, Y. Doz & A. Laurent (eds), *Human Resource Management in International Firms*, St Martin's Press, New York, 1990, pp. 7–17.

20. M. Beer & N. Nohria (eds), *Breaking the Code of Change*, Harvard Business School Press, Boston, 2000.

21. D. Dunphy & A. Griffiths, *The Sustainable Corporation: Organisational Renewal in Australia*, Allen & Unwin, Sydney, 1998, Chapter 6: 'Building corporate capabilities', pp. 140–70; S. J. Goerner, *After the Clockwork Universe: The Emerging Science and Culture of Integral Society*, Floris Books, Edinburgh, 1999, Chapter 8: 'The economic debate', pp. 323–71.

22. T. Clarke & S. Clegg, *Changing Paradigms: The Transformation of Management Knowledge for the 21st Century*, HarperCollins, London, 2000, Chapter 6: 'Stakeholders', pp. 295–368.

23. ibid., p. 295.

24. Based on an account by K. Wilber in *No Boundary: Eastern and Western Approaches to Personal Growth*, New Science Library, Shamhala, Boulder, 1981.

25. D. Turner & M. Crawford, *Change Power: Capabilities that Drive Corporate Renewal*, Business and Professional Publishing, Sydney, 1998.

Chapter 2

An organisational renaissance

Around the globe, a feeling of expectancy and ebullience was evident as clocks ticked past midnight on 31 December 1999—a new century and a new millennium were symbolically being ushered in. The quarter century before had brought groundbreaking changes and discontinuities to economies, societies, organisations and individuals; however, fashioning these discontinuities into constructive, wealth-creating change constitutes the major leadership challenge at all levels in the early decades of the twenty-first century. A similar feeling of expectancy had earlier engulfed the world during 1989 as hundreds of thousands of East Berliners surged through the walls which had separated them from their West German compatriots since World War II. The breakdown of the concrete Berlin Wall was symbolic of the breakdown of 'bounded thinking' within East and West Germany—thinking locked into political ideologies which shaped the economic, social and organisational conventions and structures of these societies. While the breakdown of the barriers was widely celebrated, managing the discontinuity which has followed has been more difficult.

These change management challenges are also true for organisations: there are many exponents of organisational change, but fewer who have the capacity to steer a course through the new boundaries, and the resulting discontinuity. The leaders of West Germany expected a quick transition: approximately 2000 billion deutschmarks of public funds was spent over the decade of the 1990s in an attempt to fast-track the process of German reunification. However, two successive German governments have discovered that true transformation is much more difficult, and takes longer than most expect.

While change is often destructive of an older order, if it is well managed it can lead to new forms of learning, or organisational renaissance. The changing themes of major international conferences are instructive—'Strategic Renaissance: The Transformation of Economic Enterprise' in 1993, had by 1999 become 'Winning Strategies in a Deconstructing World'[1] at annual conferences of the Strategic Management Society. The upbeat proposition of the 1993 conference was that the transformation of our corporations is comparable in scope and effect with the transformation of societies during the Renaissance. Information and communication technologies were releasing people from institutional control in a way analogous to the release of people from the power of the church and clergy in the original Renaissance. By 1999 there was recognition that renaissance, although positive in the result, also involves deconstruction and radical change.

Some may therefore look at the environments of their corporations and see troubling discontinuities, while others may perceive a renaissance or an awakening and, with it, opportunities. Whatever our perception, it is clear that all Western industrial economies are experiencing a succession of 'breakpoints' or 'turning points' which challenge accepted notions of how to successfully organise economic enterprise. 'Breakpoints', according to management writer Paul Strebel, are sudden environmental or opportunistic changes.[2] He contrasts them with 'turning points' (or, in our terms, transitions) which represent more gradual changes that produce significant consequences over longer periods. Whether breakpoints or transitions, the common denominator is groundbreaking change in the environment of the corporation, forcing managers to consider

The greatest danger in times of turbulence, is not the turbulence...it is to act with yesterday's logic.

PETER DRUCKER[3]

and implement change in their organisations—change which is invariably transformative in scope. Old business models are being jettisoned: experimentation with new forms of wealth creation is now endemic. This should not mean that we are irrevocably destined to become the victims of such constant change, even though we are affected by it.

What are the boundaries being challenged, reshaped and traversed in the new economy leading to such a fundamental re-evaluation of our forms of economic enterprise? There are many, but we cover four:

1. from local to global focus;
2. a new technological basis of competition;
3. convergence and breakdown of industry structures; and
4. radically changed work structures and expectations.

Boundaries under challenge

From local to global focus

By the turn of the millennium, the boundaries around the traded goods sector and the financial economies of both Australia and New Zealand had been fundamentally reshaped. Comfortable tariff walls of industry and financial protection had been successively lowered in the 1980s and 1990s by governments of all ideological persuasions in order to force greater competitiveness against countries with significantly lower labour and infrastructure costs, and higher levels of product quality. The economic consequences of these deregulatory policies are now manifested in radically reshaped industries, emergent new industries and more internationally open economies at the same time as economies around the globe have moved from paternalism to economic interdependence. We will argue later that the social costs of these deregulatory policies, which have led to this greater international orientation, have been high, not only in Australia, but also across the world. However, by the turn of the millennium it was a commonly held view that Australia had changed so dramatically that it was one of the globe's more vigorous economies. Sustained growth in its gross domestic product (GDP), substantial increases in total factor productivity and its international openness had restored it to being one of the leading OECD economies. These changing national and international contexts have major implications for enterprises across the globe.

The authors of the groundbreaking book on globalisation, *Race for the World*, write:[4]

> Today, almost 20 percent of world output—about $6 trillion of the $28 trillion world gross domestic product (GDP)—is produced and consumed in global markets. In these markets, all the world's consumers have access to all products because industry structures exist to deliver output everywhere. Most consumers, then, have limited access to 80 percent of world output because products are being delivered primarily through local or national industry structures. But this will change.
>
> Within thirty years, we estimate at least 80 percent of world output will be in global markets. By then, worldwide GDP will be $91 trillion, so the globally accessible arena could be $73 trillion—twelvefold increase in thirty years.

The greatest wealth will be accessed by those companies that either operate, or are competitive, globally. We are not arguing that global operation is the only way for managers to take their enterprises. There is still a viable place for the locally operating company. But all enterprises, whether operating globally or locally, face competition within a global marketplace. There will be few corners left to hide for inefficient local enterprises.

Globalisation opens up huge opportunities for local firms wanting to expand their operations internationally. Well known examples are Lend Lease Corporation, National Australia Bank, CSL, Hawker de Havilland and CSR's North American business. These successes, however, are hard won against tough competition from the world's other leading industry players and the wins cannot be made without a commitment and capacity for self-transformation that has been rare among many Australian and New Zealand companies.

What is the dilemma here for managers? Because of our relatively small market size, it will be the unusual organisation based in Australia or New Zealand that can take on the whole world, even in some highly specialised niche market. The choice for managers will seldom be one of being fully local or fully global but rather deciding where to compete globally and with what products and services. For example, in going international, Lend Lease initially targeted the United States, later almost withdrawing, then Asia, then the United Kingdom and then the United States again: Fletcher Challenge defined two major areas of focus—the broader Pacific Rim (Australasia, the west coast of the United States, Canada) and South America. BHP Steel targeted the Pacific Rim.[5] Going international may also involve matching or neutralising the strategies of competitors by forming alliances, as Qantas has attempted in its 'The One World' strategic alliance with British Airways, Cathay, American Airlines, Canadian Airlines and Iberian.

Globalisation also affects management's choices of its mix of products and services. Australian firms, marketing mainly in Australia, have tended to carry a broad array of products and services. Australia is a large geographic area with a relatively small population. In a globally competitive world, specialisation is increasingly the key to success. Only products and services that have distinctive competitive advantages will survive. Australian universities are a case in point. Traditionally most offered a comprehensive range of courses, but as distance learning courses proliferate, and are increasingly offered by international consortia of universities, local universities are facing a new order of competition in relation to cost and quality. Some degree of specialisation will be a necessary strategy for survival. But how much? And what should be the areas of specialisation?

So globalisation creates a new set of dilemmas for managers. Are we going to go global or try to compete only locally? If we go global, in which part of the globe will we choose to operate? Will we form alliances to extend our global reach? Which mix of products and services will we offer and how can we ensure that what we do offer is world class? Those managers and companies that choose to be bystanders, rather than drivers, on the road to the new economy will either become irrelevant or be run over. The choices are difficult but unavoidable.

Figure 2.1 demonstrates the success of Australian enterprises in the 1990s relative to the 1980s in developing operations offshore. Offshore operation represents one form of internationalisation. Another form is to export high value-added products such as wines, or aircraft componentry. Another form still is to encourage inward revenue flows from the provision of educational, professional and tourism related services. The challenge is to think globally, even if the extent of operations is primarily local.

The economic boundaries of countries across the globe are now more open as a result of global competition, as countries have progressively deregulated their trade and financial economies over the past twenty years. Simultaneously, there has been a trend towards the building of huge, relatively formalised trading blocs: the European Union (EU), the North American Free Trade Agreement (NAFTA), the less formalised trading union of the Association of South-East Asian Nations (ASEAN) and the less effective Asia-Pacific Economic Co-operation (APEC) association in the Asia-Pacific. Milton Leontiades[6] suggests that each major geographic bloc has a different

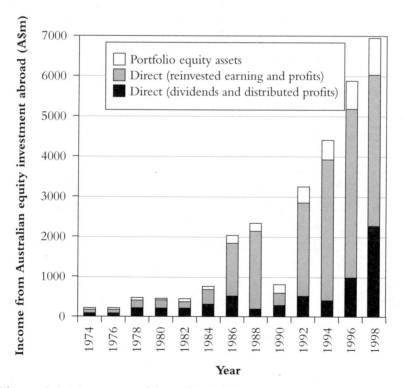

Figure 2.1 More successful on the global stage   AUSTRALIAN BUREAU OF STATISTICS/HSBC, QUOTED IN J. EDWARDS, *THE NEW AUSTRALIAN ECONOMY*, HSBC PUBLICATION, SYDNEY, 1999, P. 10

tradition of wealth creation, all of which, as single models, have been vying for supremacy. In North America and in many Western economies the system of laissez-faire market capitalism has until recently emphasised short-term year-on-year profits to satisfy shareholders. In Western Europe, the emphasis has been on longer-term balancing of multiparty concerns—on all stakeholders (owners, management and unions) managing corporations for longer-term sustainability. In Asian economies, the emphasis has also been longer term, encouraging competition between firms but often with government intervention to ensure that 'national goals' are enhanced. These three traditions of wealth creation are shown in Table 2.1.

Table 2.1 Creating wealth: Three traditions

Western Europe	United States and some Western economies	Japan/Asia
Stakeholder capitalism	*Shareholder capitalism*	*Collective capitalism*
Management balances multiparty concerns of the board, management and industrial unions **Focus on:** • skills enhancement necessary with technological change • balancing economic outcomes with environmental concerns • democratisation of the workplace	Maximising share price is management's objective **Focus on:** *Phase 1* (1980s–early 1990s) • market share • cost reduction • competitive strategy • immolation of competitors, globally *Phase 2* (late 1990s onward) • global strategy • creating the global standard	Management takes longer term view of developing an internationally competitive corporation **Focus on:** • institutional/ government and corporate co-operation • adding value to products and customisation • focus on the national interest and national competitiveness
Managing in a complex environment	*Profit focus, laissez-faire/market oriented capitalism*	*Longer-term developmental, collective focus*

Source: Adapted from M. Leontiades, Rutgers University, 'Scenarios for the nineties', paper delivered at Panel Session at the Strategic Management Society Conference, Stockholm, October 1990.

There would be few who would disagree that that decade of the 1990s was the decade of US oriented market capitalism: Western European and Asian economies and businesses have struggled against the apparent success globally of the so-called US business model. We suspect that part of the secret is the capacity of the US model to metamorphose and adapt: in the early 1990s the emphasis was almost entirely on cost cutting to create superior shareholder returns, but in the latter part of the 1990s the emphasis had moved to global dominance through alliances, technological (particularly software) superiority, and an approach to innovation that left other international competitors flat-footed, and often financially weakened.

By 2000, however, it was almost as though the excesses of American turbo-charged globalisation were being questioned from within. Unprecedented opposition to further globalisation and market capitalism found its focus in late 1999 in Seattle, one of the world's most globally influential cities (home of Boeing and Microsoft) at the summit meeting of the World Trade Organization. Over 40 000 demonstrators and rioters effectively stopped the meetings. *The Economist*, the influential global news magazine, editorialised:[7]

> The economic benefits of the greater openness—faster growth, cheaper imports, new technologies, the spur of foreign competition— that the world has enjoyed in recent years are too easily taken for granted. Greater prosperity is also the best way to improve working conditions and the environment. Yet, for all the gains that globalization brings, it can also create losers, who naturally dislike change. Their concerns should not be dismissed. But shutting out the rest of the world would make everyone worse off.

We argue that sustaining international competitiveness, and the benefits of open markets, will require new national and corporate models of wealth creation. However, in future we will be forced to draw on the stronger elements of all three of the above models, and extend them, rather than relying on one-size-fits-all business and economic models.

The more successful private and public sector corporations are now focusing on what is required to create wealth over the longer term, not just next year. Corporations must create a sustainable future, in such a way as to balance longer-term social meaning with economic wealth creation and profitability in the shorter term. This productive blending of the traditions calls for the investment of time, capital and research in developing customer centred products and services, new markets and more highly skilled workforces. It also demands a mental shift to understand how to create internationally competitive enterprises, while at the same time addressing the social and human dimensions of change.

From mainframes to dot.coms

The boundaries of technology are tumbling like the tumbling walls of Berlin, except that new walls seem to keep tumbling each year, or even each week. An international information technology executive, Peter Schavoir, assessed that in the year 1970 there were 50 000 computers worldwide; there are now far in excess of 50 000 computers of comparable processing capacity manufactured every business day.[8] Computing power is now one ten-thousandth of its cost when computers were first introduced in the 1950s. Moore's Law, the theory that the capacity of semiconductors will double and their price halve every eighteen months, is predicted to continue for at least another twenty years. In Figure 2.2 we trace the successive waves of information technology. Boundary after boundary has fallen, and will continue to fall.

In communications, new technologies are introduced and become outmoded almost before they are launched because of rapid developments in microchips, satellite technology, fibre optics, cellular and wireless technologies. The giant communication product companies know that after launching a major new product, they have barely a matter of months, if not weeks, before global competitors will have vastly upgraded products with new features for sale at a lower price.

Author Thomas Friedman in *The Lexus and the Olive Tree*[9] argues that the introduction of railroads in the late nineteenth century caused the world to 'shrink' from large to medium for traders, and for those fortunate enough to travel. He argues that the info-communication revolution of the latter twentieth and early twenty-first centuries has further 'shrunk' the world from medium to small.

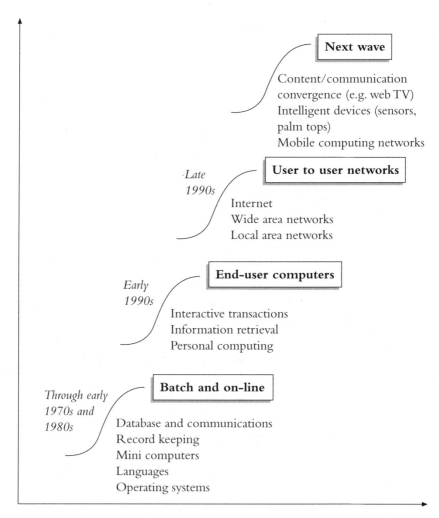

Figure 2.2 Computing technology growth cycles   PETER RULE, ERICSSON, AUSTRALIA

Indeed the marketing slogan for IBM, the information technology company, is 'Solutions for a Small Planet'. This effectively captures the new global dynamic being created by the revolution in technologies. Now that much of the developed world has sped up to Internet time, the traditional factors of production—capital, skilled labour and proximity to markets—are no longer the success factors they were. Information and its use has become the critical success and survival factor.

The phenomenon of convergence and the blurring of industry boundaries by technology innovations is one of the most powerful drivers of change, globally. Figure 2.3 illustrates how the boundaries of formerly separate industries such as telecommunications, computing, film and the media are converging to form an 'infotainment' industry. The speed of change has been breathtaking. In early 2000, only several years after the mega-merger of the Time and Warner media and entertainment titans to form Time-Warner, came the world's biggest merger deal—the acquisition of Time-Warner by America On Line (AOL), a twelve-year-old Internet company, to create a US$350 billion infotainment behemoth. The aim was to dominate markets through the effective tie up of 'content' and 'distribution' channels. In Australia, similar attempted convergence has been occurring between such companies as Telstra, Ozemail, Solution 6, Ninemsn and Sausage Software, to date with only limited success.

In the twenty years prior to the turn of the millennium, it was viable to argue that the primary force behind the globalisation of markets was politically inspired deregulation and free trade policies. As we have moved into the twenty-first century, the ubiquity of information on a global scale seems to be a primary shaping force, leading to radically reduced barriers to market entry, globally. It is almost as though deregulation per se is now a second or third order story. The Internet, powered by the worldwide Web, although only a recent commercially viable phenomenon, is emerging as a mass market platform and low cost distribution channel, particularly in the high tech services, and also in the traded goods sector. It is the most powerful force for globalisation; government policies are barely able to keep pace.

Dell Computers provides an example of the radical new business model being adopted by many companies. The company went public in 1988, on sales of US$159 million. In 1998, its sales were US$19 billion, built on a model of mass customisation, selling computers directly to customers. Dell avoids all intermediaries, making a product only when it receives an order, with a promised five-day turnaround period. For Australian markets, this includes assembly of the customised order in Malaysia, and then airshipping it directly to the customer. In this way it is able to offer the most

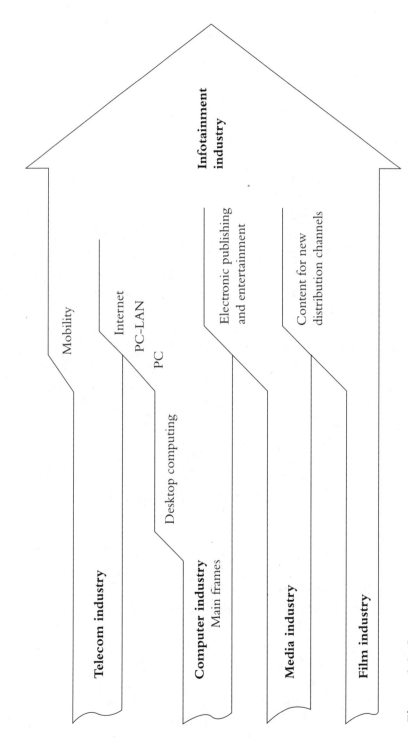

Figure 2.3 Convergence

up-to-date product, at lower cost, at a speed unheard of except for off-the-shelf products. Such customisation of products makes nonsense of traditional market segmentation theories—Dell has customer segments of one. Velocity is the key:

> *The building blocks of mass customisation have emerged over the past decade, including more detailed sales data, improved supply-chain management systems, and computer-controlled, highly flexible factory equipment. The internet ties them together, giving companies the means to take orders directly into factories and directly to their component suppliers, and giving customers the means to design their own products.*[10]

The projected growth of dot.com, electronic business (e-business) in the United States and Europe, is shown in Table 2.2. Similar proportional trends are evident in Australia.

Table 2.2 Projected growth of electronic business (US$b)

Business to business (USA)			Retail business (USA and Europe)		
Sector	1998	2002	Sector	1998	2002
Computing and electronics	19.7	319.0	Travel	2.3	15.3
Motor vehicles	3.7	114.0	PC hardware and software	2.7	11.9
Petrochemical	7.0	111.0	Books	0.8	5.2
Food and agriculture	0.3	27.0	Music	0.2	2.2

Source: 'The dot.com imperative', The World in 2000, *The Economist* Publications, London, 2000, p. 104.

This shows that the dominant applications of e-business are initially expected to be in business-to-business (B2B) transactions. The Internet is becoming a primary business-to-business communication and trading channel. In the retail sector of business to consumers (B2C) it is sensible to think of the Internet as providing a parallel distribution system, rather than a total replacement system. In many areas, consumers will still want to experience their potential purchases—there will still be a need for 'hi touch' in the midst of high tech, even though the high tech advances are of Industrial Revolution proportions. In the service economy, airline bookings and the like, the Internet will be a potent force. When the products are physical, the Internet's threat to traditional business distribution methods may be less significant.

With each successive wave of technological change (see Figure 2.2), hardware has become less important and software has become critical. This underscores the boundaries that technology and info-communications titans like IBM and Ericsson must traverse as they try to transform themselves from hardware suppliers to solutions and software driven companies. Solutions and software, unlike hardware, are not electronic technologies: they are an 'intellectual technology'. The transformation is from mainframe to dot.com, but also from mainframe to mindframe. Swedish Professor Bengt-Arne Vedin wrote:[11]

> hardware represents a paradigm founded upon the laws of nature, software is qualitatively different, since its foundation is human logic rather than the laws of nature…Technology, then, is not just technology based on laws of nature or even human thinking, but group behaviour. Several borders are therefore being bridged almost at once.

The borders are very elusive, but both software and hardware technologies are changing rapidly, and these shifts have profound effects on the functioning of organisations.

In *Powershift*, futurologist Alvin Toffler likens the functioning of organisations in the future to 'information wars'.[12] Those organisations that have the information—on customer habits, preferences, buying patterns—will succeed, those who do not will fail, and this is true for organisations in both the private and public sectors. He invites readers to 'forget, for a moment, all conventional job descriptions; forget ranks; forget departmental functions. Think of the firm instead, as a beehive of knowledge processing'.[13] The structure of that beehive, he suggests, is radically different to organisations as we presently know them. Technology is the key variable making possible, and imperative, the reinvention of the corporation.

Of at least equal significance to the high tech communication revolution are the stunning and even startling advances in bio-medical technologies. Non-invasive surgery, advances in diagnostic and pharmaceutical technologies are the observable trends. What is less known are the rapid advances in genetic research, and genetic engineering affecting both plant and animal life. The implications for humans, and eventually for organisations, are far-reaching. Explains Steve Connor, Science Editor of the *Independent*:[14]

> the first working draft of the human genome—the digital recipe of our genes—… represents a critical milestone in the mammoth international project to decode the entire genetic sequence of man. It will also mark a new era of personalised medicine in which a patient's genetic make-up is used to treat illnesses with drugs tailor-made for an individual's inherited predispositions.

The moral issues here are potentially vexing, and we expect that this area, as is already the case in the global debate over genetically modified (GM) foods, will become more significant for societies, individuals and organisations in the early decades of the twenty-first century.

From staples to services

Over almost two decades a generation of leaders and managers in our organisations has either created or marched to the tune of relentless change as a result of the global and technology trends we have already discussed. In the process many have transformed their organisations; others have achieved change by incremental means. By the turn of the millennium, a raft of external indicators showed that Australia, and many of its enterprises, were seen as credible global players. Yet, electoral and organisational moods were often skittish, if not volatile. Part of the reason for this is not only the pace of change, but also the deep changes to the structures of industries which have left few societies, organisations and individuals untouched.

Compared to the rest of the economy, emphasis on physical goods has been plateauing relative to the rapid rise in the service and knowledge industries. Table 2.3 illustrates the shift, showing that from 1950 and projected to 2010, relative world trade in services (including 'knowledge' services) will have grown from 10% to 54%, while trade in agricultural products will have proportionately declined from 42% to 7%. Minerals and manufactures have held steadier percentages of the total traded sector worldwide. Radical industry change is prevalent in all advancing economies. In 1978, 235 000 people worked in Britain's collieries and 150 000 in its steel mills. By 1998, two decades later, a mere 17 300 worked in mining and 36 500 in Britain's steel mills, although the steel industry is now 80% more productive than in the late 1970s.[15]

Table 2.3 World trade in goods and services by major commodity groups (%)

Sector	1950	1960	1970	1980	1995	2010
Agricultural products	42	29	17	10	9	7
Minerals	14	17	13	20	13	11
Manufactures	34	42	47	39	38	28
Services	10	12	23	31	40	54

Source: IBIS Information Services, 1999.

Figure 2.4 illustrates change at the macro industry level showing three eras of wealth creation. At the corporate level, the trend is illustrated by the changing composition of firms represented on the Australian Stock Exchange (ASX)—see Figure 2.5.

In 1980, nine of the top ten corporations on the Australian Stock Exchange were resource related. In order, they were BHP, MIM, CRA, CSR, WMC, Santos, Hamersley, Woodside Petroleum and Comalco. Only one, ANZ Bank, was a service company. In 2000, eight of the top ten companies are technology and service companies. The relative contributions of agriculture, minerals and manufacture to GDP are all declining relative to services. However, this should not imply that these sectors are not important to a robust economy. They are still extremely important, but their basic nature, maintains futurologist Phil Ruthven, will continually change due to:

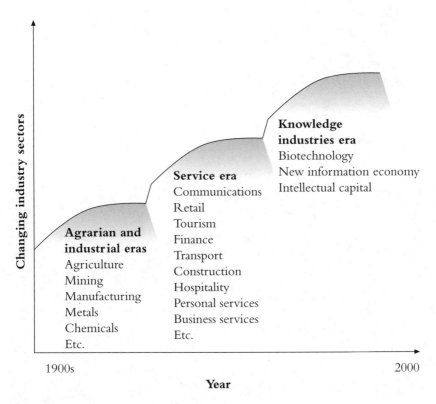

Figure 2.4 Eras of wealth creation   MCKINSEY

- increasing efficiencies—more output for less input (e.g. the use of robotics in manufacturing, and deep drilling and extractive technologies in minerals and mining);
- global market saturation for many traded goods—leading to downward price pressures in those goods (it is estimated that 40% 'over capacity' potentially exists globally for most commodities and manufactured goods);
- outsourcing of non-core activities (transferring internal service functions to the business services industry); and
- conversion of some manufacturing to retail activities—a type of instant business (e.g. photofinishing outlets, hot bread shops).

Ruthven suggests that 'manufacturing world-wide is being converted inexorably into a utility with minimal labour content. Wealth creation and jobs are emerging in new industries, as always'. Ruthven maintains that outsourcing creates new industries and new

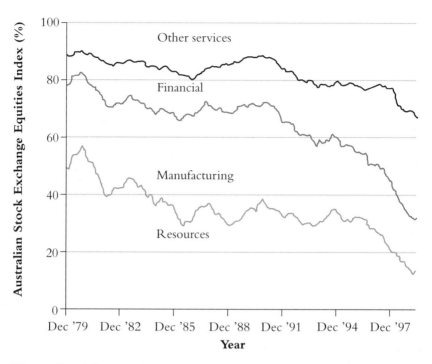

Figure 2.5 A broadening economy   AUSTRALIAN STOCK EXCHANGE

ages: 'we outsourced the growing of things to create the agrarian age industries; we outsourced the making of things to create the industrial age industries; and we are now outsourcing the doing of things, that is services, to create the infotronics or information age'.[16]

The imperative for traditional industries is to achieve cost competitiveness and sufficient scale to be viable, globally. Adding value in our agricultural, manufacturing and mining industries is also an imperative—developing the capacity to process and finesse raw materials and products rather than to export only raw commodities or to produce basic manufactured products. The development of an elaborately transformed manufacturing sector (e.g. aircraft components, car engines for world markets, biomedical technologies such as Cochlear's hearing technologies) has been positive for the Australian economy and has led to the growth in the manufacturing sector's contribution to exports from 12% in 1980 to 21% in 1997–98,[17] even though its relative contribution to total GDP is declining.

The significant shift to the service sector and the deep changes in traditional industries have been as successful as they have been painful. Edwards, commenting on an implicit global re-rating of the Australian economy, says:[18]

> the economy's resilience largely stems from a transformation in its structure that is now only starting to be widely understood. The change—15 to 20 years of vigorous economic reform in the making—has allowed Australia not only to withstand recession in the majority of its (Asian) export markets, but to maintain one of the highest OECD growth rates through the 1990s.

Nostalgia about old ways of creating national wealth must continue to be challenged, although this is not to argue for the unintelligent destruction of industries. A competitive future requires refocusing on adding value, quality and customisation in traditional industries, and continuing major leaps in thinking about how our economy, enterprises and people can be leaders in the emerging wealth-creating industries. This demands both 'renaissance' and 'deconstruction', simultaneously.

From hierarchy to competence

The greatest boundaries of all are invariably personal. People matter—and yet in the past two decades of reform, personal and professional adjustments have often been a by-product or casualty of reform, rather than a central area of concern.

Figure 2.6 illustrates the fundamental reorientations occurring in both the market and organisational focus of enterprises as they operate simultaneously across the industrial, service and knowledge economies. The first curve-style organisation was perfected in the industrial economy, and with adjustment was adapted to the early period of the service economy. Its basis was hierarchy, privileged access to markets and an in-house labour market. The second curve-style organisation has emerged particularly as a consequence of the information/Internet revolution, but aspects of it have been emerging for one or two decades. Its basis is its superior access to and networking for strategic information, its focus on global/contestable markets, and its sourcing of the best resources wherever they can be found.

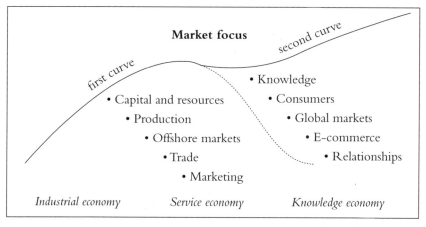

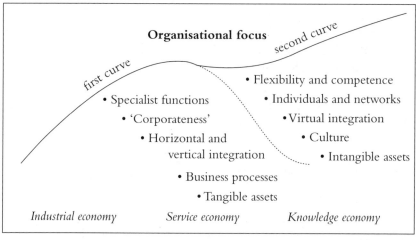

Figure 2.6 The changing enterprise ADAPTED FROM J. MORRISON, 'THE SECOND CURVE: MANAGING THE VELOCITY OF CHANGE', *STRATEGY AND LEADERSHIP*, JANUARY/FEBRUARY, 1998, PP. 7–12

Some corporations have elements of all these characteristics, prompting Dee Hock, the founder of VISA, to coin the term 'chaordic enterprise' to denote the internal tensions created by a more ordered, classical organisational form on the one hand, mixed with seeming chaos and fluidity on the other. While many traditional organisations seek to balance order and chaos, the reality is that they are often competing with new start-up organisations which commenced life on the second curve, and carry none of the legacy of the first curve.

> *The Information Revolution will do to middle management and other intermediaries what the Black Death did to 14th century Europeans.*[19]

The consequences of this for individuals have been, and are, significant. The noted American author Lester Thurow argues that the primary factors of success in the traditional economy—controlling resources, defined roles, positional authority, predictable markets— become less relevant as we move from the old to the new 'knowledge' economy. He gives three words of advice for surviving in the new economy: skills, skills, skills.[20] William Bridges, in his book *Jobshift*, goes further. He argues that the whole concept of work structures as we know them is being replaced—the job, and the positional authority which goes with it, is an artefact of history.

> The job concept emerged in the eighteenth and nineteenth centuries to package the work that needed doing in the growing factories and bureaucracies of the industrialising nations. Before people had jobs they worked just as hard but on a shifting cluster of tasks, in a variety of locations, on a schedule set by the sun, the weather, and the needs of the day. The modern job was a startling new idea—to many people, an unpleasant and even socially dangerous one…But what started as controversy (at the commencement of the industrial revolution) became the ultimate orthodoxy: we're hooked on jobs.[21]

Bridges then argues that in the emerging knowledge economy, the very conditions that created jobs—mass production and the large organisation—are fast disappearing. Public services are privatising, outsourcing and rationalising; private companies are concentrating on core business and jettisoning non value-creating businesses and functions, service and even production functions. Deirdre Macken quotes the example of the major Australian media group John Fairfax.

> Fifteen years ago, John Fairfax was a publisher that owned its own presses, its offices, car parks, garages, several residences and staff holiday spots. It employed not just its own journalists and managers but canteen staff, lawyers, accountants, cleaners, couriers, drivers, clerks, mechanics, security staff and, indeed, an inhouse barber.

Today it doesn't own its offices, or all its presses; it contracts out the canteen, security services, cleaning, couriers and many of its internal processes and professional services. It owns little property and few, if any, vehicles, and it still publishes newspapers, but calls itself an information company.

As the company moves from physical assets to intellectual assets, it will soon be simply a branded community of knowledge workers, and even that might be ephemeral, because intellectual assets have legs.[22]

For well over a decade or more, the fixed job with strongly defined functions and clear roles has been a distant memory for most workers, whether they work in core corporations, or in the multiplying smaller service enterprises which surround the larger corporations. It is as though we have gone pre-Industrial Revolution, where the best craftspeople and producers flourished, while others fell by the wayside. What is now important are personal and collective competencies, flexibly deployed, rather than hierarchical structure and jobs per se.

In his classic 1990 book, *The Age of Unreason*, Charles Handy argued that the challenge ahead would require a radical change in thinking by organisations and individuals. He saw the future of organisations as being in a 'shamrock' type of structure consisting of:

- a central company (the core) comprising a few highly committed professionals (leaders, 'project' professionals and customer-interface staff);
- subcontractors (self-employed professionals) who are paid for results, not time; and
- a flexible labour force—people whose commitment will be to a 'job' rather than to a career in a specific company.[23]

At the time Handy was writing, many organisations had barely left the hierarchical model of the industrial era. Others were downsizing, stripping out layers of management and cost to merely survive in a world where global trade barriers were falling, and where managers marched to the beat of achieving the elusive organisational goal of being world-class.

Handy's arguments at first seemed avant-garde, but attractive. But spurred by the intensity of the information revolution in the latter 1990s, companies have been forced to adopt such highly flexible and fluid structures. Handy's insights are materialising, daily.

They are indeed for many 'chaordic enterprises'. We have witnessed the positives of an Australian economy enjoying a global re-rating, and unemployment falling from 12% in the early 1990s to 6.5% by the year 2000. Simultaneously, many employees have experienced the pain of readjustment as blue-collar and traditional jobs have disappeared, layer upon layer of managers in organisations has been made redundant by the information technology revolution, and much full-time work has been fractionalised into part-time and contractual work arrangements.

The sense of impermanence covers all levels: 'in 1998...people watched as the Chief Executive of BHP and the newly graduating class of apprentices at Qantas all lost their jobs'.[24] At the top, therefore, the sense of impermanence can be as real as elsewhere in the organisation. Global technology giant Ericsson removed its CEO of fifteen months, Sven-Christer Nelsson, in 1999—citing that the company's nine months' lead on its competitors had been lost under his leadership. The company has now made up the ground. In Australia a bungled takeover of competitor GIO, and questions of personal style, led to the forced departure of AMP's George Trumbell, who had shaken up AMP and led it out of its nineteenth century paternalism.

The emerging new class of autonomous employees and leaders survive on their competence, productivity and entrepreneurial ability. The uniformity of the Australasian workplace is disappearing and in its place is a performance oriented core culture supported by a vast network of relationships with suppliers, subcontractors and knowledge workers, all of whom provide products and services to a variety of organisations.

Is such change necessary? For our organisations to survive, and prosper, yes. This is not to discount the deep pain associated with the transition. An article in *The Economist* speculated on why historically the Welsh had not progressed economically as well as other parts of the United Kingdom. The commentary was that the Welsh had seen themselves as a subnation of employees rather than as a nation of entrepreneurs. They depended on the large industrialists and the government to provide jobs.[25]

In the new world of work, we all have to be creative and enterprising. One of the results of nearly two decades of reform has been that many people have found themselves leaving the major corporations or the public sector, and participating in the growing 'personal sector' as subcontractors or part-time workers. The top graduates of many business schools and other faculties are seeking opportunities in small start-up companies, rather than in large established corporations. Over the longer term, these trends will be healthy for Australia as we become a nation of entrepreneurs, seeing many of the solutions coming from ourselves rather than being provided for us by government and large organisations. It will be essential if we are to survive and thrive in the global marketplace.

An economy is essentially energised by its private and public enterprises, by managers in enterprises and by the individuals who work in productive enterprises. The boundaries of our thinking about careers and employment are being thoroughly challenged. Government, however, has an obligation to develop and implement policies which cover both the economic and social dimensions of change.

This revolution in employment and career structures is well symbolised in the passing of a ritual of corporate life in earlier eras—the award of a gold watch to long-serving employees on retirement. As we cross the watershed of the twenty-first century, the imagery of careers and employment is more that of a Swatch—multiskilled, interchangeable, high tech...and globally acceptable.

Imperatives for organisational renaissance

It is easy to be daunted by such a period of seminal transformation in our society and organisations; however, we believe there are a number of imperatives for executives and managers as they lead their enterprises beyond present boundaries into the twenty-first century. They are:

- developing global capability;
- positioning for growth;

- relentless business improvement; and
- managing from the outside in.

We will cover each of these in turn.

Developing global capability

In the late 1960s it was Marshall McLuhan, the Canadian media theorist, who coined the notion of a 'global village' linked by powerful communication networks. Since then, the 'global village' has taken on a broader meaning to encompass the economic interdependence of nation-states, and their corporations, trading globally in goods and services, to an extent only paralleled on a proportionate basis in much earlier periods of history. A modern proverb has expressed it well: 'When the world was large we could think small: now the world is small we have to think big.'[26] Harvard Business School professor, Rosabeth Moss Kanter, suggested that the greatest challenge for large corporations in this era of globalisation was to 'learn to dance', denoting the need for strategic and operational agility. 'Thinking big' and 'learning to dance' are two powerful images of the type of strategic challenge and the type of response required for private and public corporations to create economic wealth together with the social benefits which can flow from sound economies. They are imageries appropriate not only to large, but also to medium and small organisations.

> *National prosperity is created, not inherited. It does not grow out of a country's natural endowments, its labour pool, its interest rates, or its currency value, as classical economics insists. A nation's competitiveness depends on the capacity of its industry to innovate and upgrade. Companies gain advantage against the world's best competitors because of pressure and challenge.*
>
> MICHAEL PORTER[27]

We suggest that developing global capability within organisations takes at least one of three forms:

- *Being inherently globally competitive*—the capacity to create and sustain increasing streams of wealth, or improved outcomes, at levels equal to or better than the leading firms/enterprises/bodies worldwide in:

  - products produced
  - services offered
  - return on funds employed
  - productivity levels
  - processes and outcomes

  This calls for an active search for relevant comparative data and benchmarks, and a willingness to manage the consequences of comparisons where they indicate lags. Those organisations whose sole point of comparison is domestic competition, or interstate rivals, will fall behind.

- *An export orientation*—a significantly greater number of companies and enterprises are accepting the challenge of developing value-based, competitively priced products and services for global markets. In the agricultural and manufacturing sectors, this primarily involves physical exports offshore; in the services it often involves onshore activities (for example, tourism, educational packages, financial intermediation) as well as offshore activities (software, systems, technological infrastructure).

- *Developing offshore operations/joint ventures*—many more Australasian organisations are now generating national wealth by physically operating offshore, either through wholly owned overseas operations or by joint ventures with overseas corporations, and repatriating profit streams to the home company.

Developing a global mindset

Successful leaders and managers must think globally, and push the boundaries of thinking about how their organisation can match or exceed the best, internationally. It is not 'cultural cringe', an assumption that overseas is best. Rather it is an acknowledgment that in an information-rich era, few organisations other than monopolies will survive over the longer term if what they have to offer falls significantly behind the best in class globally. In the private sector the customers will purchase elsewhere; in the public sector, the minister or the public will go elsewhere for the service. Organisations create advantage against the world's best competitors because of pressure and challenge. We readily accept this in international sport: the same principles apply to our organisations. This journey is not and never will be over, even though at the turn of the century Australia's global prospects looked more promising. The annual *World Competitiveness Report*,[28] produced after extensive surveys of world opinion leaders by the World Economic Forum and IMD, Lausanne, has rated Australia's overall position as improving to 12th position, out of 47 countries. The same survey, however, still rates Australian managers as having a significant way to go in developing a global focus. Out of 47 countries in the survey, Australian managers overall were only ranked 28th in 1999, the same ranking as in 1995. The country is doing better economically, but managers still have to lift their game, and their global focus. These ratings are shown in Table 2.4. It should also be noted, however, that some of the world's largest and most influential corporations are currently led by Australians: Coca Cola by Douglas Daft, Ford Motor Company by Jac Nasser, News Limited by Rupert Murdoch, The World Bank

Table 2.4 Australia's global competitiveness (rankings out of 47 countries)

Rating	1999	1997	1995
Overall rating	12	18	16
Factor ratings			
Infrastructure	4	8	5
Government	8	14	10
People	11	14	20
Finance	14	18	10
Domestic economy	16	22	18
Management	16	19	22
Science and technology	16	24	18
Internationalisation	28	28	28

Source: 'The World Competitiveness Yearbook—Executive Summary 2000', IMD, Lausanne, July 2000, pp. 28–9.

by James Wolfensohn, British Airways by Rod Eddington, Phillip Morris by Geoff Bible, and IBM Global Services by Doug Elix, to name several. There are scores of others at second and other levels. With sufficient global exposure, and thinking, the capacity is there.

An export orientation

There is increasing evidence that a resurgence is taking place within the Australian and the New Zealand economies in exports. In both countries new trade flows are evident in value-added agricultural products such as wine, aquaculture products, biomedical technologies such as Cochlear's bionic ear products, CSL's pharmaceutical products, vehicles exported to Asia and the United States, computer software systems, educational services (an annual A$3.5–4.0 billion input to the economy) and technology. One of the largest areas of growth, apart from the service industries, has been in 'elaborately transformed manufactures' (ETMs) which produce sophisticated products with high added value. It is also interesting that much of this export growth has come from the small to medium sized firms, rather than the large corporations. A study for the Australian Manufacturing Council found that over 90% of exporters from Australia are 'niche' players and are succeeding because of their agility, lack of bureaucratic structures, and access to inexpensive communication technologies.[29]

Offshore operations and ventures

In the area of offshore operations and joint ventures, there have been some major success stories—for example, Lend Lease, News Corporation, National Australia Bank and Westfield—and equally, difficult problems—for example, Boral, Pacific Dunlop, Mayne Nickless and the 1980s 'entrepreneurs'. We need to make the distinction here between international, and global, growth. Inter-nationalisation, on the one hand, involves either export/import or direct investments abroad with operations in one or a number of offshore countries. Globalisation, on the other hand, is a much more advanced form of internationalisation characterised by global products, global innovation and global competition.[30] Most Australian organisations have concentrated on offshore international operations:

relatively few, with the exception of News Limited and possibly Lend Lease and Fosters Brewing, have global operations. Joint ventures and strategic alliances have enjoyed varying degrees of success but represent real future opportunities if managed effectively. The demands of operating in the 'global village' are great: to do so is a challenge to leadership to think beyond domestic boundaries, to take calculated risks, and to develop within organisations a focus on global competitiveness through sustainable and profitable offshore operations.

Positioning for growth

In an earlier book, *Under New Management*,[31] we wrote of the Century of the Pacific. We made the case that a large part of Australasia's future lay in accessing markets and developing relationships with countries of the Pacific Rim rather than relying solely on traditional markets in the United Kingdom, the United States and Japan.

The financial contagion that hit the markets of Asian countries in the second half of 1997 sharply arrested the patterns of growth in Asian economies over the previous decade. As currencies and stock markets went into free fall, growth rates in the Asian economies stalled, businesses went bankrupt and inward investment dried up overnight in many Asian countries. By early 1998 non-performing bank loans totalled 25% of all bank assets in Thailand, 23% in South Korea, 20% in Indonesia and 16% in Malaysia. At one point during the crisis, South Korean banks had refused any more credit to 22 of the country's top 30 conglomerates or chaebols.

As the crisis unravelled it became apparent that Australian organisations had been partially fireproofed against such turmoil in Australia's near northern markets. Government policy had been encouraging a move away from what, in the late 1980s and early 1990s, had become almost a singular focus on the development of relationships with Asia. When the crisis came, Australian organisations seemed able to quickly diversify their focus, towards European and North American markets. A crisis for Australian organisations and the economy was averted because of an ability to respond quickly and to make adjustments. Countercyclical strategies were effectively employed.

We are still convinced, however, that Asian and Pacific Rim countries represent a major engine room for growth over the next quarter century. Perhaps not *the* engine room per se, as the popular wisdom of the 1980s and 1990s would have had us believe, but an important engine room which currently runs the danger of being neglected, to the detriment of our organisations. Some of the earlier rationale is still relevant:

- Europe is only one-quarter of the geographical size of the East Asian countries.
- The Pacific Rim has half the world's population now, and by the end of the decade will have two-thirds (Western Europe will have only 6% of the world's population).
- An emerging middle class in Asian nations is anxious to access a wider range of goods and services.
- While GDP growth plummeted in the Asian and Japanese economies in 1997 and 1998, Figure 2.7 shows continuing projected growth in the Asia-Pacific region. Indonesia, its economy ravaged by precipitous currency falls, bad business practices, and political/military tensions, does not fit this pattern of recovery. Other countries such as Thailand and the Philippines are only making slow recoveries. Japan, Taiwan and South Korea, however, are recovering well.

The relative strengths and challenges of the Asian economies could be summarised as in Table 2.5.

Table 2.5 The Asian economies

Strengths	Challenges
Commitment to *education*	Commitment to the extended family can descend into 'skewed' markets and decision processes
Commitment to increase *wealth*	
Ability to *save*	Lack of transparency in commercial laws and business processes—relationships prevail over contracts
Strong *work ethic* and long-term view	
Ready uptake of *technology*	Emphasis on quantitative versus qualitative growth

The Asian value of collectivism was once also regarded as a strength of the Asian system of capitalism, compared to other regions

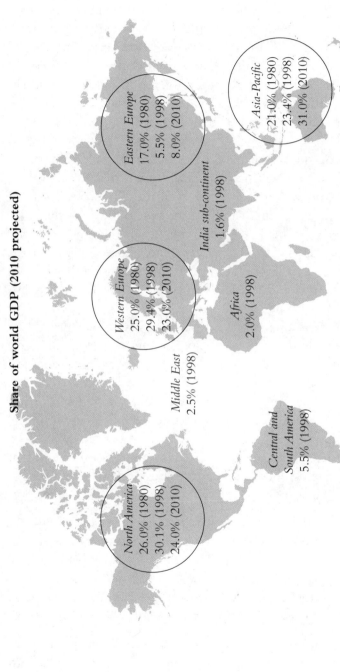

Share of world GDP (2010 projected)

Eastern Europe
17.0% (1980)
5.5% (1998)
8.0% (2010)

Asia-Pacific
21.0% (1980)
23.4% (1998)
31.0% (2010)

India sub-continent
1.6% (1998)

Western Europe
25.0% (1980)
29.4% (1998)
23.0% (2010)

Africa
2.0% (1998)

Middle East
2.5% (1998)

North America
26.0% (1980)
30.1% (1998)
24.0% (2010)

Central and
South America
5.5% (1998)

1998 World GDP, $US29.7 trillion
Note: 1980 and 2010 percentages incomplete.

Figure 2.7 Major economic regions: Growth   IBIS INFORMATION SERVICES

of the world. However, Asian policy makers now realise that the model too often leads to lack of transparency in business dealings: 'inner circles' gain privileged access to resources and information. Faced with these characteristics, world investors retreated to either the perceived 'safer' investment locations in Asia, or to traditionally advanced economies, including Australia. Since the Asian financial crisis, over 171 regional headquarters of multi and transnationals have been established in Australia, where business law and practice is more 'transparent'. A good proportion of these may once have located in Asia.

For Australia, and Australian organisations, to become complacent about current success will be to miss the point of countercyclical strategies. We must re-engage in an even more concerted way to build on our current strength and our strategic position in the Asia-Pacific time zone. The Asian economies will rebound strongly: Singapore's financial system is being shaken up with external expertise, and the island-state has agreements with three leading universities—INSEAD, Wharton and the University of Chicago—to establish campuses there to provide world-class education for executives, and competition for its own universities. Korea is in the process of radically overhauling its government and business establishment, and its union structures. Japan is at the beginning of a silent revolution where openness and transparency are slowly replacing secrecy and complacency.[32] It is imperative that Australia and New Zealand create an even stronger relationship of interdependence within the Pacific Rim economies.

Recently one of us was discussing with a senior Asian government official the packaging of educational and consulting services to Asian corporations. She said:

> The time is ripe for much more serious Australian involvement in the East Asian economies—until now it has been very skittish, half-hearted, and more related to the exotics of travel than business. The Region is desperately in need of Australia's skills and services. The Americans are too arrogant and cash-driven, but Australians are more pragmatic. As a country you have a lot to offer.

Because modern Australia and New Zealand evolved as European settlements, there are still important trade and corporate links with the European and North American economies. However, a major part of our future lies in the Pacific Rim. A global *and* regional frame of reference is therefore essential within all our enterprises if we are to continue our strong economic growth.

Relentless business improvement

Within days of the appointment of one chief executive to lead an ailing organisation, the words 'slash' and 'burn' had been stealthily etched on the walls of the headquarters building by employees fearing the new CEO's reputation for cost cutting. In another organisation, the appointment of a new CEO was met with an enthusiastic response by most employees because that person had a good reputation for building morale among employees in a previous organisation. Is productivity about reducing costs, or about maximising staff effectiveness? What are the answers in productivity?

Simply defined, productivity is the relationship between an economy's output and the inputs required to produce that output. Studies by organisations such as the Business Council of Australia in the early 1990s suggested that large gaps existed in productivity between Australian industries and best practice industries overseas, with the problem compounded by the fact that international best practice companies were increasing their productivity each year.

The challenge was heeded by many organisations, which aimed to lift their productivity levels by quantum amounts of 50–60%, and greater. Nationally, however, the overall achievements were more modest, but nevertheless Australia's national productivity increases in the decade of the 1990s outstripped the United States, Japan and major Western economies, in fact the entire group of seven nations (G7), as illustrated in Figure 2.8.[33]

Despite this comparatively impressive national performance, more creativity and effort will be required to sustain global productivity standards. This is particularly so in a relatively small economy where it is difficult to achieve efficiencies through the large scale national operations possible in the United States or the European economies.

Noted management author, Peter Drucker, predicts that the productivity of the older economy sectors, agriculture and manu-facturing, will need to increase at an average annual rate of 3–4% (as

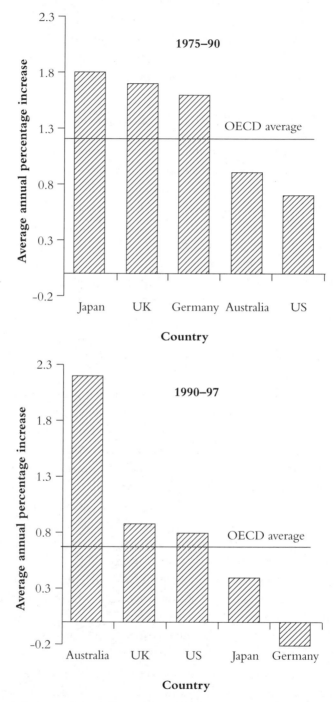

Figure 2.8 Annual growth rates in multifactor productivity   OECD/HSBC

for the past 120 years). However, he sees the greater challenge now as dramatically raising the rate of productivity of the service and knowledge industries in occupational areas such as health, law, information services, educational services, tourism and hospitality:

▶

The single greatest challenge facing managers in the developed countries of the world is to raise the productivity of knowledge and service workers. It will dominate the management agenda for the next several decades, determine the competitive performance of companies, and determine the very fabric of society and the quality of life in industrialized nations.

PETER DRUCKER[34]

Constraints on productivity can come from factors external to the enterprise, such as government policy, exchange rates or business regulations. Our view, however, is that productivity increases are primarily the domain of enterprises, a responsibility that is often overlooked by executives. The 1991 Business Council study found that 1 in 4 organisations had no efficiency or productivity targets; only 1 workplace in 10 judged itself against external standards; and less than 1 in 40 firms judged themselves against international standards.[35] In the space of a decade these figures have markedly changed for the better as a result of the increasing emphasis on global competitiveness and setting clear targets. However, much remains to be done.

Well known CEO, Fred Hilmer, has argued that a concept of productivity solely tied to labour costs is inadequate. He puts the case for the more comprehensive concept of 'strategic productivity' comprising three levels: cost, value and time productivity.[36] Cost productivity is the most basic of the three levels, focusing on the ratio of physical outputs over inputs. 'To be price-competitive, an enterprise must be cost-competitive.' The second level, value productivity, emphasises the importance of the quality or image of product and services and the depth of an organisation's core competencies. The third level, which we prefer to term 'innovation rate', involves an organisation being a first or fast mover in its markets, being responsive and timely in meeting market needs, its rate of product/service innovation, rate of technology uptake and rate of corporate reshaping.

Hilmer also says:

> Innovation rate is also intended to capture the change dynamic. If change is the only thing we can count on, then the productivity of an enterprise in making changes is itself a critical element of strategic productivity.[37]

Figure 2.9 illustrates the components of the major areas of cost, value and innovation which affect productivity. We suggest several major actions are essential for effectively spawning greater productivity:

- identify which of the components of productivity are critical to the performance of the organisation or business unit;
- identify best practice comparisons within Australasia and globally;
- introduce appropriate measurement methods and regularly communicate the comparisons, using graphs and other pictorial language, within the workplace;
- identify the management and other processes by which 'best practice' organisations are able to attain superior productivity;

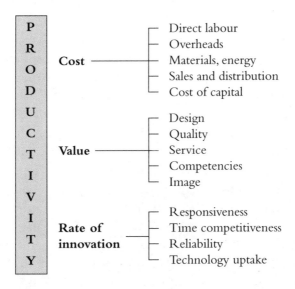

Figure 2.9 The elements of productivity

- set goals and provide leadership to close the gap, ensuring that the measures used highlight tangible factors which relate as directly as possible to the work of individuals or groups.

An Australian executive, whose Melbourne based company had compounded 20% annual increases in productivity for the previous six years, said that his company was now targeting that order of productivity increase for at least the next five to six years. It is little wonder that his company, almost closed a decade ago, is now highly profitable and exports 60% of its products globally. In a public seminar he said: 'Our company adopted a sense of urgency—we put ourselves on a wartime footing—and this is the sense which now pervades the business.' Organisations which adopt such a sense of urgency about productivity and being globally competitive will survive; those which do not, will not.

Managing from the outside in

'The customers can have any colour as long as it's black,' Henry Ford is reputed to have said of his T-model Fords. He was, of course, operating in an environment of relative product scarcity. Customers had little choice between suppliers and limited information about competitive products but could enjoy the new benefits of mass production. Product engineers and suppliers were supreme and their organisations were predominantly mass production focused.

This 'black and white mass production mentality' has become redundant in developed economies because of:

- the globalisation of markets;
- information technologies which provide instantaneous information about products or services and their comparative features;
- customers demanding choice and diversity in products and services;
- more educated communities, willing to question suppliers and manufacturers about product quality, or to demand variations that customise and build unique features into the product; and
- more ethnically diverse societies with the attendant need to provide product/service diversity to meet cultural preferences (this is a particular challenge for the organisation operating globally).

The successful organisation is therefore one that is able to amplify faint signals from its external environment into its decision processes so that it is effectively managing from the outside in, rather than from the inside out.

We will cover two major aspects of managing from the outside in:

- creating superior customer value; and
- creating superior shareholder/stakeholder value.

Creating superior customer value

Creating consistently better value for customers requires the discipline of systematically obtaining relevant external information from them and acting on this information to stimulate necessary change in the organisation. Strategists Gary Hamel and C. K. Prahalad push the boundaries further, however, by insisting that a real customer orientation is to have foresight—about customers'/consumers' future needs, and being first in the market to meet those emerging needs.[38] They maintain that customers often do not even know what they need, so merely conducting and acting on customer feedback analyses will lead to underperformance.

The organisation that survives and thrives will combine its knowledge of industry trends, technologies, emerging consumer trends and developments in competitive intelligence well enough to challenge internal thinking about the needs of the customer of the future. The organisation then positions itself to look ahead in creating new markets, products and services of which customers have not even dreamed.

At a less futuristic and practical level, the symbols of a customer orientation within organisations are many: customer-value chain analyses, service excellence programs, focus groups, customer surveys, and even talkback radio for disaffected customers. Sometimes the business aims of customer focused programs have not been well articulated or connected to the overall effectiveness of the organisation. There are legendary stories such as the hire car booking attendant who, using his initiative, chased a customer, who had just hired a vehicle, for over 50 km because the customer had left his briefcase at the counter. Temporary relief staff had to be assigned to cover the absence of the service officer. The firm was noted for legendary customer service, but at what cost? It is seldom noted that a year later the car hire firm went into liquidation through intractable cash flow problems. Is there an intersection between Hilmer's value and cost productivity, where one cancels out the other? We should quickly point out that good customer service is not always, or even usually, a cost additive factor but we offer a caution about emotionally appealing programs of customer service excellence which do not contribute to overall organisational performance. We also question the validity of 'new' customer interface services via ubiquitous call centres which hold out the importance of 'your call is important to us', but then keep the customer on the line for 15–20 minutes, furious to the point of exasperation. Call centres will have to radically lift their game if they are to convince customers that their purpose is about value productivity rather than merely another thinly veiled cost-cutting mechanism.

There is also confusion about who the customer is. There are two possibilities:

- customers who transact money for services or products provided to them (usually *external customers*); or
- internal intermediaries within the organisation who play a servicing role in providing the final product or service, but who are removed from the direct line of production or sales (sometimes referred to as *internal customers*).

Only the first of these categories is the real customer who provides the *raison d'être* for the firm. The notion of an internal customer 'value-chain' often leads to confused arguments to sustain internal organisational activities which do not add real value and, in fact, may detract from the long-term success of the firm. For example, an internal training department of 300 people in a large international bank was convinced that it was playing an important role in the value-chain for the bank; it was subsequently reduced to approximately thirty people and later to ten people without any detrimental effect on the bank. The critical issue for internal service providers is not how they use the language of customer service to justify their existence, but whether they have knowledge and data about how they add value to the organisation's key outputs, and how they benchmark their performance against best-in-class service providers for other organisations.

If customer service is primarily about external focus, key measures of progress and success are important. For example, Swissair relies on a random survey of disembarking passengers who are asked eight short questions about the journey they have had. Four responses on each of the eight questions are possible: poor, fair, good or excellent. If more than 4% of surveyed passengers say the flight was poor or fair as opposed to good or excellent, the airline explores all aspects of the flight to locate the problem. Another organisation uses a number of indices to gauge factors leading to customer satisfaction:

- phone calls answered within ten seconds—measured by a meter on staff phones;
- customer letters answered within two days—measured by an audit; and
- overall customer satisfaction above 90%—measured by an annual customer survey.

Does such an external customer focus make a difference? An important study of 500 firms in the United States was conducted to identify which of the firms, as measured by the perception of their customers, were regarded as high, medium or low service providers. Once the firms had been grouped into these three categories, a further analysis was undertaken to look at pricing strategies, market share and profitability. The results were that the high service-providing firms, relative to the low service-providing firms, charged 9% more, gained market share at 8% per annum more, and had an overall greater return on sales of 11% per annum.[39]

Clearly the firms perceived as high service providers by their customers are at an advantage in pricing, market growth and profitability. Service and product quality does pay. It is an imperative for organisational survival into the twenty-first century. With most advanced economies now surging, the danger is that the customer focus which has been so pivotal to the turnaround of enterprises and economies will recede. Hence our comment about the increasingly impersonal approach of call centres.

Creating superior shareholder/stakeholder value

The second major aspect of managing from the outside in is the capacity to consistently create superior shareholder/stakeholder value. In the private sector no company has been left untouched by the revolution in financial markets—the demand by investors worldwide for high levels of financial return for their investment, either in the form of capital growth of stocks, or healthy dividend returns. Executive teams who are unable to create such financial value are usually quickly removed from the company, or the company itself falls prey to predators. In the public sector, political and community stakeholders are equally, if not more, demanding, often leading to high rates of executive turnover if stakeholder requirements are not anticipated or met.

Economic Value-Added (EVA) is possibly one of the key techniques used by private sector companies for assessing the extent to which shareholder value, or real wealth, is being created or destroyed. EVA is an estimate of true economic profit after subtracting the cost of capital. EVA analysis techniques effectively capture and integrate all the ways that managers and employees can contribute to shareholder value: operating efficiency, growth and innovation, balance sheet management, business portfolio restructuring and financial allocations. Like customer analysis techniques, EVA is not a panacea. Rather it provides mental discipline to ensure that internal thinking is oriented towards those variables which will make the firm a net wealth generator, satisfying stakeholder requirements for their investment.

Deconstruction, or a renaissance?

It was tempting in the late 1980s and early 1990s—years of great pain for many Western industrial economies—to view that period of business volatility as a normal, if painful, dip in the business cycle. While, by the late 1990s, more buoyant economic conditions had returned, and high unemployment had decreased in most Western economies, high levels of volatility for individual businesses and organisations remained. The new volatility revolved more around surviving or thriving in a fast-moving era of globalisation and information technologies. The new discontinuities have led to enterprises deconstructing and reinventing their assumptions, strategies and business models, while individuals have had to invest in and reinvent their careers and expectations. Globally we now see that enterprises, countries and individuals that have not been able to make such a shift are struggling: witness Japan during most of the decade of the 1990s, and many old style industrial enterprises still operating in an old economy, first curve framework.

In the switch of the advanced countries from industrial to knowledge based economies, we are involved in a period of fundamental sea change, not just a dip in the normal business cycle. In a recession, organisations and economies are reshaped; in a renaissance, societies are reshaped. We are in the latter period. Organisations which stretch beyond their old boundaries and reconfigure will have a chance of surviving and adding value to society. Those which do not, will not. If handled well, deconstruction can lead to renaissance.

References

1. International Strategic Management Society Conferences, London, 14–18 October 1992, and Berlin, 16–18 October 1999.
2. The term 'breakpoints' was coined by management writer Paul Strebel in *Breakpoints: How Managers Exploit Radical Change*, Harvard Business School Press, Boston, 1992.
3. P. Drucker, *Managing in Turbulent Times*, Pan Books, London, 1991, pp. 219–24.
4. L. Bryan, J. Fraser, J. Oppenheim & W. Rall, *Race for the World: Strategies to Build a Great Global Firm*, Harvard Business School Press, Boston, 1999, p. 3.
5. D. Stace, *Reaching Out from Down Under: Building Competence for Global Markets*, McGraw-Hill, Sydney, 1997.
6. M. Leontiades, Rutgers University, 'Scenarios for the nineties', Paper delivered at Panel Session at the Strategic Management Society Conference, Stockholm, October 1990.
7. *The Economist*, Editorial, 27 November 1999, p. 13.
8. P. Schavoir, 'More market-driven through internal bridging—The IBM case', Paper to the Strategic Management Society Conference, September 1990, pp. 1–10.
9. T. Friedman, *The Lexus and the Olive Tree*, HarperCollins, London, 2000.
10. N. Shoebridge, 'Speed and agility let Dell give customers exactly what they want', *Business Review Weekly*, 16 November 1998, p. 193.

11. Adapted from B. A. Vedin, *Tumbling Walls of Technology*, Institute for Management of Innovation and Technology, Metamatic, Sweden, 1990, p. 10.

12. A. Toffler, *Powershift: Knowledge, Wealth and Violence at the Edge of the 21st Century*, Bantam Books, New York, 1990, pp. 90ff.

13. ibid., pp. 150–1.

14. S. Connor, 'The genome is published', The World in 2000, *The Economist* Publications, London, 2000, p. 128.

15. *The Economist*, 'All mod cons', 27 September 1997, pp. 45–6.

16. P. Ruthven, IBIS Business Information Services, 'Myths that hold us back', *Business Review Weekly*, 18 December 1992, pp. 18–21.

17. J. Edwards, *The New Australian Economy*, HSBC Publications, Sydney, 1999, p. 28.

18. ibid., p. 3.

19. T. A. Stewart, 'Welcome the revolution', *Fortune*, 13 December 1993, p. 8, quoting a 1958 *Harvard Business Review* article by H. J. Leavitt & T. L. Whisler, 'Management in the 1980s'.

20. L. Thurow, 'The third industrial revolution', *The Australian Financial Review*, Review Section, 2 July 1999, pp. 1–2.

21. W. Bridges, *Jobshift—How to Prosper in a Workplace Without Jobs*, Allen & Unwin, Sydney, 1995, pp. viii–ix.

22. D. Macken, 'A question of identity', *The Australian Financial Review*, 9 January 2000, p. 25.

23. C. Handy, *The Age of Unreason*, Harvard Business School Press, Boston, 1990.

24. H. Mackay, *Turning Point: Australians Choosing Their Future*, Macmillan, Sydney, 1999, p. 111.

25. 'Class in Wales: One of the boyos', *The Economist*, 24 October 1992, p. 38.

26. D. Stace, op. cit., p. xiii.

27. M. Porter, 'The competitive advantage of nations', *Harvard Business Review*, March–April 1990, p. 73.

28. *The World Competitiveness Report: Executive Summary*, World Economic Forum/IMD, Lausanne, 1999.

29. McKinsey & Company, *The Challenge of Leadership: Australia's High Value-Added Manufacturing Exporters*, Report prepared for the Australian Manufacturing Council, December 1991, p. 2.

30. D. Stace, op. cit., p. 18.

31. D. Dunphy & D. Stace, *Under New Management: Australian Organisations in Transition*, McGraw-Hill, Sydney, 1990.

32. G. van Wyngen, 'The return of the Asian miracle', *The Australian Financial Review*, 19 July 1999, p. 16.

33. J. Edwards, op. cit., p. 34.

34. P. Drucker, 'The new productivity challenge', *Harvard Business Review*, November/December 1991, p. 69.

35. Access Economics, *Developing Australia's National Competitiveness*, Report prepared for the Business Summit on 'Our Competitive Future', Business Council of Australia, Melbourne, 1991, Executive Summary, p. ix, and Appendix 1, pp. 95–106.

36. F. Hilmer, 'Coming to grips with competitiveness and productivity', *Economic Planning Advisory Council Paper 91/01*, February 1991, pp. ii–iii.

37. ibid., p. ii.

38. G. Hamel & C. K. Prahalad, *Competing for the Future*, Harvard Business School Press, Boston, 1994, p. 277.

39. T. J. Peters quoting a Strategic Planning Institute PIMS study in the video *A World Turned Upside Down*, 1987.

Chapter 3

Choosing the strategy and structures

I n 1803, the British deployed a military detachment to stand on the Cliffs of Dover to watch for Napoleon. It was not until 1927 that the detachment was disbanded, long after the original rationale for the strategy had disappeared. Strategy is the search for directions which energise the life of an organisation; structures provide the social organisation needed to facilitate the strategy. Strategic positioning and restructuring cannot be once-a-century, once-a-decade or even a periodic phenomenon, for both involve a constant process of alignment with, and influencing of, the external business environment. Strategy and structure need to be constantly re-examined and realigned to be effective.

Strategy: Creating the change agenda

Major changes in corporate strategy will often require structural change so that the new strategy can be effectively implemented. However, making changes to strategy or structure as if they were independent variables will generate a confused approach to organisational change. Noted author C. K. Prahalad[1] talks of three simultaneous agendas which need to be enacted by leaders and managers on a continuous and simultaneous basis. The first of these he calls the *intellectual agenda*: the vision, 'strategic intent' and business strategy positioning of an organisation. The intellectual agenda stretches the limits of thinking about the value the organisation is able to add for stakeholders, customers and the society as a whole. The second is the *management agenda*: this is concerned with building appropriate structures and networks, introducing appropriate technologies and systems, and having the courage to shift resources between competing needs. The third is the *behavioural agenda*: this focuses on creating corporate values and ethics, developing appropriate leadership styles, learning systems, competencies and skills, reinforcement and rewards for appropriate employee behaviours.

In managing change, it is important for leaders and managers to operate on all three agendas, rather than only one or two. Many remain fixated on the management agenda in particular: their preferred means of change is to 'have another restructure' or to reallocate resources once again on the premise that 'any change is good change'. This is limited thinking, for important as these elements of change are, they only constitute a small part of the leader's job. Leading change involves more than simply pursuing the management agenda: it involves constant attention to the intellectual and behavioural agendas as well. This chapter focuses primarily on the intellectual agenda; we discuss what it is and how it is formed. But we then also examine the implications of strategic change for the structuring of organisations. Later chapters explore more fully both the management and behavioural agendas.

Change must be linked to and driven by an organisation's strategy, otherwise it becomes change for change's sake. We show such a pattern of linked relationships in our model in Figure 3.1. Here the 'content' (where and in what direction to lead the organisation) and the 'process' (how to get there) are connected and interact; they are not treated as independent variables. This is important in change programs. All too frequently we see change interventions and people management practices introduced into organisations with little connection to what executive management is doing in the area of vision and strategy—that is, with the intellectual agenda and positioning of the organisation. It is not surprising therefore that so many strategic plans and visions fail, and equally why so many

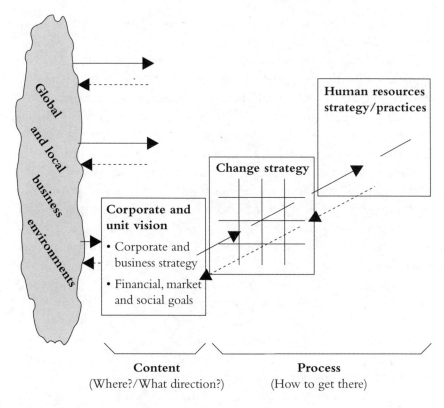

Figure 3.1 Integrating vision, change and human resource strategies

change programs fail. There must be a clear conceptual connection between 'content' (the intellectual agenda) and 'process' (how the strategy is enacted through the management and behavioural agendas). We have previously written of some generic patterns or linkages,[2] but in this book we deal in a more directly practical way with the concepts and techniques in integrating vision, change and people management strategies.

Strategy, not just planning

There is a popular misconception that planning equates with strategy: executives often assume that a strategy will somehow materialise if they engage their corporate planners or outside strategy advisers, put together a well researched, well documented strategic plan, and then communicate it across the organisation. This we call 'strategy by edict'. While useful in selective turnaround situations, it will not engender strong internal support if used as an ongoing process. Alternatively, the top team may spend time away at a strategy conference and produce an appealing statement about directions. These can be useful exercises, but if the end object is only a planning document and a 'once or twice only' communication about new directions, we can safely say that the organisation will not have a credible strategy over the longer term. Strategy has to 'go live' in, and become an instinctive reference point for, the entire workforce.

Strategy is therefore not a planning document: rather it is a purposeful process of engaging people inside and outside the organisation in scoping out new paths ahead. Gratton makes this point very effectively in her recent book, *Living Strategy: Putting People at the Heart of Corporate Purpose.*[3] The aim is to engender the intellectual, emotional and behavioural commitment of all stakeholders to a challenging new view of the future, and stretch the limits of the organisation's ability and resources to achieve success. Strong leadership of the process is essential, as strategising or 'strategic conversation' is not about finding consensus, it is about energising and crystallising the best ideas, based on sound analysis, which will challenge and motivate the organisation. Strategy may be partially captured in a series of documents—the vision, the strategic intent and the business plan—but the documents are not the strategy. The strategy is that set of embedded understandings that daily guide the directions and behaviour of the organisation. Further than that, effective strategy is about the leaders' ability to shape the business environment and to create 'space' for the corporation. Ailing organisations have no 'space'; they are always in reactive mode. Successful organisations, in contrast, are out in front of events—they create 'space'.

Strategy usually involves planning, but not always. We have previously noted that Paul Strebel talks about breakpoints, or radical changes in business conditions such as market gyrations, rapidly changing technologies, changing community and customer attitudes and shifting political frontiers.[4] Strebel says that such breakpoints may be handled in one of three ways: by anticipating the breakpoints, by exploiting the breakpoints or by creating breakpoints. Active anticipation of breakpoints so that the organisation can respond is the minimum response possible if the organisation is to remain viable. It is achieved by actively scanning the business environment and then developing strategic responses and business plans which create stretch for the organisation as a whole. This is the minimal level of strategic readiness.

However, adept organisations go beyond anticipation by exploiting breakpoints, leapfrogging on external events and, in an opportunistic way, seizing new opportunities. This demands an entrepreneurial approach, with the caveat that the opportunism is exercised within a broad vision and overall strategy for the organisation. Exploiting breakpoints is often an intuitive process.

Finally, an organisation can itself generate breakpoints by creating the competitive discontinuities which define the playing field for others. This was the type of potentially high-risk strategy played by Lend Lease Corporation when, as a project management organisation, it made a dramatic move into the financial services industry through its acquisition of MLC in the 1980s, a move which changed the playing field for the rest of the funds management and project management industries by creating a new form of integration between major projects and their funding. The creation of breakpoints is one of Lend Lease's regular business practices. Global companies such as Dell Computers, Microsoft, 3M, Charles Schwab and General Electric have all created their success by defining the playing field in ways that have reshaped their industries.

While these three types of strategy formulation in fact constitute strategy, only the first resembles 'normal' strategic planning. In discussing strategy we are therefore not only talking about astute strategic planning and scenario building, but also about calculated risk taking, and certainly about exercising strong strategic leadership. At the very least, strategy is about achieving 'fit'—that is, anticipating the emerging environment and adjusting corporate action accordingly. However, by going beyond mere adjustment to the environment through exploiting and creating breakpoints, effective leaders provide 'maximum sustainable strategic stretch' for their organisations.

In Table 3.1, we illustrate that strategy changes in its levels of specificity from corporate to business strategy levels. We also introduce the new term 'insta' strategy to encompass the emerging phenomenon of rapid-fire strategic positioning and adjustments as the 'new' and 'old' economies interact together. While the logical sequence is for the process to be sequential between the corporate and business strategy levels, increasingly in a fast-moving environment the processes are iterative: what happens on a virtual basis, at insta strategy level, can have a powerful influence on the overall strategic architecture of the enterprise. The classical economic model of industry analysis, followed by competitive business positioning, advocated by writers such as Michael Porter,[5] provided a useful framework for many executives and leaders in the decades of the 1980s and 1990s as they unscrambled companies which had lost their core focus, had became involved in unwieldy, unrelated

Table 3.1 Types and levels of strategy

Types of strategy	Level and major characteristics
Corporate strategy	
Longer term directions of the total enterprise Which industries? Which businesses? What geographical reach, or countries of operation? Longer term corporate objectives	Agreed to, or endorsed by, boards and owners (The broad 'strategic architecture' of the enterprise)
Business strategy	
How will we play the game? (e.g. low cost producer, differentiation or hybrid competitive models?) What business model? (e.g. outsourcing, alliances) Customer strategy (e.g. the customer value proposition; customer service strategy) Specific business goals for profit and other tangible outcomes	Developed by executives/business unit managers/key internal players (The tactical competitive approaches used to satisfy the growth objectives of the enterprise)
'Insta strategy'	
Nimble adjustments and opportunistic moves within a broad strategic framework Agility, and an intuitive feel for the business landscape	At all levels in the enterprise (The difference between thriving and merely surviving)

diversified businesses or had little concept of the key competitive forces in their industry. However, in the twenty-first century it is clear that industry boundaries themselves are under challenge. The phenomenon of 'convergence', dealt with in the last chapter, creates a challenging canvas on which to sketch a strategic future for rafts of enterprises: many events, such as rapid technological developments or the actions of aggressive competitors, are creating opportunities or discontinuities at the insta strategy level which, over the longer term, will have major influences on their corporate directions. In strategy, the relationship between corporate 'architecture' and business tactics is now stronger than it has ever been. Over recent years this has prompted a new stream of literature stressing the need to reinvent the 'industry boundaries' of the enterprise and to create the future.[6] Our view is that sustainable strategy demands a two-way approach— one more analytical and structured, the other more intuitive and creative. Neither top-down nor bottom-up approaches will be sufficient on their own. The important point is that strategy is about insight, energy and calculated risk taking rather than about documentation per se.

A framework for strategy

So strategy goes beyond planning but this does not preclude disciplined, analytical strategic thinking. Our research case studies in over thirty organisations, and our consulting experience in scores of others, have revealed a variety of processes used by various organisations to energise their strategic thinking. To espouse one best way would be inappropriate, but the generics can be distilled. Figure 3.2 provides such an overview. Here we see that strategy does not start with vision, mission and capability, with positioning in relation to one's competitors, or with profit ratios. It starts with an analysis of the future, based on scanning the strong, weaker or almost imperceptible signals in the environment. Visioning and environmental scanning are therefore closely intertwined and interactive activities which allow executives and managers to make the mental shifts required for anticipating, exploiting or creating emerging business breakpoints.

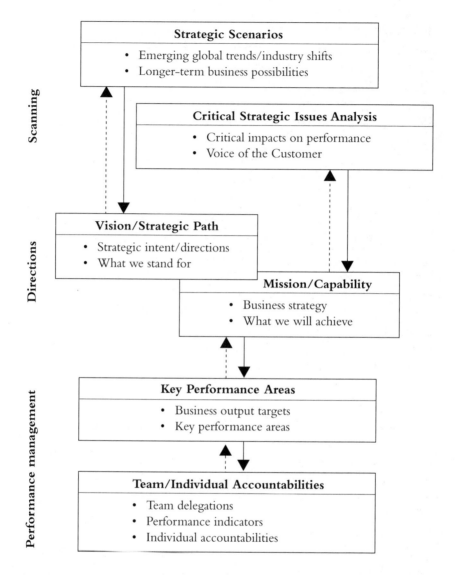

Figure 3.2 Strategy development framework © STACE MANAGEMENT NETWORKS

Figure 3.2 also illustrates that <u>performance targets must flow from the vision and mission,</u> otherwise they become comfortable tactical targets relatively unconnected with the 'strategic stretch', or overall ambition for the organisation. Alternatively, they can become unrealistic bottom-up targets which exceed the capacity of the organisation to provide resources for them. Performance management systems must therefore be integrated with, and responsive to, the vision, strategic imperatives and change dynamics of the organisation.

In the following sections, we will examine in turn each of the major elements and components of the strategy development framework—specifically:

- scanning the environment;
- vision and 'Strategic Intent' (corporate strategy);
- mission and organisational capability (business strategy); and
- performance management.

Scanning the environment

Environmental scanning is as much about a way of thinking as it is about systematic processes. It is the capacity to manage from the outside in, and involves a healthy splicing of intuition and numerical analysis. Until the late 1920s Henry Ford achieved heady business success based on a formula of standardisation and process efficiencies; however, his business was almost swamped by General Motors in subsequent years: General Motors had sensed that customers wanted choice, and proceeded to offer customisation of design and colour in competition with the black T-model Ford. Leaders of organisations who do not regularly revise their assumptions, on occasion radically so, are unlikely in today's business environment to perceive the warning signs of environmental change. There are several key components of environmental scanning, as we will see in the following three sections.

Strategic Scenarios Analysis (medium to longer term)

Faced with the possibility of widely gyrating oil markets in the 1970s, the global petrochemical firm, the Royal Dutch Shell Group, moved away from extrapolation of the future from the past, using single-line graph projections. Shell found that it needed more sensitivity in its analyses of future business conditions. Out of this arose the sophisticated approach to analysing future business conditions and internal capabilities known as **Strategic Scenarios Analysis**.[7] This methodology is used by Shell and countless organisations worldwide. In the United States, the greater proportion of Fortune 500 industrial companies use scenario planning.[8]

In Strategic Scenarios Analysis, the organisation engages in a broadly based process of strategic analysis to create alternative, internally consistent and reasoned 'stories' of how the organisation's environment or an issue may develop over time. The time period is longer term (5–15 years) or even longer. The analysis usually covers possible future scenarios in areas such as:

- industry structure;
- clients/consumers/markets;
- technologies;
- products/services;
- workforce/structural issues;
- stakeholders/shareholders;
- resources; and
- competitors.

In its simplest form, both a 'least change' and a 'high change' scenario are then developed for each of the areas chosen. This methodology provides a structured process of intra-organisational dialogue, forcing people to think beyond the business plan, beyond current resource constraints, to challenge their own mental maps and to create a new set of strategic parameters for the organisation. More sophisticated approaches are available, many of them described in an extensive literature on Strategic Scenarios Analysis. In Australia 'Scenarios for Australian Business to the Year 2015',[9] commissioned by the Australian Business Foundation in 1999, is a good example of the use of the scenarios technique. In this exercise four major scenarios were developed as discussion frames for the future of Australian business: these frames were entitled 'First Global Nation', 'Sound the Retreat', 'Brave Old World' and 'Green is Gold'. Detailed scenarios were developed under each of these broad themes. Ericsson Australia has also conducted a similar exercise involving over 200 of its managers: the aim was to search for the new engines of company growth, while challenging the mental maps of leaders and managers in the company. Author Peter Schwartz says: 'Scenarios are not about predicting *the* future, rather they are about perceiving futures in the present...the end result is not an accurate picture of tomorrow, but better decisions today about the future.'[10] Strong leadership of such processes is essential, otherwise the dialogue becomes merely discussion, and an opportunity to act on valuable views to explore and reshape strategic directions is lost.

Critical Strategic Issues (CSI) Analysis

It is also essential to develop an understanding of the potential external or internal issues which could critically impact on business performance. While Strategic Scenarios Analysis focuses on the longer term (typically 5–15 years ahead), a method known as Critical Strategic Issues (CSI) Analysis is often used for assessing shorter term (12–24 months) issues. Developed by Igor Ansoff, a leading strategy and planning writer, CSI provides a structured method of analysing issues which have the potential to affect the performance of the business. They may be issues that are negative or positive, inside or outside the organisation or business unit, and be current or future. They are usually issues which will potentially impact on the organisation's ability to meet its objectives in the next 12 to 24 months.

Critical strategic issues are therefore performance related issues and, because the time frame is usually shorter, they represent the stronger signals in contrast to the weaker or barely perceptible signals analysed in the longer term Strategic Scenarios Analysis method.

Detailed descriptions of the concept of CSI, and the method, are described elsewhere,[11] but the method can be briefly summarised as follows:

1. Each member of an executive team (or a business unit team) identifies four to five issues falling within the definition above.
2. These issues are pooled, forming an initial list of twenty or so issues.
3. This initial list is then reviewed for any obvious overlaps, and the group then accepts the discipline of reducing the list to six to eight issues considered overall to have the greatest potential to affect the business, positively or negatively, in the time period nominated.
4. Working from the reduced list of six to eight issues, the group then makes two assessments on each issue:

- What is the potential impact of this issue on business performance (low, significant or major)?
- What is the urgency that the issue be resolved (low, significant or pressing)?

The three factors on impact, and the three on urgency, can be represented as a three by three matrix. Each issue is then positioned on the matrix at the intersecting point once its assessed impact and urgency has been agreed upon. It is a powerful methodology in that it forces an assessment of issues on both the potential impact of those issues, and their urgency. Without this type of methodology, managers frequently expend inordinate amounts of attention on urgent issues, some of which may have little impact on the performance of the business. CSI Analysis provides a sharper focus on the critical issues than does the traditional SWOT (strengths, weaknesses, opportunities, threats) analysis used by some organisations. In CSI analyses, six to eight issues are the maximum; in SWOT analyses, groups typically end up with thirty to forty issues, too many to usefully provide a sharp focus on the core performance issues of the business.

While Critical Strategic Issues Analysis is one of the preferred means of scanning for shorter term business issues, there are others. Many enterprises have planning processes which involve a segment titled the 'Voice of the Business', in which the issues arising from shareholders, financial institutions, government, community and employees are examined. This process involves using a sequential method as follows:

1. listing all the critical issues relating to the business on self-adhesive notes (brainstorming);
2. grouping the issues on a whiteboard into similar categories (affinity diagram);
3. identifying primary causal factors for related issues (relationship diagram); and
4. organising the primary issues on the whiteboard into a diagram of cause and impact on the business (systemic diagram).

This is a process similar to that used in many Total Quality Management systems. Whatever the method, the important point is that perceptual judgments about the changing business (environment) are mixed with disciplined processes of analysis, involving leaders and their reporting team leaders at each level in the organisation.

Customer analysis—Voice of the Customer

An important element of these processes is the capacity to ground the analyses/intuition into an understanding of the customer—those who ultimately pay for products/services, or influence those who do. As organisational hierarchies have flattened, lines of communication have become less cluttered. In the leading organisations, there is effective two-way communication between executives and the workforce about strategy, and between product/ service areas and executives about changing customer needs and preferences. The key questions about customers are: What does the customer think? What does the customer need? What does the customer want? What is the customer likely to require in the future? Many organisations utilise systematic processes to ask these questions of customers and to collect and analyse the resulting data.

Exit surveys from aeroplanes, hotels and retail outlets are one means of such scanning, but the information is of limited value because it typically relates to past purchases or service interactions. What of the future? Qualitative research on social and market trends such as that offered by credible social researchers may also be helpful.

One of the most comprehensive approaches we observed in our research was the 'Voice of the Customer—Customer Needs Analysis' approach, used by a product manufacturer, which draws on a methodology first developed by Qualtec Inc. As part of the business-planning process every year, each of the manufacturer's plants undertakes a rigorous analysis of Direct Quality Requirements (what customers want) and Quality Elements (an assessment of plant capabilities). These analyses are constructed into two lists which are cross-referenced and related to each other on a matrix. This becomes a process of matching the strength of the relationship between what the customer requires against what the organisation can provide. Customer analysis of this kind, and customer satisfaction surveys, are a basic discipline for organisational success. However, on their own they are rarely enough, as customers themselves often do not have foresight or the ability to articulate their future needs. Akio Morita, Sony's visionary leader, is quoted as saying 'our plan is to lead the public with new products rather than ask them what kind of products they want. The public does not know what is possible, but we do…we refine our thinking on a product and its use and try to create a market for it by educating and communicating with the public'.[12] The point is that a basic level of 'satisficing' of customer needs is essential, as is an understanding of what they perceive their future requirements will be. The truly visionary organisation, however, will create the products and services required by customers and consumers of the future—before competitors do. The concept is equally applicable to public sector organisations, as the competition in the public sector is often competition for influence, rather than direct service/product competition. Effective public sector leaders understand that they need to be out in front of stakeholders without subverting them. What is required is analysis, insight and the ability to take calculated risks in a drive to create the enterprise of the future.

Vision and 'strategic intent' (corporate strategy)

When Louis Gerstner took over as IBM's Chairman and Chief Executive Officer in 1993 the company was still staggering from its failure in the early 1980s to grasp the strategic importance of software to the information technology industry. IBM in the 1980s, at over 400 000 employees worldwide, was still dominantly a mainframe company: it had allowed Microsoft to control PC software and Intel to supply microprocessors. IBM struggled into the 1990s under Chairman John Akers, trying to regain its dominance in the industry. Gerstner, an outside appointee from American Express and Nabisco, came to IBM without the legacy of 'mainframe' thinking. He faced a company losing US$8 billion in 1993, capping a three year loss of nearly US$16 billion. The early period of his leadership involved radical downsizing of 35 000 employees, in addition to 50 000 who had already left under Akers, removing board members and introducing a bottom–line imperative across the company. This was quickly followed by the articulation of IBM's new and compelling vision, 'Solutions for a Small Planet'.

The new vision was an essential element in creating an aspiration, in the middle of the painful process of turnaround. The intent was to move IBM to become a more nimble information services company, competing with the best of the Internet and 'new economy' companies. The vision, still a powerful force within the company over half a decade later, provided the strategic framework for the allocation of 50% of IBM's US$5 billion research and development budget in 1999 to Internet related projects, and to the establishment of IBM's outsourcing business, IBM Global Services. Without the vision, it would have been difficult to achieve a sustainable transformation of the company. By 1999 the company's share price had quadrupled and its profit turned around to US$6.3 billion per annum. An essential ingredient in this was the emphasis on creating rather than destroying hope, through a period of business difficulty.

In describing strategic vision, management writers Gary Hamel and C. K. Prahalad use the term *strategic intent*, virtually as a parallel of 'vision'. They make the valuable point that 'whereas the traditional view of strategy focuses on the degree of fit between existing resources and current opportunities, strategic intent (or vision) creates an extreme misfit between resources and ambitions'.[13] Vision and strategic intent involve taking the organisation far beyond its comfort zone, to create 'stretch' between current positioning and resources on the one hand, and future ambitions on the other. Or, in the words of other authors, 'successful companies do not just add value, they reinvent it'.[14]

The process of establishing the vision involves critical considerations of what businesses the firm should be in. Answers to questions such as 'Is the firm in banking, bank assurance or financial services intermediation?' can lead to a qualitatively different view of its future. In the info-communication industry, these choices revolve around whether the focus of the corporation is to be in a single business (for example, the Time publishing business), a set of businesses which have strong generic relationships (for example, Time-Warner information and communication systems), a converging industries business (for example, America On-Line merged with Time-Warner) or a set of businesses whose only common factor is their common ownership (for example, a holding company with investments in a range of generically unrelated businesses, such as Bond Corporation in the 1980s). The vision must be able to give a strong sense of what the areas of business focus are. Incorrect choices made in this area are potentially fatal for the enterprise. For example, many single-business firms not only 'stuck to their knitting', but in doing so stuck to yesterday's knitting (for example, railroads) or, alternatively, diversified to such an extent that they lost their way through lack of focus (for example, US tobacco companies which unsuccessfully diversified into trucking, vineyards and real estate).

A vision is an ambition about the future, articulated today; it is a process of managing the present from a stretching view of the future. If it is intellectually rigorous, and well conveyed, such a vision helps to create an impelling sense of urgency for achieving major change within the enterprise, quickly.

Other organisations have expressed equally compelling moves about their future. For well over a decade British Airways's vision of 'The World's Favourite Airline' provided a powerful slogan. The airline was transformed through the 1980s and early 1990s from a laggard in a globally deregulating airline industry to arguably a leader in global aviation, stripping out costs and arcane work practices. Simultaneously the airline underwent a revolution in its customer service practices, in the process establishing new industry standards for service innovation. During the 1990 Gulf War, with global airlines suffering severe downturns in passenger loads because of safety concerns, BA stunned the industry by offering all its seats, on all worldwide routes, free for one day. Inundated with calls, it not only filled its planes, but created a rich data bank of customers.

Similarly, General Electric's vision to be 'position number 1 or 2 in all businesses and markets' provided both a challenge, and an effective measure of achievement. Led by the legendary Jack Welch, GE has become one of the world's top two or three firms by market capitalisation. A key component of the turnaround from the ailing organisation of the early 1980s was Welch's use of an educative and strategic discourse process with thousands of managers, throughout the company, at GE's Leadership Centre at Crotonville. Known as 'Work Out' sessions, managers were given the chance to explore ideas about the changing business environment, learn management techniques and interact with Welch in small groups. The vision of

'Being position number 1 or 2 in all businesses and markets' provided the framework for lively dialogue about the company's future, and the part of GE's people in it.[15]

Success is not always guaranteed, however. BHP's 'Growth, Globalisation and Generational Change' (known as the three Gs) was developed to provide much needed focus for the company in the early 1990s. The company was still recovering from the damaging takeover battle with corporate entrepreneur, Robert Holmes à Court. All elements of the three Gs provided strong directions for BHP's future—to grow rather than stagnate, to expand into global operations, and to introduce a new generation of thinking into a company that had previously rested on its blue chip status. However, the requirement for 15% per annum growth in all businesses eventually led to ill advised, overpriced acquisitions, such as the US company, Magma Copper, and to 'growth' projects which fell far short of business objectives. A crisis of confidence by shareholders followed, leading to the early exit of Chief Executive John Prescott, and to traumatic times for the company through most of 1998 and 1999. It is a good example of how vision, and stretch goals, can lead to excess. We also suspect that the vision was more a slogan than a living intellectual framework in the company.

At the level of nations and jurisdictions, it is possible to create a strong ambition. Singapore is a good example: for over twenty years, its vision of becoming 'The Intelligent Island' has provided a challenging framework for its economic, educational, technological and social policy. In a similar way, in 1999 Australia's Northern Territory government created a detailed but motivational view of the future for the Northern Territory in the first decade of the twenty-first century in its 'Foundations for Our Future' strategic process. Public sector organisations in the Territory use the six

> *The visionary leader is a transformer, cutting through complex problems that leave other strategists stranded. Visionary leadership encourages innovation—fiction becomes experiment. Visionary leadership inspires the impossible—fiction becomes truth.*
>
> FRANCES WESTLEY AND HENRY MINTZBERG[16]

major platforms of the strategy to stretch their own thinking, and as a framework for their strategy.

Part of the essence of leadership is therefore a capacity to gather the weak and strong signals from the business environment, to tap into the ambitions people have for their organisation or, alternatively, to develop that ambition, and then to articulate a key message or set of understandings about the vision in a credible way. If written, the vision should apply uniquely to the particular organisation; it should be succinct and contain an appealing sense of challenge and urgency. The important element, however, is that the strategy and vision must 'go live'. Executives in organisations who perpetuate a state of myopia through lack of vision or an insufficiently stretching vision will not survive the renaissance sweeping our private and public sector corporations.

One caveat is necessary. Visioning is not about uninformed dreaming; it arises from strong, credible analyses derived from the environmental scanning processes of the organisation, together with the exercise of strong leadership, calculated risk taking and effective intuitive judgment. Some elements of the environmental-scanning processes we covered earlier will, over a period of years, affect the way in which the vision is enacted. On occasion, the strength of the emerging economic, social, technological and political trends may be such that they require a fundamental change in the vision itself. An illustration of this was the change in Westpac's vision of the early 1990s from being 'Australia's World Bank' to a more focused vision through the latter 1990s of being a highly profitable, regional bank.

Mission and organisational capability (business strategy)

The terms 'corporate strategy' and 'business strategy' are often confused, although in practice there is considerable overlap between corporate strategy (the where) and business strategy (the how). As shown earlier in Table 3.1, corporate strategy is about longer term directions, or the strategic intent of the enterprise, while business strategy is about providing a sharp competitive focus, or a mission and direction which is more specific. Typically some of the considerations in business strategy are:

- How do we compete on service, quality and price?
- What is our desired market positioning?
- What technologies and business models are required to meet our business imperatives?
- What strategies and tactics are our competitors adopting?
- How do we add value to customers, and to the business overall?
- Where are we placed in 'best practice' benchmark comparisons?
- What are the appropriate financial ratios by which we will measure success?
- How can we maximise the use of our resources?
- What competencies are needed to develop the business?

Answers to questions like these impel the organisation's operational strategies in areas like customer service, financial allocations, investment policy, information technology decisions, people management strategies and environmental practices. Decisions taken in these areas affect how the intended corporate strategy is enacted; the organisation's 'intentional strategy' does not become the 'realised strategy' if operational mission and capability are not aligned with the vision.

The vision represents the 'inspiration'; the mission represents the 'perspiration'. One vocational educational institution developed a vision statement which read: 'To make a measurable contribution toward a competitive and skilled Australia.' However, they also developed a mission statement titled 'Our Commitment and Core Values', which gave more extended definitions of how the vision would be achieved through:

- partnerships and networks (professional and resource links to the outside world);
- a team environment (the desired internal environment);
- relentless improvement (in productivity, technology, service delivery and financial viability); and
- creating a learning organisation (a capacity to upgrade competencies and service delivery, and to see change as a way of life).

The 'Commitment and Core Values' statement of approximately half a page was used as one means of communicating internally the business imperatives driving and supporting the vision. It is not essential to have a mission statement; it is essential, however, that managers provide intellectual leadership in helping staff to operationalise the emerging business strategies of the organisation.

The role of Strategic Benchmarking

In Chapter 2 we looked at the imperatives for organisational renaissance, two of which were the need for corporations to develop a 'global mindset' and the need for all corporations to manage the cost, value and innovation elements of productivity. There is a close relationship between the two, as productivity comparisons are now made on a global basis between nations and between corporations. An example of the former is the World Competitiveness Index created annually by the World Economic Forum/Institute of Management Development comparing the 'competitiveness' of nations, mentioned in Chapter 2. At the level of corporations, Benchmarking is one of the means of obtaining such comparative information to assist in establishing stretching performance goals. Benchmarking can therefore be used at a variety of levels, but for discussion, we break it into Strategic (policy) Benchmarking and Process Benchmarking.

Strategic Benchmarking involves making comparisons with external organisations on measures that have implications for organisation-wide performance. Examples of strategic benchmarks are key profit ratios, comparative productivity levels, percentage of funds spent on research and development, pricing policy and customer service satisfaction levels. These are key pieces of information which are integral to exercises such as the 'Voice of the Customer', Strategic Scenarios and Critical Strategic Issues analyses—that is, to critical phases in determining the organisation's strategy.

Process Benchmarking, on the other hand, relates to the comparison of operational efficiency in plants, offices or service facilities, in the use of technology, in work processes and in productivity comparisons with best practice competitors. Most organisations practising Benchmarking indicate that the ratio of Strategic Benchmarking to Process Benchmarking is approximately 1:9, indicating that while Strategic Benchmarking can help in clarifying the direction and focus of the firm's efforts, the major effort in performance improvement comes from process improvement. We will cover Process Benchmarking in greater detail in Chapter 7.

In the real world, Strategic and Process Benchmarking often merge. For example, Motorola and General Electric worldwide have comprehensive systems of Process Benchmarking which take place at all critical levels of the businesses—in work teams, business units and in the company overall. The aim is to reduce error rates, continuously improve the end product, and relentlessly strive for higher levels of customer satisfaction as key elements of improved company business performance. Motorola initially established a company goal of improving product quality 10 times over 5 years, 100 times 2 years later and of Six Sigma capability as the ultimate goal. Six Sigma is derived from mathematics, and is used to denote a maximum defect rate of 3.4 parts per million in each step of company processes. Six Sigma quality goals in Motorola and General Electric are in fact strategic benchmarks which impel their processes and operational goals.

As the era of industrial capitalism recedes, it is evident that the strategic benchmarks of organisations are changing. In the classical era of industrial capitalism, strategic benchmarks were nearly all expressed in financial or market terms: the typical measures were net profit, return on investment, return on earnings and market share. Organisations compared themselves and were driven by these or similar ratios. It was as though the unwritten law of each organisation was to become the biggest and the most profitable, quite often by immolating competitors. Today, we are witnessing a sea change. Why? Because shareholders are not the only organisational constituents of the firm: stakeholders, customers, network and alliance partners are just as important. We see evidence of this in the organisations that now have strategic benchmarks in key areas such as those shown in Table 3.2.

The new strategic benchmarks demand a refocus of organisational aspirations. The first curve organisation that worked to the older strategic benchmarks is often ill suited to work to the new second curve-type benchmarks. In the latter part of this chapter, we examine some of the implications of this for the structure of the emerging organisation. However, organisations that merely use Benchmarking to catch up will rarely be leaders in their fields. The organisations which create the future are those that leapfrog the performance of others—and define new standards and playing fields.

Table 3.2 The old and new strategic benchmarks

The old strategic benchmarks	The new strategic benchmarks
Profit	Total economic value created
Market share	Global market reach
Return on equity	Customer satisfaction
Production targets	Quality indicators
Capital investment ratios	Intellectual property, brand value
Company expansion	Sustainable growth

Performance management

In all cases, the higher to medium performing organisations in our research had developed systematic processes for assigning accountability at the corporate, unit and individual levels. The systems for performance management we reviewed divide into two types:

- *Goal-setting systems*—systems that allow managers and staff to negotiate and set business and behavioural goals based on strong professional judgments about how individuals and units can add value to the business. Some goal-setting systems such as this are linked only tenuously to the business plan.
- *Business performance-planning systems*—systems that involve structured participation by managers in developing the business plan, leading to the establishment of business unit goals, and cascading these down to personal goals relevant to the business plan.

The first of these, the goal-setting approach, is more effective in professional environments where much of the developmental and strategic thrust of the organisation comes from individuals within the professional units. In this case, strategy is more an emergent process, a bottom–up approach. The potential flaw is that the internal focus can often leave the organisation working at a comfortable level rather than at the level of 'maximum sustainable strategic stretch'.

The second, the business performance-planning approach, is more of a top-down process, with allowance for two-way influence. Our research shows that this form of performance management is more dominant in volatile business environments, allowing executives to progressively adjust the strategic focus of the organisation. This is then followed by a process of internally aligning the internal goal-setting processes with the strategic changes in the organisation.

Performance management systems per se will not deliver effective strategic implementation, but the best of such systems provide a systematic process of analysis and communication among team members about how the vision and mission can be translated into sequences of action to which individuals can commit and for which they are accountable.

The essence of strategy

The approaches outlined above provide a guide rather than a rule book. In fact, while systematic approaches to strategy are mandatory in the majority of organisations, creativity and intuition are key parts of successfully positioning the enterprise. It is the combination of these systematic and intuitive processes that leads to strategic agility. Overall, we would summarise the following characteristics of effective strategy. To be effective, strategy must:

- have intellectual rigour;
- create a gap between ambition and currently available resources;
- create strong emotional appeal;
- be memorable and communicable; and
- create a sense of urgency.

Strategy provides the driving force for change.

Recreating organisational structures

Traditional structures: Machine bureaucracies and divisional structures

Changing strategies usually has considerable implications for structures. The command and control pyramidal model, the once familiar corporate hierarchy with ten or more levels, served first curve-style organisations well in the unproblematic economic era of industrial expansion. The pyramidal model has now crumbled in all but the most traditional of organisations. It had two main forms: first, the machine bureaucracy, a specialised departmental structure with work narrowly divided into functional specialist areas; and second, the divisional structure in which there was separation of 'policy' in corporate headquarters from operations carried out in field/area divisions. Both had advantages and vulnerabilities, as illustrated in Figure 3.3.

Both of these models were variants of each other in that typically the divisional structure was enacted in larger organisations which

Traditional structures	Features	Vulnerabilities
Machine bureaucracies 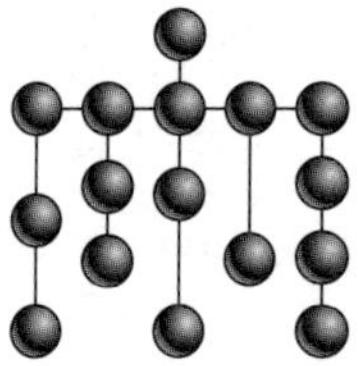 • Mechanistic structure • Specialised departments	• Efficiency • Control, stability • Work specialisation • Executive decision making	• Low adaptability and minimal innovation • Difficulty of cross co-ordination between specialist areas • Difficulty of identifying accountabilities and performance outputs
Divisional structures 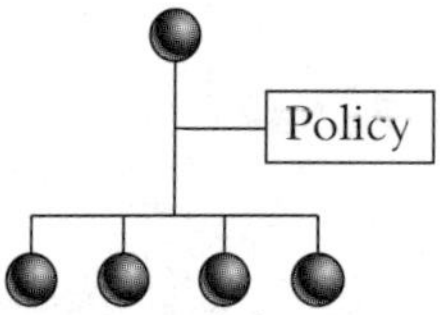 operational divisions • Separation of policy from operations • Product/area decentralisation	• Separation of strategy and operating divisions • Clear accountabilities for line divisions • Managerial decision making • Corporate policy setting	• Conflict over long-term versus short-term goals • Corporate headquarters far removed from customer and customer trends

Figure 3.3 Traditional organisational structures

had a broad geographical spread, or where different divisions concentrated on specific products. However, the division in many cases built up its own hierarchy, often replicating the previous corporate hierarchy. The problem then became one of sorting out the new complexity created by the overlaying corporate and operational hierarchies. In the post-World War II era of industrial growth, this was not a major problem as organisational resources were usually available to create new executive, managerial and supervisory positions to co-ordinate and control the lengthening hierarchies. Spans of control became narrower—in many instances one person supervising only several others, or even one.

In one large traditional organisation included in our research, the formal reporting relationships read like a military organisation: chief executive, chief general managers, general managers, chief managers, manager (levels 1, 2 and 3), middle managers, supervisors, team leaders, senior staff, junior staff and customers. In fact, this was never an organisational structure: it was really a career structure which passed for an organisational structure.

The real structure worked on much less hierarchical and informal lines; it had to for the organisation to survive. In all organisations, except monopolies, the decades of the 1980s and 1990s witnessed this formal structure being radically reshaped, a process involving the elimination of many executive, managerial and supervisory positions.

These forms of organisation could not survive into the twenty-first century, for several reasons:

- Tall functional hierarchies had too narrow and specialist a focus, and were unable to grapple with the complex, myriad influences facing corporations; in such organisations people thought compartmentally rather than seeing the whole, and protection of one's hierarchical position often became more important than adding value.
- Radical global business shifts demanded rapid responses which tall hierarchies were unable to provide. Speed of response is vital to surviving and thriving in a hyper-competitive world.
- Lengthy communication chains became dysfunctional in transmitting strategic shifts to staff, or transmitting information

upwards about customer attitudes and responses to the organisation's executive about products and services. Key messages and
feedback from the initiators, top or bottom, only effectively
reached the first or second levels.

• The functional hierarchy and the divisional structure became, in
time, career structures rather than effective organisational
structures. People became more concerned about their career
progression than about getting the job done.

Newer structures

Newer structural forms have emerged. As organisations focus on
their core business, develop new channels of distribution, change
their business models, or search for growth in global markets, the
emphasis has been on identifying and implementing new forms of
structure to deliver their new strategies. In addition, the basis of
competition changed dramatically in the latter 1990s, progressing
from the cost driven era associated with radical downsizings and
rationalisation towards the new arena of competition—innovation.
The key factors in innovation are market knowledge, speed of
response, flexibility, product/service innovation, technology adoption, and the development of highly skilled, committed employees
or partners. These strategies require more flexible structures. This
does not imply that innovation replaces cost competitiveness: the
challenge is to manage cost and innovation concurrently. Hence
structures often tend to be in a state of flux, as expressed in the term
'chaordic enterprise' quoted in Chapter 2. On the one hand, cost
reduction strategies will require strong accountabilities at line levels,
and a minimum of corporate overheads, while innovation will
require partnerships, alliances and consortia arrangements. We will
discuss several of these new structural forms, under the headings of
'Structures for cost reduction' and 'Structures for innovation'.

Structures for cost reduction

The main structure we discuss here is the Strategic Business Unit
(SBU). Wishing to empower their executives and managers to run
their part of the corporation as an accountable profitable business
centre, many organisations have stripped out multiple levels of the

corporate hierarchy, delegated financial, personnel and operating decisions to SBU executives, and created a climate in which local decision making is expected and encouraged. In its most extreme form this structuring allows the corporation to become almost a holding company, providing strategic directions for the corporation overall, but enacting its real success at the plant or service office level.

SBUs became almost a dominant approach in the late 1980s and early 1990s—the era of corporate turnarounds. Recent examples, however, include the radical centralisation of strategy, and the equally radical decentralisation of operational authorities in BHP, CSR and AMP, all of which have been recently involved in corporate turn-arounds. Organisations such as Pacific Dunlop have used such a structure for well over a decade, although with mixed results. In their case corporate headquarters comprises a small headquarters staff of 30 for a 30 000 employee organisation: corporate headquarters decides overall group strategy, acts as group treasurer and provides investor relations programs. Pacific Dunlop's product divisions have maximum freedom (and accountability) to develop their business and to create profits.

In BT Funds Management, investment managers are empowered to make their own decisions on all matters after strategy has been corporately determined. However, the approach to implementing strategy can vary: in one of BT's SBUs change is implemented using a very consultative approach with staff; in another, a very tough, directive stance is used. Both approaches are successful in yielding strong investment performance.

This type of structuring usually works best where the SBUs cover dissimilar service areas, or are separated geographically. The structure, in its pure form, works least well where there are critical interdependencies between divisions, such as in banks or airlines where the whole organisation must work towards a common set of strategic imperatives and, in the case of airlines, must meet a critical operational schedule on scores of tarmacs each day, demanding full integration of a wide range of organisational capabilities.

The SBU structure has been extremely effective for many organisations. However, too much empowerment of individual SBUs has sometimes led to disasters, such as in some of the major banks where corporate-lending departments were set up as profit account-able SBUs. The feeling of empowerment was obviously very motivating, but the 'drift' by SBUs from the emerging new strategic imperatives of the financial services industry often led to their failure. Overall, the great strength of the SBU structure is the emphasis on accountability for results, and on stripping away layers of corporate bureaucracy which do not add value to the bottom line or to the overall product and service delivery of the corporation. Some of the characteristics of the SBU are summarised in Figure 3.4.

Newer structures	Features	Vulnerabilities
Strategic business units • Fully accountable profit units within a larger corporate structure	• Full delegation and autonomy to operational units • Performance oriented, competitive • Focus on bottom line	• SBU 'drift' from corporate thrust • Loss of cross-corporate synergies • Managerial career blockages
Strategic networks • Alliance partnerships • Joint ventures • Product/market development links • Technology sharing • Financing consortia	• Ability to draw on and leverage up strategic intelligence • Maximises cross-corporate synergies: development is co-operative rather than combative • Resource efficient if high development costs are shared	• Firm may lose its 'intellectual' technology to competitors • Strategic networks can be transient, and volatile

Figure 3.4 Newer organisational structural forms—corporate level

One variant of the SBU is the franchise, such as Colonial State Bank's franchised bank branches. In this case, the corporate organisation takes responsibility for orchestrating the critical interdependencies and systems, while local operations are run by business lessees, the franchisees.

Structures for innovation

In this section, we deal with structures at three levels: strategic networks, resource networks and internal horizontal networks or work teams.

Strategic networks

Four hundred years ago a trading colossus, which was an early model of some of the more innovative structures appearing today, was founded. In 1599, four ships of the Far Lands Company returned to the Netherlands loaded with riches from the fabled Spice Islands, the Meluccas. To develop and regulate the subsequent trade, six Regional Chambers of Commerce came together in 1602 to form the Dutch East India Company, known by its Dutch initials V.O.C. This powerful alliance lasted 200 years, aided by its collective strength, its access to the best charts and ships, and a willingness to think beyond traditional boundaries of ownership.

Several simultaneous trends are now leading to a new surge of collaborative structural forms, such as strategic alliances, joint ventures, financing, technology sharing and product/market development consortia arrangements:

- Globalisation has opened up huge new market opportunities, and few potential players have the size, resources and local knowledge to attempt the slower path of organic expansion. Alliances are a way to build critical mass and market power, quickly.
- The rapid rise of new industries is reconfiguring markets constantly, demanding new blends of complementary strategic advantages. Alliances are a way to develop a broader range of corporate capabilities.
- The speed of change means that it is risky to rely on internal research and development alone or, alternatively, pay the large

costs of acquiring firms with promising new technology, products or services. Alliances and networks can enhance innovation and increase speed of response and so energise market opportunities.

▼

To fully exploit the opportunities open to it, a company today must have an ability to conceive, shape, and sustain a wide variety of strategic alliances.[17]

The goals of such alliances often involve working with potential competitors rather than competing head on; to seek complementary strengths, by combining the unique resources of different organisations, and enhancing corporate learning through the exchange of ideas and systems. From the start, it is important to identify:

- how a new alliance will enhance, rather than decrease, performance;
- whether the primary purpose is to reduce costs, or foster innovation; and
- the potential benefits for all partners.

Some of the most notable alliances have been formed in the airline industry. Commencing over a decade ago with the joint sharing of global reservations systems, Sabre and Armadeus, these alliances are now multifaceted, underlining the point that contemporary alliances are often multiple rather than simply bilateral. For example, the 'The One World' alliance encompassing Qantas, British Airways, American Airlines, Canadian Airlines, Cathay Pacific and Iberian Airlines provides a primary level of collaboration between airlines, potentially offering a seamless customer loyalty program across the globe. However, at a secondary level, each airline itself has a complementary range of alliances with car rental companies, credit card partners, travel services and accommodation chains. Other examples of strategic networks and alliances are the relationship formed between competitors, IBM and Apple, and the vast array of alliances between Microsoft and smaller potential competitors. In the latter case Microsoft has in effect externalised much of its innovative capability, while Microsoft itself defines the global standards, in much the same way as JVC did in the battle to establish the VHS video standard over the Beta format in the 1980s. The most innovative companies are not always the best resourced, but they have a long term view which is compelling enough to attract alliance and network partners. The features and vulnerabilities of strategic networks and alliances are shown in Figure 3.4.

Resource networks

A complementary form of structure to both strategic networks and the SBU is the resource network, where the organisation (or SBU) focuses on its core activities, is resourced primarily for those core activities, and subcontracts other resources and capability as required. This form of structure has arisen as organisations have reduced layers of management and have replaced them with a co-operative network of external relationships to achieve better product/service outcomes, and a greater rate of innovation at radically reduced costs. Examples of this are: the subcontracting of most supply functions (for example, component manufacture), service functions (for example, payroll, computer services), or distribution functions (for example, sales franchises) to outside organisations. Management writer Raymond Miles says that many new corporations will resemble a 'switchboard'—a small communications centre managing a network of relationships.[18]

The resource network is focused on efficiency, is results oriented and seeks extra leverage into products or markets by virtue of a cross-flow of ideas, resources and capabilities from network partners. Rosabeth Moss Kanter[19] says that this type of organisation:

- minimises ongoing overheads and maximises options. It helps keep fixed costs low by using variable or contingent means to achieve resourcing goals;
- provides leverage through influence and dedicated resources. It derives power from access to, and involvement with, the network organisations rather than control or total ownership of them; and
- encourages 'churn'—or constant improvement. It keeps things moving, and relies on turnover of people and ideas.

Resource networks may still fail despite this compelling logic. Research by Raymond Miles and Charles Snow[20] has shown that there are several common causes of failure in networks:

93

- Customers, suppliers, subcontractors and distributors may rapidly become part of a stable network with the core firm. In itself, this may not become a problem, but it can lead to staleness.
- The key elements of the network may become too dependent on the core firm, become too customised in their approach to meet the core firm's needs, become overspecialised—and so lose the advantage of working at the innovative edge for several, equally demanding core firms.
- Larger organisations which try to convert themselves into 'internal networks', providing services to their operating divisions and to outside organisations, find that the politics of internal pricing and marketing becomes dysfunctional. They then move either to an external network arrangement by radically downsizing the business, or revert to an older hierarchical form. IBM worldwide faced this challenge, as it moved to an external network of alliances, franchises and supply relationships in place of a system of internal 'producers'. This left IBM's core business intact, but created a very flexible periphery. As a result, the company was able to eliminate tens of thousands of jobs which were once considered to be core.

The creation of both strategic networks and resource networks is underpinned by two very powerful and interrelated phenomena: first, the desire by many employees to take more control of their work and careers; and second, the capacity provided by information and communication technology to structure a firm differently.[21] In economically developed, industrialised societies, most highly educated employees want emancipation from rigid organisational controls and, in fact, more highly educated professionals have the capacity, desire and confidence to work on a more independent basis. This is the social manifestation of the organisational renaissance. The second phenomenon, that of technological innovation, makes such emancipation possible. The pyramidal hierarchy provided a form of control, career structure and a physical set of communication channels, but the latter function has now been overtaken by fibre optics, silicon chips and computer generated memories. For example, three London firms of stockbrokers now network with a Dunedin based computer-processing firm. All of their computer processing is done overnight in Dunedin and transmitted via satellite more cost effectively than if it were done in London. The physical location of work is no longer important for many projects of this kind.

In manufacturing, the phenomenon is the same. For example, over the past twenty years the automobile industry has been radically reshaped. Previously huge car makers with highly integrated design, component-manufacturing, production and marketing functions in each country have been reshaped in one of two ways.

In the first case they have become a series of much smaller core firms, networking with myriad smaller networks to design and deliver component supplies. Previously, where components were purchased, this was done on a system of competitive bidding where the lowest tenderer received the contract. But changing suppliers based on cost competition led to problems of quality assurance. The new system seeks to build a series of more stable supplier networks, providing components to the core firm using the Just-In-Time system. Christian Berggren, a Swedish researcher, identified the lack of continuity in such networks in the automotive industry as one of its greatest challenges. He argued that the automotive industry needs to replace the pattern of shifting buyer–supplier relationships with a more stable, globally co-ordinated, complete supply chain to reduce costs and improve quality in the industry.[22]

In the second case, a system of external network partners co-exists with the creation of an internal sourcing network within the global firm itself. Ford is an example where the major elements of car manufacture—design, engines, transmission systems—are allocated to 'global centres of excellence', selected country operations in Ford's global network which have demonstrated superior competence in particular areas, and which then deploy this capability globally. The completed product is then assembled in a variety of country operations across the globe.

The network firm is not just another supplier; it becomes part of the enterprise with the core firm, but is not entirely dependent on the core firm. In manufacturing enterprises like Tubemakers, key educational programs are focused inwards towards core staff, but also include special educational programs every six months for suppliers, subcontractors and other network organisations to share the vision of what Tubemakers is trying to achieve. In service enterprises such as Lend Lease, constant relationship building with subcontractors and service networks is part of the firm's working ethos.

At every level of organisation—transnational, national firm and Strategic Business Unit—the network is one of the most common forms of structuring.

Newer structures	Features	Vulnerabilities
Resource networks • Relationship contracting • Project/venture structures with outside organisations	• Flexibility in use of best available resources, inside or outside • Cost-effective control over outputs • Network suppliers, distributors more responsive/relevant than comparable internal resources	• Network resources are potentially transient • Capacity must be negotiated with outsiders, and contractually committed • Network can become too stable and non-innovative
Horizontal work teams goal A goal B goal C • Semiautonomous work teams • Parallel task forces • Project teams working across functional boundaries	• Work is organised around changing key goals rather than historical functions • Teams complete whole tasks rather than fragments of tasks • Greater work satisfaction	• May lead to confused accountabilities • Costly, if overlaid on a functional structure • 'Teaminess' may cloud a real output orientation

Figure 3.5 Newer organisational structure forms—divisional and team levels

Horizontal work teams

Where the network organisation focuses on external interdependencies, the horizontal organisation focuses on how the core organisation works internally in structuring workflows. It seeks to provide a cross-functional emphasis in which work is primarily structured around a small number of business processes or workflows which cut across functional or even network boundaries. It is similar to a parallel structure, in which staff members may 'belong' to a unit, but the actual work they do is organised on a project basis, often involving staff from several units working in cross-disciplinary teams. Horizontal work teams, however, comprise only cross-disciplinary 'project' teams organised around key performance objectives, such as 'Design, build and commission Project X', 'Reduce cycle time' or 'Increase percentage sales for $ expenditure'. The assumption here is that work is intrinsically a team activity rather than an individual or specialist activity. While this is true in some manufacturing and process oriented service environments, it may not be true of highly professional work such as specialist advisory services or, for example, in some branches of medicine. To this extent, horizontal work team structures do not have universal applicability.

Frank Ostroff and Douglas Smith[23] have sketched out the following principles of structuring horizontally:

- Organise around process, not task, by linking workflows and relying on teams rather than elevating individual contributions.
- As hierarchy arises from the division of labour, flatten hierarchy and minimise the tendency to subdivide workflows into narrow functions.
- Assign ownership of processes and process performance to teams, not individuals.
- Link performance objectives and evaluation of work processed directly to measures of customer satisfaction.
- Combine managerial and non-managerial activities to encourage self-management rather than positional authority. The team leader should be a value-added specialist, rather than a distant generalist.
- Treat multiple competencies and multiskilling as the norm, as it encourages flexibility.

- Maximise supplier and customer contact with the team.
- Reward individual skill development, but also reward team performance.

Few organisations have introduced this type of structure in its pure form, but variants of it are seen in semi-autonomous work teams in which the normal command-and-control routine is disbanded in favour of virtual self-management within the work team. The galvanising force is the set of key performance objectives the team sets itself. In the State Library of NSW, cataloguing is performed in this way, with work functions shared and rotated, and jobs broadened. National Mutual, MLC, NRMA, Colonial and the Australian Tax Office are all reported to use small work teams which have the skills and authority to handle every aspect of a client's business, rather than different pieces of the client's work being undertaken in different functional areas of the organisation.[24] Technology, and the availability of critical information, has been pivotal in this type of work autonomy.

When a customer telephones with an enquiry, a unit member can access the client's details on a computer screen and can usually answer a question by talking to another member of the group. At Colonial, the groups no longer use 'customer response forms' which were designed to elicit answers from remote departments within twenty-four hours. They simply deal with the issues directly themselves.[25]

A similar variation on the concept is the use of parallel task force teams often seen in conjunction with Total Quality Management programs. While the organisation is still organised by functions such as production, marketing, personnel and finance, much of the implementation of the organisation's new strategies is achieved through special 6 month, 12 month or longer term task teams drawn from across the functions. These teams have specific briefs, such as to improve product quality as measured by rejects/returns by x% per annum, or to reduce operating costs by 25% in year 1 and then by 6% per annum compounding.

This type of internal 'horizontal' structuring of work has become more common with the increasing pervasiveness of information— both the information held by customers, and information which cuts across functional boundaries within the organisation. Functional areas can no longer treat specialist information as exclusively theirs to protect; hence the breakdown of much of the fabric of the older hierarchy into self-managing teams, autonomous work groups, task teams and project groups. The gains are greater flexibility, the potential for better customer responsiveness, greater staff involvement, and satisfaction.

The potential weakness is unclear work/reporting accountabilities, which may become a serious impediment in difficult economic environments when bottom-line considerations are paramount, particularly if adequate control systems are not built in to track actual performance. We provide more extended discussion of this and other forms of flexible work organisation in Chapter 6.

The 'Prudent Mechanistics' have staying power

Figures 3.4 and 3.5 summarised the major forms of the new organisational structures. Most readers would recognise these or variants of these structures in their own organisations. However, despite the logic behind these newer structures, there is some evidence from our research of the re-emergence of a variant of the older mechanistic, machine bureaucracy in some organisations. These newer mechanistic organisations we term the Prudent Mechanistics— organisations that are primarily structured into functional specialist departments or divisions, and are very tightly controlled by the central executive. These organisations are prudently, even conservatively, managed, and successful. They show little of the flamboyance of many firms which have experimented with newer corporate structures, yet they are still innovative in product and service development.

We summarised the features of the older mechanistic structure in Figure 3.3; its newer form contains fewer overall levels of hierarchy, and is more accommodating of cross-divisional co-operation than its predecessor. In earlier research two such organisations were the NRMA (one of Australia's most successful motorists' and insurance organisations) and the Commonwealth Bank. At the time of our earlier research, the NRMA was extremely successful, but very stolid, quite unlike many seemingly more venturesome banks and insurance companies. However, while the NRMA's macrostructure was organised functionally, internally there was an overlay of task teams as part of the NRMA's Total Quality Management approach—almost an internal horizontal organisation. The Commonwealth Bank, at the time of our earlier research a decade ago, was not rated highly as a performer by independent industry analysts, and certainly had not adopted many of the more aggressive strategies and the more organic structures of its competitors. Yet the continuing shakeout and rationalisation in the financial services industry demonstrated that this more traditionally structured and managed organisation not only survived, but by the latter 1990s had become one of the highest performers in the financial services industry.

This provides an important caveat to much of the thrust of new management thinking. In a changing business environment, it is easy to conclude that the only organisations that will succeed will be those that make changes which mirror the leading-edge experimentation of so-called exemplary organisations. Change can become change for change's sake, an organisational fashion show, rather than a well thought through set of strategies customised to the needs of the organisation. There are dangers associated with such an uncritical approach to change.

Making intelligent choices

The message is clear. While there are broad trends in organisational structuring, strategy and management methods, all of which we describe in this book, they are only trends. Our view is that the most successful Australian organisations practise 'eclecticism'—a pragmatic approach to finding their own solutions in strategy and structure. They do not slavishly follow one model or trend. The Japanese 'model' of the 1980s and the US model of the 1990s were only adopted in full and uncritically by less successful organisations. No one managerial system is universally appropriate, notwithstanding the current fascination with the so-called US business model. We would also add that no one organisational structure is universally appropriate, despite the success of, and fascination with, Strategic Business Units, networks, alliances and horizontal work teams.

Some of the best moves may at times be countercyclical, going against the trend. In our next chapter we describe how different organisations have approached the task of change in quite different ways, some against the prevailing wisdom of the time, but with substantial success.

References

1. C. K. Prahalad speaking at a Harvard Change Colloquium 'Breaking the Code of Change', Boston, August 1998.
2. See D. Stace & D. Dunphy, 'Beyond traditional paternalistic and developmental approaches to organisational change and human resource strategy', *International Journal of Human Resource Management*, 2, 3, 1991, pp. 263–83; and D. Stace & D. Dunphy, 'Translating business strategies into action: Managing strategic change', *Journal of Strategic Change*, 1, 4, 1992, pp. 203–16.
3. L. Gratton, *Living Strategy: Putting People at the Heart of Corporate Purpose*, Prentice-Hall, London, 2000.
4. P. Strebel, *Breakpoints: How Managers Exploit Radical Change*, Harvard Business School Press, Boston, 1992.
5. M. Porter, *Competitive Strategy: Techniques for Analysing Industries and Competitors*, Free Press, New York, 1980.
6. G. Hamel & C. K. Prahalad, *Competing for the Future*, Harvard Business School Press, Boston, 1994.
7. K. van der Heijden, *Scenarios: The Art of Strategic Conversation*, Wiley, Chichester, 1996.
8. P. Shoemaker, 'Multiple scenario development: Its conceptual and behavioural foundation', *Strategic Management Journal*, 14, 1993, pp. 193–213.
9. Commissioned Report, 'Alternative Futures Scenarios for Australian Business to the Year 2015', Australian Business Foundation, North Sydney, 1999.
10. P. Schwartz, *The Art of the Long View*, Doubleday, New York, 1991, p. 38.
11. I. Ansoff, 'Strategic issue management', *Strategic Management Journal*, 1, 1980, pp. 131–48.
12. G. Hamel & C. K. Prahalad, 'Seeing the future first', *Fortune*, 5 September, 1994, p. 76.
13. G. Hamel & C. K. Prahalad, 'Strategic intent', *Harvard Business Review*, 67, 3, 1989, pp. 63–76; and 'Strategy as stretch and leverage', *Harvard Business Review*, 71, 2, 1993, pp. 75–85.
14. R. Normann & R. Ramirez, 'From value chain to value constellation: Designing interactive strategy', *Harvard Business Review*, July–August, 1993, pp. 65–77.
15. N. Tichy, *Control Your Destiny or Someone Else Will*, Stratford Sherman Press, New York, 1999.

16. F. Westley & H. Mintzberg, 'Visionary leadership and strategic management', *Strategic Management Journal*, Vol. 10, 1989, p. 31.

17. Y. Doz & G. Hamel, *Alliance Advantage*, Harvard Business School Press, Boston, Mass., 1998.

18. Raymond Miles quoted by R. Moss Kanter, *When Giants Learn to Dance*, Simon & Schuster, New York, 1989, p. 351.

19. R. Moss Kanter, op. cit.

20. R. Miles & C. Snow, 'Causes of failure in network organisations', *California Management Review*, 34, 4, 1992, pp. 53–72.

21. D. Limerick & B. Cunnington provide extensive discussion of networks and strategic alliances in their book *Managing the New Organisation: A Blueprint for Networks and Strategic Alliances*, Business and Professional Publishing, Brisbane, 1992.

22. C. Berggren, 'Changing buyer–supplier relations in the Australian automotive industry: Innovative partnerships or intensified control', *Working Paper 025*, Centre for Corporate Change, Australian Graduate School of Management, Sydney, 1992.

23. F. Ostroff & D. Smith, 'Redesigning the corporation: The horizontal organisation', *The McKinsey Quarterly*, 1, 1992, pp. 148–68.

24. P. Roberts, 'Service companies go Japanese', *Australian Financial Review*, 3 June 1992, p. 32, quoting John Mathews, *Colonial Mutual Life Australia: Service Quality Through Self Managing Teamwork*, Industrial Research Centre, University of New South Wales, Sydney, 1992.

25. ibid., p. 32.

Chapter 4

Translating business strategy into action:

Transitions, Transformations and Turnarounds

Qantas: A decade of renewal

The appointment of James Strong as CEO of Qantas in October 1993 signalled the beginning of what has been a process of continuous transformative change. Qantas had had a long history and a distinguished record of corporate achievement. Prior to 1993 it was essentially an arm of the Australian government, the country's flag carrier first, and a business second. As such, it was an Australian icon, but had all the characteristics of a traditional government organisation, including tall hierarchy, deliberative decision making and high-cost structures. Employee loyalty was high, employees had secure jobs and excellent conditions, and often spent their whole careers in the organisation.

However, Qantas was living in a fast receding era. From the early 1980s, the global airline industry was being deregulated and privatised. In Australia it was not until the period 1991 to 1993 that the domestic airline market was deregulated and the Australian government abandoned its two airline policy. Australian Airlines was sold to Qantas in late 1992, and in 1993 British Airways purchased 25% of Qantas. It was subsequently announced that Qantas was to be fully privatised.

Qantas was initially slow in responding to the accelerating deregulation of the industry, while the globalisation of business was bringing more airline travellers, but also more competition. Before 1993 many attempts were made to reduce costs and restructure the airline, but these were not sufficient to inspire the government with confidence that the airline would be cost competitive against large global competitors into the future.

In 1993, the government appointed a new board chaired by ex-Brambles CEO, Gary Pemberton. In May 1993 Qantas and Australian Airlines were merged, and in October 1993 the board appointed James Strong to carry out the far-reaching changes thought necessary. The charter was to create a privatised airline with the financial viability to attract shareholders, and an ability to grow shareholder capital.

James Strong had previously been CEO of Australian Airlines (formerly TAA) and had had remarkable success in transforming that airline into the leading domestic airline, effectively taking the major share of the business traveller's market from Ansett.[1] James Strong's appointment as CEO of Qantas signalled the advent of a tough new approach designed to transform the airline. He began by replacing all but one of the senior executives reporting to him. He replaced them with new appointees whom he believed had the commitment and capabilities to undertake the changes he thought were necessary for the airline to compete in a period of intense global competition. Maintaining financial viability during this period was essential.

The changes subsequently initiated a time of turmoil in the organisation, exacerbated by the problem of integrating the culture of Qantas and Australian Airlines—the 'red tail' and the 'blue tail' ways of working. Major structural changes were initiated, and significant cost cutting took place as management adopted a directive 'crisis management' leadership style.

When the most significant cost cutting was behind them, the senior team, including James Strong, modified their leadership style, moving to encourage more participation by employees in decision making and to emphasise cultural rather than structural change. The pace of radical change slowed in 1995 as the changes were absorbed and consolidated.

But in 1996, the government announced the full privatisation and floating of Qantas on the sharemarket. This necessitated further cost cutting to reassure the market that the airline would operate profitably and make returns to shareholders. In August 1997, Qantas was able to announce a record $253 million profit—a major Turnaround from a position of mediocre financial performance.

With the float concluded, the senior executive group again turned its attention to cultural change, with an emphasis on customer service. A range of new initiatives were launched, including: Total Quality Management, Benchmarking, Re-engineering of Work Processes, leadership training, the introduction of organisation-wide service standards (Service 2000), face-to-face focus meetings with major customers, and the introduction of a competitive tendering process in the baggage-handling and customer service areas. In addition, Qantas and BA continued to add new airlines to their 'The One World' Alliance, potentially providing greater global reach. This comprehensive change program involved a set of 'bundled interventions', rather than attempting to achieve change with a single intervention such as TQM or Re-engineering.

This process of change was widely interpreted by the financial markets, customers and employees as successful in the period of 1993–99. The share price more than doubled and Qantas was able to wrest further market share away from its major domestic rival, Ansett. It was also travelling well against international competitors.

Leadership, however, will always be under challenge. By 2000 the Qantas business environment had again changed dramatically. International competitor Virgin Airlines had announced its entry into the Australian market; a previously struggling Ansett had been sold to Air New Zealand, backed by the financially strong Singapore Airlines; and Qantas itself was defending the quality of its brand caused by several aircraft 'incidents'. By mid-2000 its share price had fallen by 40% from its twelve-month high, and its core value of safety was being tested. New approaches to leadership became necessary in order to create stakeholder confidence, internally and externally, during this period.

What the Qantas story does highlight is the necessity of using different change leadership approaches in different business periods.

Situational strategies for change

During the past decade, the research we have undertaken to determine how corporate Transformations can be successfully managed has shown that there is no single path to successful change implementation that holds in all situations. However, we have found that we can define a small number of viable routes to success, each of which works in particular circumstances.

The central models of organisational change arising from our research are shown in Figures 4.1 and 4.2. Figure 4.1 is our original conceptual model of change, showing four levels for the scale or intensity of change, and four levels for the style of change management (that is, the way in which an organisation's executive leadership or dominant elite leads the process of change).[2]

Figure 4.2 shows the areas of the change matrix 'utilised' by the twenty sample organisations for their change strategies, based on our research of them. This was based on ratings by executives, middle managers and team leaders whom we interviewed. They rated their organisations at two time periods.[3]

Our research results show that, even in higher performing organisations, more differentiated successful change strategies exist in practice than are often portrayed in the management literature. Overall, the predominant approach to corporate change identified was not that of participative evolution or even the charismatic transformation so widely advocated by management theorists; we found that medium to high performance can be maintained by leading the corporation using either a consultative or a directive management style. As to scale or intensity of change, maintaining a minimal level of change (which we refer to as 'fine tuning') appears overall to be a non-viable change strategy. Such minimal change is unable to deliver enough adjustment for the organisation to sustain high performance in a rapidly changing business environment.

The findings also suggest that the near universal advocacy of participative forms of leadership may have the effect of leaving executives confused and ill equipped to handle the demands of leadership in a difficult business environment. However, we do not

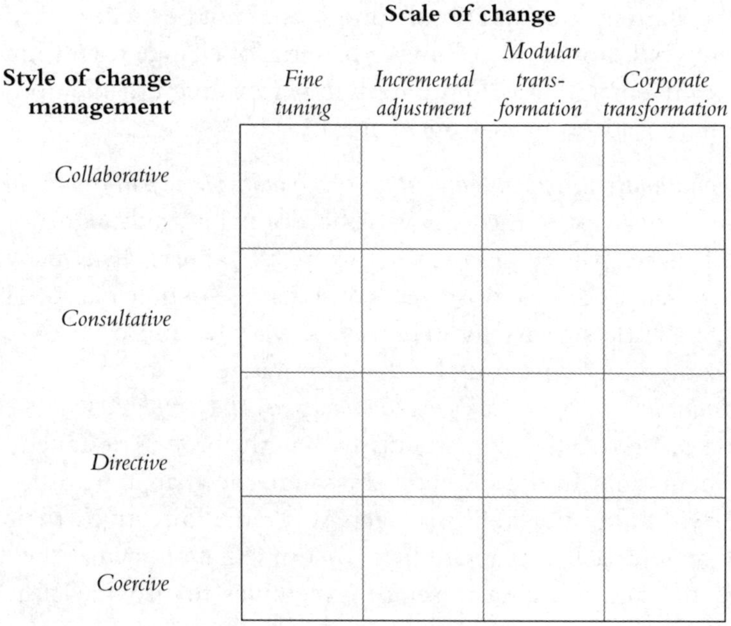

Scale of change

Style of change management	Fine tuning	Incremental adjustment	Modular trans- formation	Corporate transformation
Collaborative				
Consultative				
Directive				
Coercive				

Figure 4.1 The Dunphy–Stace change matrix

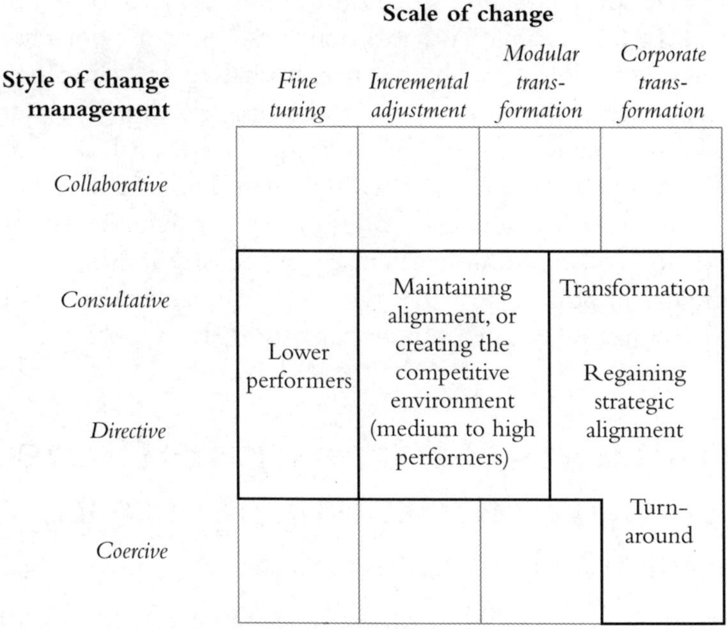

Scale of change

Style of change management	Fine tuning	Incremental adjustment	Modular trans- formation	Corporate trans- formation
Collaborative				
Consultative	Lower performers	Maintaining alignment, or creating the competitive environment (medium to high performers)		Transformation
Directive				Regaining strategic alignment
Coercive				Turn- around

Figure 4.2 Dominant patterns of corporate change

suggest that participation or consultation should not be used. In fact, our research has shown the following patterns of change leadership most typically emerge in medium to high performing organisations at two different levels in the organisation:

- *A predominantly directive change style at corporate level, particularly in times of business volatility* This was the dominant, although not the exclusive, pattern. However, where the approach used by the corporate executive was rated 'consultative', middle managers and team leaders generally expressed a wish for more decisive and strong direction setting by the corporate executive.
- *A consultative change style between managers and employees at the business unit level* This was particularly so in the process of strategy implementation. In the several cases where the change management style of business unit managers was rated 'directive', their directive approach was an attempt to compensate for what they saw as the failure of more senior executives to provide clear leadership.

This suggests that attempts by many change agents to develop a uniform style of leadership throughout an organisation are misdirected. In fact, it appears that the successful organisations use a blend of styles, alternating between consultative and directive, and vice versa. Executives may need to be strongly directive, but the message has to be translated by managers and team leaders to their staff in a much more consultative manner. This also does not exclude coercion by executives in cases of major realignment, nor does it exclude collaboration, particularly at the unit level.

The important point is that the style of change, and the scale of change used, must be attuned situationally to organisational needs.

Transitions, Transformations or Turnarounds: Which approach to corporate change?

In Figure 4.3 we develop the model further, overlaying on Figure 4.2 major categories of change observed in our research. The four categories of change successfully used by organisations are shown in Figure 4.3 as:

- Developmental Transitions (constant change);
- Task-focused Transitions (constant change);
- Charismatic Transformations (inspirational change); and
- Turnarounds (frame-breaking change).

A fifth category, Taylorism, is also shown on the model. Our research has consistently shown that, unless the organisation operates in a monopoly structure, lower performance tends to be associated with fine tuning and paternalistic approaches to change management. Similarly, overuse of Turnaround strategies (frame-breaking change) for periods longer than two to three years can lead to lower performance; in this case, management fails to regain control of a

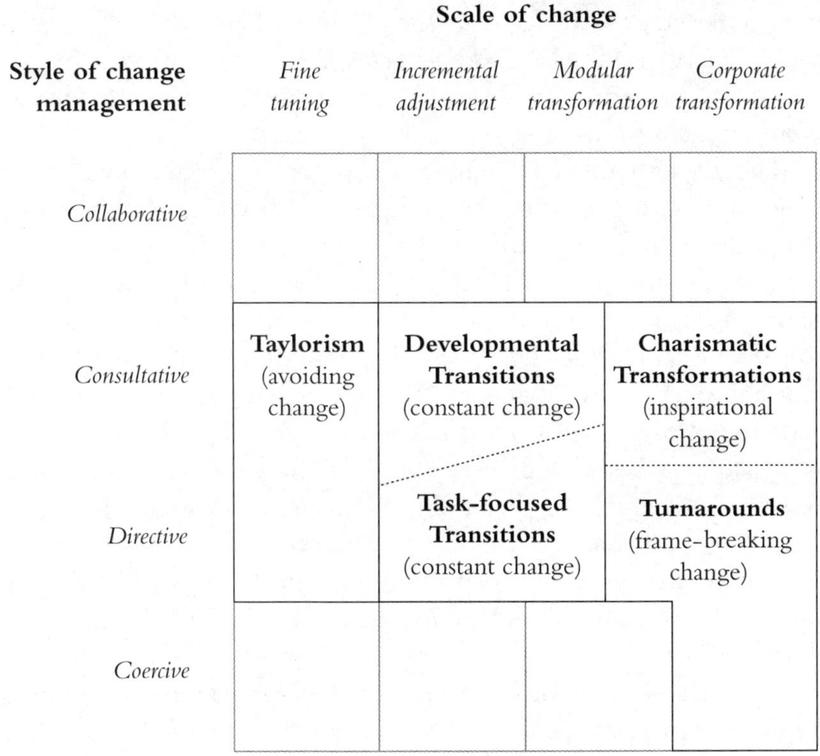

Scale of change

Style of change management	Fine tuning	Incremental adjustment	Modular transformation	Corporate transformation
Collaborative				
Consultative	Taylorism (avoiding change)	Developmental Transitions (constant change)	Charismatic Transformations (inspirational change)	
Directive		Task-focused Transitions (constant change)	Turnarounds (frame-breaking change)	
Coercive				

Figure 4.3 Which approach to corporate change? © DOUG STACE AND DEXTER DUNPHY

shattered, demoralised culture. We do not propose to make any further analysis of the Taylorism category of change here.[4]

We will take up an analysis of the four approaches to corporate change where organisations are either maintaining their alignment with their business environment, or are actively in the process of regaining alignment. We provide an overview of the characteristics of each of these approaches and then illustrate their application by reference to Australian corporations identified from our research as being case examples of each approach.

Developmental Transitions

The Developmental Transitions approach to corporate change represents constant change. Organisations use this approach when they are able to maintain their strategic alignment with the environment, or actively create the playing field to which the rest of the industry must adapt. Regeneration can be achieved over a sustained period through the constancy of change; the pot of change is simply kept simmering.

The Developmental Transitions approach is often evident in collegial-type organisations or in organisations which feature strong team development and corporate culture-building activities. Corporate-wide Total Quality Management, service quality and team-building programs are often a feature of this type of organisational change. Leadership is primarily consultative in style. The approach is often evident in the service industries rather than in production organisations, but not exclusively so.

Macquarie Bank is an excellent example of a highly successful organisation which has been able to maintain strategic alignment using this approach; the Bank has maintained a constant incremental adjustment process (not fine tuning) for almost two decades despite operating in a rapidly changing environment. One executive described it this way: 'We never stay still, but we don't change in quantum leaps—our corporate culture would preclude that; running a business on partnership concepts means that policy decisions are not too dramatic, they evolve.' From a 200 person organisation in 1978, Macquarie now has 4000 staff globally. Fast and successful evolution indeed.

As the greater size and complexity at Macquarie created increased complexities of co-ordination, the obvious answer was to create additional structures, systems and controls, but this was foreign to the collegial values of the Bank, which is staffed mainly by highly qualified professionals. The answer chosen was to produce a 'goals and values' statement, an articulation of deeply held values about cultural and business behaviour, including how the process of change should be managed. The values statement is essentially a set of values and norms—that is, internalised controls that substitute for external control systems. Despite its size, Macquarie's values still provide a strong corporate 'glue', although more emphasis on structures and systems is now evident.

In a dynamic business environment, how has the Bank been able to maintain an incremental strategy and achieve such outstanding performance? Its success appears to have been mainly a function initially of its size relative to other banks, but more recently of a culture of constant innovation combined with a loosely coupled flexible organisation. Its short communication chains, modular structure and collegial workforce culture have led to considerable flexibility in responding to changing market demands. These are strengths that many larger organisations seek to emulate through the formation of decentralised Strategic Business Units.

Task-focused Transitions

In this approach to organisational change, the process of strategy formation is strongly driven from the top, while business unit leaders are given considerable autonomy in strategy implementation and in operational matters. In the business units themselves, the approach to change management is likely to be more consultative than at the top. There is a strong financial bottom-line orientation associated with this approach to change; 'let the managers manage, but hold them accountable for results' is how it could be characterised.

The positive feature of this type of change is its potential for making rapid changes in the strategic direction of the enterprise. The potential downside is that the translation between corporate intent and the implementation of corporate strategy at business unit level can become disjointed if there is inadequate leadership at this level. The approach is also heavily dependent on effective management systems in areas such as workforce planning, job design and process oriented Total Quality Management. While this approach to change is more heavily dependent on systems than on voluntarism, within business units and work teams a consultative approach to strategy implementation is often in evidence. Team loyalty within business units is paramount.

Australia's Lend Lease Corporation has used this type of tough, directive, results oriented approach to strategic and workplace change in its core project management business for over twenty years. It is an approach not highly recommended by a large proportion of change agents and management theorists, yet for Lend Lease it has led consistently to high profits, a strong balance sheet, and a workforce culture which shows cohesion and discipline. Through 'forced evolution' and a 'no big shocks' approach, Lend Lease appears to respond to, and influence, its environment. It is an organisation which has a strong strategic 'control posture'.

The Task-focused approach was also seen in our study of the previous Lend Lease subsidiary, MLC Life Limited, after the initial period of Turnaround. Having come through traumatic, frame-breaking change in the mid-1980s when taken over by Lend Lease (40% workforce reduction, 85% of executives retrenched), MLC moved back to a mid-range, directive–transitional style of change. After the trauma of the takeover, the emphasis was on restructuring work and work teams within business units, job redesign, process re-engineering and practical skills based training. MLC became an organisation in which performance and reward for achievement were key features. The organisational culture could not be described as collegial, as in the Developmental Transitional approach. Rather it was results oriented and pragmatic, and focused on providing high value to customers and stakeholders. There is a high degree of business unit autonomy within MLC but the overall strategic directions were corporately determined and driven.

MLC has been highly successful in business terms. Revenues and profits have risen consistently for over fifteen years. With the organisational Turnaround successfully completed, the symbol of the new dynamic high performance culture has become their refurbished open plan office building in North Sydney with its emphasis on provision for innovation and dynamic flexibility. MLC is an example of an initially coercive transformation which then utilised a Task-focused Transitional change strategy at the corporate level. (In Appendix 4B we illustrate how MLC has changed its approach once again, with good success.) It is profit driven, people oriented and focused on quality products and service to meet the needs of the energy customer of the twenty-first century.

Charismatic Transformations

Radical corporate transformation contrasts with constant transition. This is revolutionary change, used when the organisation is radically out of strategic alignment with its environment, where there is little time for extensive participation in decision making, but where there is support for radical change within the organisation. The executive, exercising a charismatic style of leadership, is able to engage the intellectual, emotional and behavioural commitment of staff to a comprehensively new view of the organisation. This often involves new business strategies, new structures and new systems, and acceptance of new external appointments into key positions. Many 'new' economy companies, or 'old' economy companies moving into the new economy, are led by such transformative leaders.

Some Organisational Development (OD) theorists[5] who previously viewed participative evolution as an almost universal panacea to change, have more recently espoused Organisational Transformation (OT) as the preferred model of change if the amount of change required is major and speed is vital to survival or success. The primary need in this type of change is for the executive to provide clear information about the ends, and consultation about means, even if the speed required for organisational change precludes extensive participation in the decision-making process itself.

The positive feature of this type of change strategy is its capacity to create a radically new order with majority staff support in a short period of time. However, optimum business conditions are pre-ferable; it is a strategy which works well in growth situations. The downside is that the strategy is heavily dependent on the personality and style of the chief executive, on his or her capacity to articulate a vision and capture the hopes and aspirations of the majority of staff members. Charismatic leaders also frequently leave the organisation abruptly, and too soon, before the transformational task has been completed. Bob Mansfield's tenure as CEO of Optus and Fairfax is a good example of this. The departure of a charismatic leader leaves a leadership vacuum, and the potential for a new leader to use a completely different and less motivating approach to change.

Charismatic Transformations typically occur in start-up situations or as attempts to initiate voluntary commitment by organisational members to a Turnaround strategy. With the initiation of a range of new IT and biotechnology companies, we have witnessed many examples of charismatic individuals, often very young, drawing enthusiastic and innovative people to them, and launching new enterprises.

The approach is less often used and not as successfully in large corporate Turnaround situations or, if it is, it is often accompanied by directive or coercive change at other levels. This is because in large traditional corporations, some interest groups will resist change, seeing it as unnecessary or destructive of entrenched privilege.

Telstra provides a clear example of charismatic leadership.[6] When Frank Blount was appointed CEO in 1992, he perceived that transformational change was necessary. Typically, the transformational leader emphasises the development and transmission of a new vision for the future of the organisation. Blount quickly established such a vision, and then aimed to motivate and empower lower level managers to develop a new cadre of leaders throughout the organisation. He used the Employee Relations group within the organisation as active change agents to work with the selected leaders to bring Telstra's vision into reality. Blount identified the major problem as 'behavioural'; in his view managers were not exercising leadership, not focusing enough on the clients, not problem solving. He saw the root causes of this issue as 'lack of ownership, lack of focused accountability and supervisers/managers not understanding and living their roles'.[7] Managers were typically concerned with a particular narrow functional, usually technical, area and were unable to see the importance of much emphasis on the behavioural aspects of Telstra's change. How, therefore, could Telstra executives create a powerful commitment to leadership throughout the organisation?

At Blount's instigation in 1996, an internal process was used to develop Telstra's 'Organisational Principles', a set of simple statements defining important fundamentals of leadership and the management of people.

Several specific initiatives emerged from the principles, designed to create a readiness for change and an environment where leaders could begin to lead.

- A new structure of six levels of management replaced the existing structure of twenty-three levels. Each level provided focus by defining very explicitly the roles for managers at that level.
- A new system of reporting relationships was developed (Employee Relations Authorisations). This gave managers the authority to select their direct reports so that they could be held accountable for their work.
- A raft of approximately 25 000 unfilled positions were removed. (In 1995 there were approximately 75 000 people working for Telstra but over 100 000 nominal positions.)
- New workplace agreements were put in place to increase organisational flexibility and to encourage a culture of customer service.

All this was part of Blount's vision for a new Telstra, but the vision had to be shared by others. So Blount conducted 'Front Line Forums' where he met with over 1400 managers and supervisors. These CEO 'roadshows' were an attempt by Blount to reshape competitive business strategy by providing an inspiring vision. CEO roadshows of this kind carry a risk of increasing cynicism and disillusionment if the CEO seems insincere or fails to follow up the rhetoric with credible and relevant action.

Blount's use of this channel of communication to his new leadership cadre was, on the whole, effective. He possessed credibility in Telstra because of his engineering background, his established track record, his evident honesty in responding to questions, and his willingness to put in place the reforms he saw as being necessary.

The 'Front Line Forums' were just one of several key interventions used in this period of 'Charismatic Transformation'. They can be, however, an important vehicle for conveying a new vision for change throughout the organisation and gaining the commitment of change agents throughout the organisation. Communication and the development of trust, or 'faith', are key to successful Charismatic Transformations.

Turnarounds

Organisational Turnaround is revolutionary change too, used when the organisation is radically out of strategic alignment, or where there have been large scale strategic shifts in the environment. In these situations there is no time for extensive participation in decision making and often little support within the organisation for radical change, but nevertheless radical change is vital for organisational survival. In its most extreme form, the strategy could be characterised as extremely coercive, but the executive style can also be modified to be top-down directive/directional rather than coercive.

This approach involves the major reshaping of corporate and business strategies, significant revision of the macro-organisational structure, stripping out layers of management, downsizing staff numbers and removing redundant operating systems. The emphasis is on breaking the old frame and creating a new structure, with particular focus on new appointments to key executive positions. The turmoil created in General Electric corporation in the United States by incoming CEO, Jack Welch, is illustrative of this approach to change. Hundreds of businesses were sold off, hundreds of thousands of employees left, and lifelong employees looked back wistfully at seemingly more caring days. But the business environment had changed, and GE had not kept up. In a similar way General Colin Powell, Chief of Staff for the US Forces, faced a problem of even greater proportions following the meltdown of the Cold War. Faced with no real alternate superpower, Powell had no alternative but to adapt a Turnaround strategy.

The positive feature of this change strategy is that it is an attempt to change structures and systems through decisive leadership and, as such, is not as dependent, initially, on attitudinal changes across the workforce before major strategic gains can be made. The downside is that, if not handled carefully, this approach can be used on an ongoing basis by an executive team as a reflexive approach to managing change, irretrievably breaking an organisational culture and putting nothing new in its place. On its own, this approach does not usually generate behavioural change until there is a subsequent modification to the Task-focused Transitional approach where the process of rebuilding the organisation can take place. Our research shows that a period of up to two years is the maximum an organisation can stay in the Turnaround mode of change without generating cynicism and lack of commitment in the majority of employees. The message is clear: if major organisational surgery is required, act decisively and quickly, but then moderate the approach so that a new business culture can be developed.

Many prominent Australian corporations—including BHP, CSR Ltd, Pacific Power and the New Zealand and Victorian public sectors—went through major Turnaround episodes in the 1980s and 1990s. Perhaps the most noteworthy and recent case was the confrontation on the Australian waterfront between Patrick Stevedores and the Maritime Union of Australia (MUA). On 7 April 1998, Patrick Stevedores, headed by CEO Chris Corrigan, sacked its entire MUA workforce. The MUA (led by National Secretary, John Coombs) and the union movement responded by mass picketing Australian ports. The issue became even more controversial as the federal government took a strong position: the Prime Minister and the Minister for Industrial Relations made strong public statements supporting Corrigan, against the unionists, and were accused of being implicated in attempts to train a substitute non-unionised workforce in Dubai. (The attempt failed.)

The dispute was 'resolved' when Mr Justice North of the Federal Court ordered Patrick to reinstate the stevedores, who also undertook not to continue their industrial action and to sacrifice salaries to enable the company to trade out of insolvency. Patrick appealed to the High Court, which ruled in the MUA's favour. Despite these rulings, Patrick persisted with a tough stance, and finally won through, tripling the company's share price in the process. It could well have gone the other way.

The case illustrates that a coercive approach to change is a high-risk strategy. Putting aside the ethical and legal issues involved in this case, in simple power terms, the case shows that the direct confrontation of interest groups can have high costs for all parties involved, can exacerbate existing conflicts which sometimes escalate out of control, and can dramatically complicate the process of change.[8]

The Turnaround change strategy is not a panacea for success. Toughness for its own sake is an insufficient rationale for this type of change. It is often emotionally painful for both the leaders and the workforce. However, if an organisation's external environment moves rapidly, or if the organisation is at a low level of performance, and if support for major change is low, it may be kinder to act decisively than to linger on over many years trying to make changes incrementally. For the Turnaround change strategy to work, decisive leadership must be linked with an incisive analysis of the strategic directions needed to return the organisation to high performance, or the organisation can be decisively led the wrong way. We have several examples of this from our research; the result is continuing low levels of corporate performance and a demotivated, cynical workforce.

Like the other approaches to corporate change, the Turnaround strategy is successful when used as an intelligently chosen approach to assist the organisation to strategically reposition itself within its business environment. The process of change does not drive the business strategy; rather it is an iterative relationship between strategic positioning and a coherent and well thought through change strategy.

Linking business strategy and change

In earlier work[9] we demonstrated the links between four generic types of business strategy (Miles and Snow's Defender, Prospector, Analyzer and Reactor) and the 'types' of change illustrated in Figure 4.3 and described in this chapter (Developmental Transitions, Task-focused Transitions, Charismatic Transformations and Turnarounds).

In Figures 4.4 to 4.7, we take this further by summarising the key features of those linkages. We relate the four change categories to examples of Australasian organisations which have used the approach, in each case summarising the common features of their approach to change and strategic positioning.

Developmental Transitions

Case examples

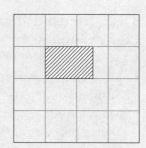

- Macquarie Bank (continuing)
- State Library of NSW (early 1990s)
- Many leading professional service firms
- MLC (late 1990s)
- SPC Cannery (mid-1990s)

Business strategy

- Dominantly product/market innovator (Prospector), or
- Successful low-cost producer of high-quality products (Defender)

Change strategy

- Constant, relentless mid-range change (change as a way of life)
- Executive leadership which operates on a collegial, consultative basis
- Team leadership which is sometimes directive, to balance the consultative executive style
- An emphasis on changing dominant values and mindsets in order to change the organisation

Business planning

- Primarily 'bottom-up' planning, within corporate parameters—business units strongly influence corporate directions

Conditions for use

- Use when markets are growing and product/market innovation is desired. Organisational change strategies must create cross-organisational synergy, and a 'market leader' culture. Strong emphasis on individual development, corporate culture management, developing a strong internal labour market and team skills.

Figure 4.4 Linking business strategy and Developmental Transitions

Task-focused Transitions

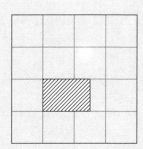

Case examples
- MLC (early 1990s)
- Lend Lease (project management business)
- Many public sector enterprises, after a process of Turnaround
- Rio Tinto, and many large product manufacturers
- Electricity industry

Business strategy
- A focused strategy; cost containment in some business areas, product/market innovation in others (Analyzer), or
- Successful low-cost producer of high-quality products (Defender)

Change strategy
- Constant improvement and relentless mid-range change
- Executive leadership which operates on a decisive/strongly directional basis
- Business unit leadership is mostly consultative, but within a strong framework of well organised systems
- Focus on improving structures and systems

Business planning
- Clear statement of corporate 'strategic intent'—implementation cascading down to business units. Mixture of 'top-down' and 'bottom-up' business planning

Conditions for use
- Use when markets/products/services are undergoing major change and 'niche' exploratory strategies are prevalent. Organisational change strategies must deliver the capacity for rapid structural, systems, skill and cultural changes. Strong emphasis on business unit autonomy, maximum devolution and outsourcing, workforce redesign

Figure 4.5 Linking business strategy and Task-focused Transitions

Charismatic Transformations

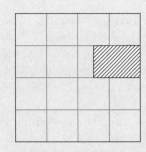

Case examples
- State Library of NSW (late 1980s)
- Qantas (mid-1990s)
- Optus (early 1990s)
- Telstra (mid-1990s)

Business strategy
- Product/market innovator (Prospector)

Change strategy
- Rapid, radical redefinition of the business, or creation of the new business domain
- Reshaping of corporate strategies and competitive business strategies
- Executive leadership which provides an inspiring vision, and generates the respect and support of staff

Business planning
- Entrepreneurial, not systematised
- Strong emphasis on intuitive thinking and calculated risk taking

Conditions for use
- Use when the business environment changes dramatically, or when a radical repositioning of the organisation is necessary to meet future business challenges. Organisational change strategies must help to create a new vision and organisational mindset, where changes to a new business culture are welcomed by the majority of participants

Figure 4.6 Linking business strategy and Charismatic Transformations

Turnarounds

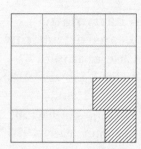

Case examples
- Patrick Stevedores (latter 1990s)
- CSR (latter 1990s)
- Victorian public sector (most of 1990s)
- BHP (late 1980s and again in late 1990s)
- Fairfax (late 1990s)

Business strategy
- Dynamic refocus on the core business and selected business areas, adoption of a focused, niche strategy (Analyzer) having previously been either low performers (Reactors) or medium performers and losing 'alignment' with the business environment

Change strategy
- Rapid, radical redefinition of the core business
- Divestment of non-core business areas
- Successive corporate and workplace restructures, downsizing and retrenchments
- Restructuring/abolishing traditional systems
- Chief executive welds together a strong top team
- Decision making is recentralised

Business planning
- Top team holds frequent retreats to consider strategy
- Major focus on creating a new corporate plan and negotiating this with external stakeholders
- Business unit planning strongly influenced by the corporate plan

Conditions for use
- Use when the business environment changes dramatically and when the organisation is not aligned with its environment. Organisational change strategies must break redundant and ineffective frameworks of thinking, refocus the organisation on fundamentally new strategies and seek a new fit for the organisation in a changing business environment

Figure 4.7 Linking business strategy and Turnarounds

We have not covered in any way, other than by inference, a fifth category of change illustrated in Figure 4.3—Taylorism. This is a type of change which our research has consistently shown is associated with low performance—characterised by tall hierarchical structures, aversion to risk taking, a centralist mentality and rigid approaches to work and job structuring. In the rare cases where this approach survives, it is usually associated with highly regulated monopolies. Even in the public sector, few real monopolies now exist and those that do are usually under the active scrutiny of parliaments. In the business conditions of the twenty-first century, Taylorism—avoiding change or consolidating—does not produce sufficient momentum in the organisation to maintain strategic alignment.

This chapter therefore provides an overview of the options available in strategic change, the rationale for using different approaches, and some guidance on the overall patterns, linkages and interventions possible. We make the case for an intelligent analysis of the choices available, rather than relying on recipes from the past, or inappropriately targeted change 'packages'. A change strategy is a key strategic variable required for the organisation to anticipate, exploit or create the breakpoints in its environment. Managers and leaders must be clear in analysing when to employ a specific change strategy and approach to effect the repositioning required.

We need a theory of change

Why do we need a theory of change? Perhaps this question is best answered with a real life example.

In 1994, David Mortimer, the head of TNT, then a large Australian transport company, appointed Richard Osbourne to bring together a number of TNT's transport businesses and amalgamate them into the General Freight Division. The aim of this exercise, the first wave of change, was to take what had been a collection of smaller carriers which tended to duplicate and compete with each other and to achieve higher efficiencies through centralisation and economies of scale. The change strategy chosen by Osbourne focused on structures, capital restructuring and financial reporting.

Within six months the hoped for synergies were not being achieved. In the new General Freight Division, the amalgamated firms still failed to cooperate, morale was low and the Division lost its customer focus. Several key clients left TNT for competitors. Eleven months after the formation of the General Freight Division, Richard Osbourne realised that the human relationship and cultural issues had been ignored and in fact had to be dealt with if the Division were to be turned around.

So, with a new senior management team, Osbourne took time out to plan a new change initiative. The team came up with a future vision and set of action plans which they called 'TNT Gold'. Consultants Booz Allen and Hamilton were brought in to help in order to reduce costs further, but also to improve customer service and build a new culture of commitment. 'TNT Gold' had eight performance-enhancing projects in which people and cultural issues were central. By March 1996, the new program had achieved no noticeable bottom-line results, although the few months that had passed since 'TNT Gold' was launched was a minimal time period in which to bring about significant cultural change.

However, the board was losing patience with the lack of progress, and Osbourne was transferred to the Marketing Department. A new CEO for the Division, Ian Fraser, was appointed. Fraser initiated the third wave of change. He abandoned 'TNT Gold' and decided to attempt to turn the Division around by decentralising. However, before detailed plans could be completed, the board decided to divest the Division. By 1997 TNT itself was in dire trouble, and was eventually acquired by a Dutch company, and delisted from the Australian Stock Exchange.

The TNT Freight Division case illustrates the need for a coherent theory of change. The board and managers involved appear to have shared no consistent theory of change from which they could derive a meaningful and workable strategy. Just as a fish, landed on the end of a line, flip flops from one spot to another, desperately hoping that the next jump will solve its problem, TNT tried centralising and decentralising, financially driven and culturally driven change alternately. Like the fish, jumping from one place to another failed to solve their problem.

Effective change managers have theories which guide their action. The theories are not always explicit; some managers cannot articulate their theory clearly but nevertheless their actions show a consistent and meaningful pattern of response which produces a powerful trajectory of change.

In this chapter we have identified a theory of change comprising a small number of implementation models which leaders and managers can use to reposition their organisations strategically in maintaining a process of continual adaptation to a changing environment. In the following chapters we examine some of the choices available in leading the implementation process, alternative approaches to effecting change in the workplace and some of the specific tools or change 'interventions' that can be used successfully to effect Transitions, Transformations and Turnarounds. Preceding this, in Appendix 4, we illustrate several different approaches to change using the change model.

References

1. See D. C. Dunphy & D. A. Stace, *Under New Management: Australian Organisations in Transition*, McGraw-Hill, Sydney, 1990, pp. 5–8.
2. The overall results of our research have been described in detail elsewhere: see D. C. Dunphy & D. A. Stace, op. cit.; also D. A. Stace & D. C. Dunphy, 'Translating business strategies into action: Managing strategic change', *Journal of Strategic Change*, Wiley, London, 1, 4, 1992, pp. 203–16; also D. C. Dunphy & D. A. Stace, 'Strategies for Organisational Transition', in R. T. Golembiewski (ed.), *Handbook of Organisational Consultation*, Marcel Dekker, New York, 1992, pp. 191–203.
3. The modal score of all interviewees was used for the purpose of 'positioning' an organisation on the change matrix.
4. See our paternalistic human resource strategy type in D. A. Stace & D. C. Dunphy, 'Beyond traditional paternalistic and developmental approaches to organisational change and human resource strategies', *International Journal of Human Resource Management*, 12, 3, 1991, pp. 263–83.
5. See, for example, J. M. Bartenuk & M. L. Louis, 'The interplay of organisational development and organisational transformation', *Research in Organisational Change and Development*, 1988, 2, pp. 97–134; P. H. Mirvis, 'Organisation development: Part 1—An evolutionary perspective', *Research in Organisational Change and Development*, 1988, 2, pp. 1–57; P. H. Mirvis, 'Organisation development: Part 2—A revolutionary perspective', *Research in Organisational Change and Development*, 1990, 4, pp. 1–66;

J. I. Porras & R. C. Silvers, 'Organisation development and transformation', *Annual Review of Psychology*, 1991, 42, pp. 51–78.

6. Telstra, 'Our Future', No. 261, 1996, p. 1.

7. We are indebted to three AGSM MBA students—Michael Martin, David Kan and Jonathon Herma—for much of the material regarding the Telstra case. We have drawn from their unpublished paper 'Organisational Change at Telstra', 1999.

8. For a detailed review of this case see 'The Economic and Labour Relations Review', 'Symposium on the Waterfront Dispute', Vol. 9, No. 2, December 1998, pp. 155–245.

9. D. A. Stace & D. C. Dunphy, 1992, op. cit., pp. 203–16.

Appendix 4

Case studies in change

I n this section we illustrate some of the paths to change taken by different organisations operating in different sectors of the economy. The cases demonstrate a rich variety of approaches to change being used by organisations as they seek to shape their futures, and to survive against global competition.

4A Going global to grow: The case of Lend Lease Corporation
4B Innovative twenty-first century workplaces
   Ericsson Australia's 42nd Precinct
   Campus MLC
4C Transforming a traditional workplace: The case of ICI Botany

Readers have the opportunity to explore the application of the change model in more detail by reading these studies.

Appendix 4A
Going global to grow: The case of Lend Lease Corporation

In the latter 1990s Lend Lease's executives were, with few exceptions, located in Sydney running one of Australia's most consistently successful corporations—in the project development and funds management businesses. By 2000 the situation had changed dramatically: the Chief Executive, Chief Financial Officer and Global HR Executive were located in London, the Director of Information Technology worked out of Boston, the Global Real Estate Executive worked from Chicago, while the head of Lend Lease's Australian business and the head of Lend Lease Bovis, Lend Lease's global project management business, worked from Sydney. This executive meets formally six times per year, alternating in different international locations, and conducts an extended fortnightly executive meeting by telephone conference stretched across Asian-Pacific, European and North American time zones. The 'midnight shift' for these fortnightly executive meetings is rotated. 1999 marked the transition for Lend Lease—from an Australasian business with some international interests to an internationally and globally focused corporation. Lend Lease's Chairman is now Jill Ker Conway, an Australian, who lives in Boston.

Decisive strategic shifts

Lend Lease was established by immigrant Dick Dusseldorp in the 1950s as a project construction business for the Snowy Mountains Hydro-Electric Scheme, and was subsequently built into a project management and funds management powerhouse under the leadership of Chief Executive and later Chairman, Stuart Hornery. Over its lifetime Lend Lease has been a dominant and shaping force among Australian corporations. It has created the playing field in many areas, including:

- the establishment of the ACTU-Lend Lease Foundation in the 1970s, a groundbreaking move in the militant construction industry;

- a radical diversification of business focus in 1983 with the acquisition of the moribund insurance business MLC Limited, prior to building it into a leading funds management enterprise. This was followed by successive acquisitions of financial services institutions, including Capita Financial Group, Australian Eagle Insurance, and substantial interests in Westpac Banking Corporation in the 1990s;
- steps to create offshore business—Property Services in Singapore in 1975; Property Construction in the United States in 1987; development of an Asian strategy from 1992–93; commencement of the A$1.5 billion Bluewater Centre development in the United Kingdom in 1994.

Through the early 1990s there was a realisation that to continue its historical pattern of growth, Lend Lease would have to aggressively seek offshore growth. The domestic Australian market in property services and financial services was saturated with capacity. Lend Lease's concerted move into Asia from 1993 was seen as at best a long-haul strategy, arrested to some degree by the 1997 Asian financial crisis.

Throughout the early 1990s strong emphasis had been placed on cost cutting and rationalisation in both the project management and funds management businesses. The move into Asia was part of an aspiration to move the company beyond its domestic roots: 'We needed a dream, a focus on creating new value, rather than constant cost cutting,' said one executive. Although the move to establish a strong Asian business did not provide Lend Lease with the quantum shift it required, it provided important experience in internationalising the corporation. In addition, the success of the Bluewater development in Kent, United Kingdom, provided an emphatic establishment of the Lend Lease brand in northern hemisphere markets.

A series of major moves in 1999–2000 continued the pattern of decisive strategic shifts which have become one of Lend Lease's hallmarks. In a period of a little over six months Lend Lease bought or acquired major interests, totalling A$1.6 billion, in:

- British construction company, Bovis;
- Boston Financial Group;

- Canadian Eastern Life, a substantial operator in the Hong Kong life insurance market;
- parts of Amresco, a US real estate developer and financier; and
- shopping centres in Spain and Portugal.

In this series of moves, it grew from a 4500 to a 12 000 person company. In an equally decisive move in April 2000, Lend Lease announced the sale of its MLC funds management business to Australia's largest banking group, National Australia Bank, for A$4.6 billion, involving the transfer of 2000 staff.

A changing value chain

The strategic shifts briefly described are part of a pattern of Lend Lease looking to create new value. This can be illustrated as in Table 4A.1.

Table 4A.1

Period	Business focus	Value proposition
1950s–1970s	Development and construction	Industry leadership in major project developments
1970s	Project management	The integrator and project manager of prestigious development projects
1980s–mid-1990s	Project management Funds management	An innovative force in the new financial services industry, linked with project management and funding of major projects
Late 1990s	Global real estate management services Project management Funds management	A new value chain linking funding with property development, with real estate investment and fund management services

The divestment of MLC in 2000 removed the funds management arm of the company on the rationale that, unlike the 1980s, capital for projects was much more readily available, freeing funds for the company to pursue its emerging global position in real estate management and investment services.

Change: Lend Lease's distinctiveness

Our research into Lend Lease, and particularly into its funds management arm until 2000, MLC Limited, spans fourteen years over four major research projects. What allows a company to make such major changes in strategy, while maintaining an unbroken record of profit increases for twenty-five years? In our view there are three primary factors:

1. a culture of innovation and relentless improvement;
2. minimal formal structure, and the ability to quickly modify structures to emerging business requirements; and
3. considered opportunism, and an ability to quickly change strategy while communicating openly with employees about changing business directions.

The ability to change, without major internal dissent, represents in our view Lend Lease's core distinctiveness. Change for Lend Lease appears to be a unifying, positive force even though different styles have been used in different eras of the corporation. We illustrate this from research in Lend Lease/MLC using the change matrix (see Figure 4A.1).

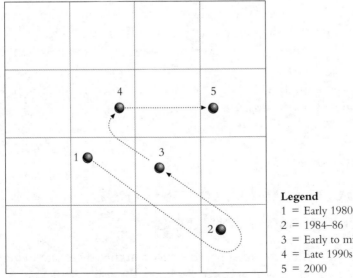

Legend
1 = Early 1980s
2 = 1984–86
3 = Early to mid-1990s
4 = Late 1990s
5 = 2000

Figure 4A.1 Change in Lend Lease/MLC

The matrix in Figure 4A.1 illustrates the following characteristics of Lend Lease's/MLC's approach to change:

1. classic Lend Lease change approach in the early 1980s—directive, incremental adjustment;
2. takeover and Turnaround of MLC Limited—coercive, total corporate transformation;
3. continued focus on cost productivity, efficiencies—directive, continuing transformation to a leadership role in financial services;
4. workplace innovation is institutionalised via the campus MLC concept—a process of involving employees in designing a twenty-first century workplace; a more consultative leadership style, still involving major change; and
5. once again, major change for MLC as it is divested to a new parent, National Australia Bank. The management team remains intact, as it is projected that the new owners wish to mainstream some of MLC's innovative culture into the parent organisation.

MLC has now left the Lend Lease fold, but from its acquisition by Lend Lease in the 1980s, we see how a moribund organisation had been enriched by the innovative Lend Lease culture, to the extent that MLC itself had become a test bed for workplace innovation within the Lend Lease group by the latter 1990s.

The Lend Lease of the early twenty-first century is now venturing globally in search of growth. Its new partners are experienced operators in their northern hemisphere markets. Lend Lease brings to the table its capability as an integrator and innovator—capabilities it will now need in order to sustain and grow its global operations.

Appendix 4B
Innovative twenty-first century workplaces

We illustrate in this section approaches to workplace change being trialled by two organisations as they address the joint challenges of increasing the rate of project/service innovation, while at the same time engaging and motivating a new emerging class of 'knowledge worker'.

Ericsson Australia's 42nd Precinct[1]

In 1997, Ericsson Australia established its Blueprint 2002 strategy— a major repositioning of the company's operations in Australia from being a supply oriented telecommunications equipment organisation, to a technology and solutions based info-communications company. Through a series of cross-functional business leadership programs, scenario development teams, Blueprint implementation teams and relentless refocusing in its customer units, the journey begun in 1997 was, several years on, starting to pay dividends. The Blueprint process, and the metamorphosis into an info-communications company, was occurring at the same time as Ericsson globally was undergoing major, but successful, change.

Part of the transformation involved the establishment of Ericsson's 42nd Precinct in Melbourne—an innovative cross-functional development hub designed to provide a less corporatised environment to deliver faster, more integrated solutions in multimedia, data, info-communications and Internet global applications. Where European equipment manufacturers such as Ericsson had dominated the telecommunications supply industry in earlier eras, new North American competitors such as Cisco, Nortel and Lucent provided serious competition in the latter 1990s. Initially Ericsson had not been as adept as they in anticipating the 'convergence' phenomenon—the virtual melding of computing/ Internet, telecommunications and media technologies.

Bluepoint 2002 provided the strategy to fight back: the 42nd Precinct was a manifestation of that strategy. The precinct is situated high above Melbourne's CBD on the 42nd floor of Ericsson's Australian headquarters. Initially conceived by Peter Rule, Ericsson's Strategy and Marketing Director, and strongly supported by the then Managing Director, Kjell Sorme, and his successor Karl Sundstrom, the precinct was an opportunity to set up a floor of innovators across a mix of technologies: a formalisation of 'skunkwork' teams by putting them together on a single floor and allowing cross-fertilisation between teams. The Melbourne centre is the third and largest international site of its kind, joining Ericsson 'cyberlabs' in San Francisco and New York.

Physically and organisationally, the Precinct is distinctive. The physical fit-out gives the floor a 'techno' feel. It features street signs, logos and slogans etched on glass partitions, and open plan spaces with futuristic meeting rooms. It also features a cybertheatre and the 'e-home'—a concept loungeroom demonstrating how emerging technologies would impact on the home. The cybertheatre is a room equipped with the latest technology, including two giant flat computer screens to display content from laptops. The décor is very high-tech, with metallic surfaces resembling electronic circuits.

Organisationally, the 42nd Precinct has no managers: each of the 100 strong team reports formally via their pre-existing channels of management. Peter Rule has been 'appointed' as Mayor of the Precinct, and on occasion wears mayoral robes and chain in a

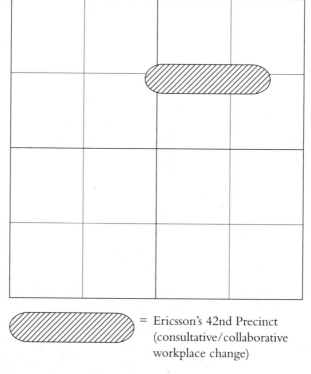

= Ericsson's 42nd Precinct (consultative/collaborative workplace change)

Figure 4B.1 Innovation in Ericsson

symbolic gesture. He regards his role as establishing 'centres of influence'—a guiding rather than a management role. The Precinct now hosts about eight innovation teams, with a backlog of teams wanting to move in. The rule so far is that once a product concept gets to the stage where it can stand alone, it moves out of 42nd Precinct and back to the product/service unit.

The 42nd Precinct is a radical departure for Ericsson, which traditionally has had a somewhat conservative corporate reputation. The facility has an informality that is designed to get people from disparate technology disciplines talking and becoming more productive. It is a good example of the type of experimentation taking place in our organisations as we move across the watershed of the twenty-first century. It is a reference point in change, not necessarily a recipe. We illustrate its positioning on the change matrix in Figure 4B.1.

Campus MLC

The ubiquitous open-plan office of the 1990s has taken a different turn with MLC's 'Campus MLC' concept. Open plan can be just as hierarchical and inconsiderate of human needs as the floor to ceiling office spaces they replaced. MLC, under the guidance of Rosemary Kirkby, MLC's General Manager (People), has experimented with a different approach. Hers has been an emphasis on melding:

- people (the twenty-first century knowledge worker);
- plan (creating a village-like workplace environment); and
- process (to achieve sustainable cultural change).

Her leadership was strongly supported by MLC's previous corporate parent, Lend Lease. MLC is now seen as a lead site for mainstreaming cultural change by its new owner, National Australia Bank.

Kirkby stresses that Campus MLC is not an overnight phenomenon. It started well over a decade ago with some of the points along the journey including the following:

- In the latter 1980s a new financial services skills base was built in what had been an hierarchical insurance organisation. 'We had to get rid of the tea lady, cardigan and dark panelled-office mentality.'

- In the early 1990s almost 70% of employees were given the chance to participate in cross-functional programs exploring MLC/Lend Lease's place in the rapidly globalising business environment. This was followed by the establishment of a team based Enterprise Agreement process, the results of which cast MLC as a clear leader in the financial services industry for innovative practice and flexible work design.
- The mid-1990s were difficult years of re-engineering in which MLC's product line was radically rationalised, the business restructured and 40% of costs cut out of the business.

Faced with the pressures of global financial service giants at Australia's doorstep, MLC realised that its initial approach to cultural change and to restructuring had merely helped it to stay in the game, even though it was regarded as a clear market leader at home. There was also the realisation that to attract and retain the best talent, MLC would have to create a work environment which 'connected' with the professional and social needs of an emerging information technology literate, younger and more highly educated workforce in an extremely competitive globally oriented industry. Says Kirkby, 'As salaries, benefits and career structures have became less of a differentiator, workplace culture and lifestyle have become increasingly important points of difference in the endeavour to become the employer of choice—this ultimately is a people, and "knowledge" business.'

Campus MLC was born from this history and these concepts. Key features of this new workplace concept include the following:

- *No personal office space* No one in the new environment, including the CEO, has an office. Space dedicated for individual use has decreased, with communal areas increasing. The provision of space is based on need rather than seniority.
- *More meeting spaces* Campus MLC acknowledges that meeting spaces are vital for the modern office, especially in a project based culture. However, research has shown that 90% of meetings are held between four or fewer people. Therefore, Campus MLC features a wide variety of formal, informal and flexible meeting spaces.
- *The 'vertical street' and staircase* Running through the core of the building is a 'vertical street' linking floors and featuring meeting and communal spaces. A new open glassed stairway has been

built into the building, a critical element in the vertical integration of MLC's business units and a key physical mechanism for creating the sense of community in the building.

- *More relaxation and recreation areas* Each floor incorporates a civic area which encourages interaction between employees from all business units.
- *Themed floors* Following input from MLC people, each floor features a theme.

What started off as a building refurbishment moved on to become a business refurbishment, with widespread involvement of employees in developing the themes for their floors.

Level 1 is called 'The City' and offers traditional boardroom-style meeting rooms in investment banker style. Level 3 is the Japanese inspired 'Zen Den' (complete with bean bags, giant tropical fish tank

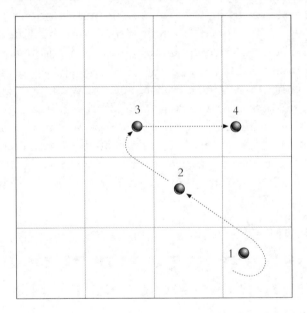

Legend

1 = Mid-1980s takeover of MLC by Lend Lease
2 = Early to mid-1990s, Process Re-engineering, cost focus
3 = MLC 2000, consultative, mid-range change
4 = Projected change 2001–2002 at MLC: fast paced, consultative change (technology platforms, global linkages)

Figure 4B.2 Change in MLC

and raised floor. Socks and stockinged feet are common in this space). Level 4 is called 'The Table', because at its heart is a large timber 'kitchen table' with full commercial kitchen facilities. Level 5 has the cinema and multimedia facilities. 'Café Six' has a commercial café which will ultimately be extended to the roof. 'The Gallery' promotes a sense of change and renewal with displays of art; and the top level, called 'Fifty Seven', mimics the atmosphere of a Qantas Club.

Some MLC-ers describe the new workspace as 'in your face…transparent…egalitarian…a community'. Kirkby is quick to point out that while the early readings are very positive, not everyone is comfortable with the idea of community and what she calls 'collaborative-space'. There is often an unspoken tension between the new generation, free-form, laptop workforce, and the more regular system oriented workforce.

Our research in MLC among a representative sample of team leaders revealed a strong focus on a performance oriented 'can do' culture. When questioned about the future, some held the view that MLC was about to undergo another major period of change—but change in which MLC and its employees would play a strong leadership role, rather than being merely recipients. Within weeks of completion of our research, the acquisition of MLC from Lend Lease by National Australia Bank, at a price premium, was announced. Indications are that the new parent was prepared to pay a premium for both the MLC brand, and its performance oriented workplace culture. We illustrate its positioning on the change matrix in Figure 4B.2.

Appendix 4C
Transforming a traditional workplace: The case of ICI Botany

ICI is a UK based chemical manufacturer which established a number of plants in Australia. The major Australian manufacturing site at Botany in Sydney was established in 1941. This account of twelve years of change at the plant from 1986–98 has been drawn from a PhD thesis by Tony Mealor.[2]

The case describes the transformation of a corporate culture based on traditional adversarial industrial relations to a strong partnership between management, unions and the workplace. In the process, the core work processes were also transformed, productivity increased dramatically and costs were slashed. The case is particularly informative because:

- detailed longitudinal studies of corporate change such as this are seldom undertaken;
- the author had access to all company records, including productivity data;
- in the ten years covered by the study, almost every historical change initiative (such as TQM and Business Process Re-engineering) was included in the ongoing change program;
- the site originated a number of radical innovations in employee relations (such as the twelve hour shift system, annual salaries for hourly paid workers and self-managed team structures) which subsequently diffused widely through Australian industry generally;
- the changes kept the site viable at a time when extreme competition threatened it with closure.

The background to change

The Botany Plant, when the case commences in 1986, was a complex of ten distinct operations, producing products such as polypropylene, PVC and carbon tetrachloride halocarbons. The site culture was traditionally dominated by a paternalistic Tayloristic work ethos stemming from the values and training of the UK engineers who set up the site. Workers on the site were unionised, with five unions strongly represented. Their shop stewards met on a regular basis and were united in viewing management as the enemy. Over the years 'a panoply of overtime lurks, dargs,* perks, backhanders and bribes became embodied in the custom and practice of the ten factories on site as socioeconomic work norms to maximise income'.[3] In reality, workers, rather than managers, controlled most of the plant's operations.

---

* A 'darg' is an Australian term for an informal restriction, imposed by the workforce on production. It is aimed at maintaining employment, reducing effort and increasing overtime.

The change program on the Botany site went through three major phases or 'waves' of change: Figure 4C.1 outlines these waves.[4]

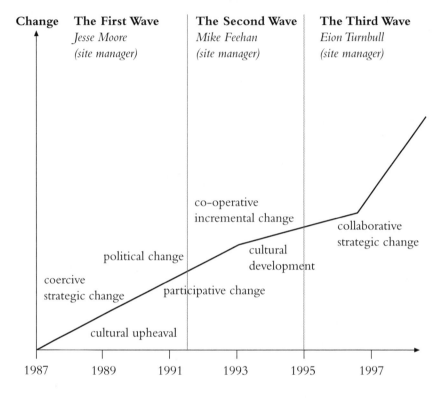

Figure 4C.1 The waves of change at ICI Botany, 1988–98   MEALOR (1999), P. 77

The First Wave: Top-down strategic change, 1987–91

In December 1986, the board of directors decided to 'take on' the unions in order to regain control. The immediate stimulus was tariff reduction by the federal government. This threatened the plant's viability by subjecting it to global competition. Management's aim was to eliminate or substantially reduce union power so that future productivity improvements would be possible. Management presented a set of demands to the workforce addressing issues of downsizing, restrictive work practices and organisational change ('The Green Paper'). The workforce, led by the union shop stewards, rejected these demands and initiated a period of 'industrial anarchy'.[5] A major strike in February 1989 crippled the company's operations and led to ICI suing key union delegates for $26 million. However, the unions threatened to close the plant if the writs were enforced, so a standoff ensued. ICI calculated its losses through the industrial confrontation at $134 million. Clearly a coercive approach had foundered on the realities of power.

There were subsequent changes in management ranks, some of the union hardliners left and the remaining union representatives adopted a more pragmatic approach. Both sides were frustrated with the situation that had developed and, out of their frustration and falteringly at first, a new way of working together was forged. Figure 4C.2 shows the dramatic impact of the resulting changes on the incidence of industrial disputes.

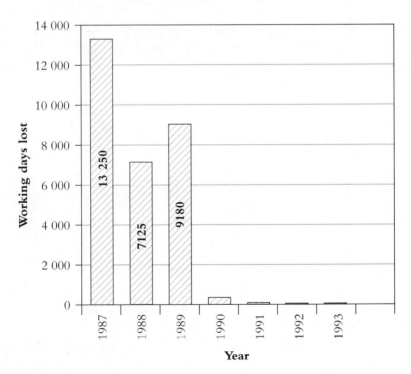

Figure 4C.2 Strikes at ICI Botany, 1987–93   MEALOR (1999), P. 81

A critical group in developing a new approach to change on the site consisted of thirty members of FEDFA (the Federated Engine Drivers and Firemen's Association), who worked in the site Utilities section providing essential services to the whole site. In 1986 they had researched, redesigned and negotiated their own twelve hour roster system, introduced a new computerised distributed control system (DCS), organised themselves into self-managed teams and moved from an hourly paid contract to annualised salaries. In September 1988, they entered into negotiation with management and, in August 1989, they negotiated these changes into the first enterprise agreement on site.

In the protracted negotiations involved in drafting and adopting the new enterprise agreement, management and union representatives worked conjointly on problems, debating this bundle of interventions and their potential consequences. As this debate took place, trust was being tested and slowly building. The original confrontation had created a catalyst for change, demonstrating that continuing conflict would make the plant economically non-viable. Both sides were therefore testing out whether a more collaborative approach could be developed while being fearful that agreements might be subverted or sabotaged. The model agreement developed with FEDFA subsequently spread through the plant and in phase 2, by 1993, formed the basis of a combined site agreement. The initial FEDFA pilot program showed what could be achieved by a more collaborative approach and led to workers in other parts of the plant pressuring their representatives to negotiate similar conditions and work redesign. Management also saw real benefit in the changes.

What were the interventions agreed on by management and unions, and what impact did they have on the workplace and workplace culture? Two interventions had an immediate and dramatic effect on work organisation, on the attitudes of the workforce and on their behaviour. The first was a move from an eight hour to a twelve hour shift roster, and the second a move to annualised salaries rather than hourly paid work. The old eight hour shift system disrupted workers' social life and allowed them only one weekend off a month. As a result, absenteeism averaged 20%. The twelve hour system allowed two long weekends off each month. The annualised salary eliminated paid overtime, absorbing it into the pay package; in return, workers agreed to undertake overtime required by business needs, managing it themselves.

The impact of these changes on behaviour was dramatic for process workers. (See Figure 4C.3 and note that payment of annualised salaries commenced for process workers in January 1990.)

Maintenance workers did not enter into an agreement which included annualised salaries until July 1991, but nevertheless the cultural change had a progressive impact, and their absenteeism also reached a low by late 1991. Without significant overtime and with two long weekends a month, workplace members were now developing more satisfying social lives outside work and work itself was a more satisfying place to be.

This created new openness to management's initiative to upskill the workforce significantly. Under a new agreement with TAFE (Department of Technical and Further Education), a systematic set of courses was provided to increase competency levels. The increased competency levels strongly supported the effective functioning of the new multiskilled work teams being instituted across the plants.

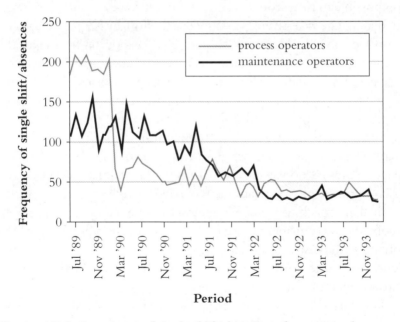

Figure 4C.3 Frequency of single shift absences of process and maintenance operators   ICI BOTANY HRM DEPARTMENT, IN MEALOR (1999), p. 92

And what impact did this set of 'bundled interventions' have on productivity across the site? First, it is important to realise that with a $100 million plant any downtime is costly. The changed culture eliminated strikes and dramatically reduced downtime. Measuring productivity is difficult and had not been seriously attempted at the time. Different parts of the plant had very different operations and so productivity had to be measured differently in each. But Mealor was able to find measures of the impact in several locations. The measures show substantial productivity improvements. For example, in the Olefines plant before the change program, 9% of product had to be recycled because it did not reach specified quality standards. After the change, in 1989, this figure was halved and improvement continued subsequently. The introduction of teams, skill based training and quality control concepts were having a significant impact on the bottom line. One reason for this was that the workforce now had a career path and payment for higher skill levels acquired and used.

The key lesson to be learnt from the First Wave of change is that it is possible to turn around a situation of extreme conflict. However, such a change takes time and concerted effort by all parties to build trust and solve problems collaboratively. In addition, it is clear that changing the workplace culture can best be accomplished by using a selected set of mutually reinforcing interventions. There is no simple fix or quick gimmick. It is also clear that real cultural change requires opportunism and strategic planning.

Strategic planning can only become a useful and central characteristic of a change program when the organisation is basically healthy and in good shape. If there is major conflict and workforce discontent, employee relations may have to take precedence over a rational approach to strategy. Only when the major discontents are resolved can confrontation be replaced by collaboration on problem solving with positive productivity gains. Successful strategic planning depends on the consent and commitment of an informed, skilled and co-operative workforce.

The First Wave of change demonstrated that industrial peace could be created and that positive gains could flow both to the workforce and shareholders. The First Wave therefore laid the foundation for future change.

The Second Wave: Co-operative incremental change, 1991–95

Following on from the turbulence of the First Wave, the organisation moved through a period where new senior managers were appointed, including a new site manager, Mike Feehan. Through this period structural changes, including plant closures and workforce reductions, were made on the site. However, instead of these issues recreating industrial unrest, management and union representatives moved into a strategic alliance to address these issues. This was only possible because of the trust established in the First Wave.

But not all initiatives succeeded. By mid-1990 industrial relations at the site had improved to the extent that the senior strategists in the company thought it was a good time to introduce quality concepts to the workforce. A US package had been bought and was being strongly pushed by the global company. The quality program was imposed directively on the site and was not integrated into the selected bundle of complementary interventions being managed collaboratively. By the end of 1995, the quality program was floundering, quality management teams disintegrated and management was no longer driving the quality program. Clearly, a new approach to quality that fitted the overall ongoing change program on site was needed.

In July 1991, a team of twelve unionists and managers formed what became the Botany Site Productivity Council (BSPC). This group carried out research into productivity measurement and gain sharing and for the first time plant and site productivity was measured in a rigorous way.

During this Wave, three plants were closed and a manpower review, which resulted in 112 positions being eliminated, was initiated. The unions were involved in making these decisions and in their implementation. Over time the BSPC evolved into the Botany Improvement Team. This was a smaller group consisting of seven managers and five union delegates. This team achieved cost reductions of $14 million in 1993–94 while maintaining production levels.

By 1995, robust systems had been established in the areas of Human Resources, Manufacturing, Quality and Safety and Reliability. Costs had been reduced, the new DCS technology had diffused over large areas of the site and industrial relations had never been better. For the first time productivity measurement was being carried out with rigour. New competencies had been developed, both technical and around the management of change, and the collaborative culture seemed strongly entrenched. In 1992 a new CEO, who strongly supported the site initiatives, had been appointed to the Australian company. It was a far cry from the confrontational politics of 1986–87.

The Third Wave: Collaborative strategic change, 1995–98

The catalyst for the Third Wave of change was the appointment of a new site manager, Eion Turnbull, in May 1995. Eion was a chemical engineer with a Cambridge PhD who undertook a world trip to benchmark the industry and estimate the extent of future competition. In Mealor's words: 'What he found was disturbing. Even with all of the improvements which had taken place and the dramatic change in culture, to one of cooperation and collaboration, the site's productivity was well below the world's best—especially in terms of labour costs per tonne of product and plant reliability.'[6] This profile needed dramatic improvement if the Botany site were to attract the necessary investment to underwrite ICI Australia's planned thrust into Asia. The lesson to be learnt here is that a change program can bring about substantial improvements in performance but still leave the organisation far behind competitors.

Eion's favoured management style was consultative and he had no wish to engage in another major confrontation with the site unions. Instead he took the senior management team and the site union convenors away for a weekend of strategic planning. The two groups returned to the site with an agreed strategy to reduce labour costs but minimise the negative effect of this on the workforce and the organisation's core capabilities. The group also planned a range of other initiatives designed to turn ICI Botany into a world-class chemical producer.

The proposal outlined a plan for downsizing—perhaps the first and only time in Australian history when union members have actually argued for this. But this was downsizing with a difference: new requirements for commitment to safety, flexible work practices, meeting high work standards and upskilling were also outlined. Those who were not prepared to work to the new requirements were asked to accept a redundancy package but, before they could go, they were required to pass on their skills and knowledge to the relevant people remaining in the workforce. In this way, there would be little loss of the intellectual capital and experience base of the workforce.

Other interventions included:

- the formation of a site leadership team (the 'White Team'), comprised of section heads and three senior union officials. This team was responsible for streamlining the site's management and consultative process;
- initiation of a review of the use of contractors on site;
- formation of a communication team to keep everyone informed; and
- formation of a single site union by amalgamation of the unions represented on the site.

Over the next year, 186 people left the site and their skills and knowledge were passed on to the work teams. Eventually, through a process of merger, a site union was created.

In 1995, Plant Composite Review Teams (PCRTs), made up of representatives from the maintenance and process workforce and management, were formed. These teams were particularly concerned with improving the efficiency of core work processes within their plants and across the site. Each PCRT was an integrating forum for the three subteams needed to run a modern petrochemical plant efficiently: the Operations Team which runs the process; the Reliability Team which maintains the equipment; and the Process Improvement Team which provides engineering and infrastructure support for improving performance.

What effect did this wave of change interventions have on performance?

Between 1994 and 1997 workforce numbers were reduced from 1061 to 758. People cost per tonne of product dropped from $165 per tonne to $125—a 24% increase in labour productivity. This figure was enhanced by an increase in volume of product produced, with record production levels achieved. Safety also improved substantially. Reliability of performance (such as machine uptime) showed dramatic increases on a variety of measures. Overall, the cultural changes on the Botany site now penetrated deeply into the workforce culture, transforming the way work was performed, turning conflict into commitment and ensuring that the company stayed in the petrochemical business at a time of heightened international competition. The company also reinvested in the plant.

In 1997, ICI decided to divest itself of ICI Australia in order to help fund its acquisition of the Unilever Group's global specialty chemicals operation. Mealor's case study ends at this point but, of course, change at the plant continues.

Change programs take time, are complex, involve creating mutually supportive and relevant interventions and rely for success

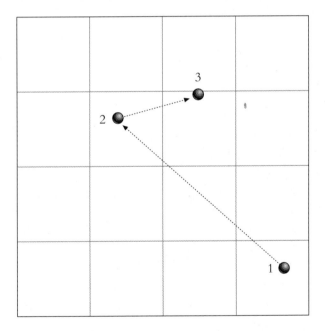

Legend
1 = The First Wave: Top-down strategic change, 1987–91
2 = The Second Wave: Co-operative incremental change, 1991–95
3 = The Third Wave: Collaborative strategic change, 1995–98

Figure 4C.4 Transforming the workplace at ICI

on building commitment and momentum. They are long-term political processes in which single change interventions seldom lead to sustainable workforce change. This study illustrates especially that transforming an industrial workplace is not achieved overnight. While dramatic changes did occur in short time periods on the Botany site, a fundamental reorientation of workplace practices took at least ten years. A workforce culture which has taken decades to evolve may take a decade to transform. The study also illustrates the progressive upskilling of the workforce in technical, supervisory and managerial skills as discussed later in Chapter 6. We recommend readers consult the thesis for further details.

References

1. Parts of this case are drawn from Jennifer Marshallsea, Malcolm Munro, Susan Rushworth & Grace Tonich, 'The Story of the 42nd Precinct', unpublished study, Swinbourne Institute of Technology. We gratefully acknowledge their work.
2. T. Mealor, 'Catalysts, Continuity and Change: Workplace Restructuring in the Chemical Industry', PhD Thesis, Australian Graduate School of Management, University of New South Wales, June 1999; see also T. Mealor, 'Transforming Employee Relations from Adversarial to Problem-Solving: ICI Botany', Case Study D, in G. L. O'Neill & R. Kramen (eds), *Australian Human Resources Management: Current Trends in Management Practice*, Volume 2, Business and Professional Publishing Pty Ltd, Warriewood, Australia, 1998, pp. 115–24.
3. ibid., p. 76.
4. ibid., p. 77.
5. ibid., p. 116.
6. ibid., p. 119.

Dedication

This case study is dedicated to the memory of

TONY MEALOR BSocSci (Hons) PhD, who died in January 2000

Shipwright, seaman, bus conductor, metal finisher, copper miner, fitter, smelter hand, crocodile hunter, wine bar manager, maître de, furniture store manager, milkman, carpet salesman, commercial traveller, sales manager, managing director, foreman, food refinery operator, maintenance officer, steam engine driver, union organiser, academic researcher, change agent and loyal friend.

'He lived a life worthy of a human being.'

(Michael Johnston, Former Human Resources Manager, ICI Botany Operations)

Chapter 5
Taking charge of change:
Coaches, Captains, Charismatics and Commanders

Leadership: Sustaining and shaping corporate success

In late 1999 Pricewaterhouse Coopers and the Australian business magazine *Business Review Weekly* hired the research company A C Neilsen to survey the CEOs and chief financial officers in Australia's 100 largest organisations to determine the most admired business leaders and companies in Australia.[1]

The resulting list of most admired business leaders showed that their reputations were based primarily on success in managing major change in their corporations. For example, Don Argus headed the list for his leadership in cementing National Australia Bank as the country's foremost bank and a force in the global consumer banking market. Argus is now Chairman of BHP. Next on the list was James Strong of Qantas, there for his leadership in managing Qantas's successful privatisation during the deregulation of the industry and global reorganisation. Similarly with others on the list, such as Dennis Eck of Coles Myer who challenged the highly successful Woolworths Turnaround of some years earlier to replace Woolworths as the most admired company in the retail industry. Leadership in today's corporations consists in the ability to reshape the organisation for future success.

In Chapter 4 we introduced the changes made to Qantas under James Strong. It has been a mixture of hard (structural) and soft (cultural) change. Until 2000 the fact of Qantas's transformation seemed unquestioned and, despite difficulties encountered in 2000, there is a lot we can learn about change leadership from the story of Qantas, and from James Strong.

There are several clear principles. A long-term organisation-wide change program shifts emphasis significantly over time. In successful change programs these shifts are not random fluctuations or the trial and error approach of the TNT example we discussed in Chapter 4. Rather they are mindful, strategically planned responses designed to reposition the organisation to take advantage of new environmental opportunities and challenges.

Such significant shifts in implementation strategy must be planned and led. The Qantas case shows Strong and his executive team taking a series of initiatives, each of which modifies their leadership style and/or the scale of change. In the early crisis period, where the financial viability of the airline was under threat, this style was coercive initially (removing senior managers and executives, and dictating structural change). When the financial crisis was past, the pace of change was maintained but the style of leadership was modified, becoming more consultative, encouraging participation. Strong's 'Staff Forum' sessions became legendary, involving widespread commitment and engagement of staff.

As new business challenges emerged (the sharemarket float), the leadership style reverted to directive again, and so on. We show this in Figure 5.1. One of the remarkable characteristics of James Strong in Qantas and other organisations has been his broad repertoire of leadership styles and the flexibility with which he can move his style as the situation requires it. In 2000–2001 this capacity was being tested again.

This sets the theme for the rest of this chapter, which deals with the way in which managers translate strategic vision into action. We discuss real people taking initiatives in actual organisations. Our aim is not to canonise a few iconic figures but rather to illustrate that effective change is run by people who share the limitations of normal human beings. They are simply people like us who have

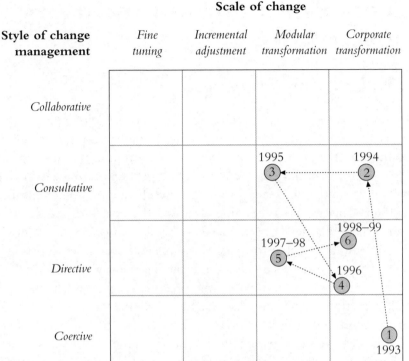

Figure 5.1 The path of change implementation for Qantas

dared to show courage in the face of their fears, conviction despite their doubts and the doubts of others, and who prefer to be actors rather than powerless bystanders in the unfolding drama of corporate change. Their motto might well be the old organisational adage: 'It's better to be forgiven than forgotten.' They are risk takers, but the risks are calculated.

Leadership, communication and culture

The leadership of change

In this chapter, we will focus on three critical elements in the process of translating strategy into action: the leadership of change, communication strategies and strategies for cultural renewal.

Current management literature places great importance on the role of executive leadership in corporate change implementation.[2] In the last decade it has become clear that the boards of listed companies share this view, as evidenced by the increasing trend to remove CEOs who are unable to marshal the resources of an enterprise to deliver profits and success. Effective change is led, and led by executives; without executive leadership, organisational change is chaotic, lacks direction and is simply reactive to environmental pressures rather than becoming an active force in shaping the environment. The central task of management today has become the leadership of change. In the case of the Qantas change process, Strong and his team adopted an energetic and visionary approach to the external pressures that then threatened the airline. They perceived that the increasingly competitive global environment demanded a fundamental change in the way Qantas did business and they used that challenge as a launch pad to ensure that it became successful against other airlines which were increasingly adopting a global, competitive ethos.

Leadership does not always arise at the top of organisations; the critical leadership for change sometimes comes from below and can be blocked or diverted by strong executives with a stake in the status quo. However, ideally, strategic change is either led from the top, or executive leadership provides support and co-ordination of the change initiatives of others in the organisation. Change led in this way typically achieves results. The conflict that always occurs in change programs is more likely to be resolved productively when change is being sought and supported by a senior executive group which has developed a clear understanding of the environment, can work as a team, and which shares an understanding of the new strategies they wish to pursue. However, leadership at the top is not enough. Managing the implementation of strategic change also involves identifying and developing a cadre of other leaders and change catalysts throughout the organisation who act in a purposeful and co-ordinated way to create the energy and momentum to bring about a new order.

In his book, *A Force for Change*, Harvard Professor John Kotter[3] documents the critical shift that has occurred in the roles of executives and senior managers from concern with managing ongoing operational tasks to leading change. Table 5.1 summarises Kotter's view of the shift.

Table 5.1 Comparing management and leadership

Management	Leadership
Planning and budgeting	*Establishing direction*
Establishing detailed steps and timetables for achieving needed results, and then allocating the resources necessary to make it happen	Developing a vision of the future, often the distant future, and strategies for producing the changes needed
Organising and staffing	*Aligning people*
Establishing structures for accomplishing plan requirements, staffing the structure with individuals, delegating responsibility and authority for carrying out the plan, providing policies and procedures to help guide people, and creating methods or systems to monitor implementation	Communicating the direction by words and deeds to all those whose co-operation may be needed in order to influence the creation of teams and coalitions that understand the vision and strategies, and accept their validity
Controlling and problem solving	*Motivating and inspiring*
Monitoring results versus planning in some detail, identifying deviations, and then planning and organising to solve these problems	Energising people to overcome major political, bureaucratic, and resource barriers to change by satisfying very basic, but often unfulfilled, human needs
Produces a degree of predictability and order, and has the potential of consistently producing key results expected by various stakeholders (e.g. for customers, always being on time; for stockholders, being within budget)	*Produces change,* often to a dramatic degree, and has the potential of producing extremely useful change (e.g. new products that customers want, new approaches to labour relations that help make a firm more competitive).

Source: Adapted from J. Kotter, *A Force for Change*, Free Press, London, 1990, p. 6.

Increasingly we see leaders delegating operational responsibilities to line employees, first to create space for leadership, and second to empower a workforce which is becoming more skilled and articulate. This demands a shift from the routine bureaucratic role of an operational manager to the often unfamiliar roles of change agent and change leader. But what is a change leader? And what does change leadership involve?

Communication strategies

One of the central tasks of leaders of change is to generate the new strategic directions which will guide the organisation into a viable future. However, these directions, often in the form of a vision or strategic intent, must be communicated effectively so that they are eventually translated into the concrete actions of the members of the organisation. The creation of the directions themselves demands communication and two-way engagement throughout the whole organisation, with significant numbers of employees at all levels being involved in providing feedback and input on early core ideas. Alternatively, the directions are developed at the top and communicated authoritatively throughout the organisation. Later, as the new strategies are put in place, the directions typically evolve and take on form through being fleshed out in the plans and actions of the various divisions, strategic business units and work groups which make up the organisation. Communication is vital to this phase of the change process and often involves feedback cycles between critical segments of the organisation.

Different types of change programs require managers to use contrasting communication strategies, and in this chapter we describe these distinctive communication strategies. However, first we outline in Figure 5.2 the key issues involved in designing a communication strategy for any organisational transition. Then later in the chapter we discuss how these issues are handled in four differing approaches to leading organisational change.

Strategies for cultural renewal

The longer term goal of change leadership is to regenerate an organisational culture to support continuing high-level performance

1. **What are the goals of the communication?**
   That is, what is the communication strategy designed to achieve in terms of changed awareness, knowledge, attitudes and/or behaviour?

2. **Who is to be involved in the communication process?**
   What parties are to be involved in the communication process? Who will be the key communicators who represent the points of view of the critical parties?

3. **What kinds of issues are to be addressed in the communication process?**
   That is, what is to be the message content, both explicit and implicit, and what coverage of issues will be attempted?

4. **Through what channels will communication messages flow?**
   In what directions will the flow be? That is, will the communication be one-way, two-way or multiway? Will it be downwards, upwards or lateral? What will be the timing and sequencing of communications?

5. **What will be the balance of power and influence between the parties to the communication?**

Figure 5.2 Key issues in the design of a communication strategy for an organisational transition

in the strategically repositioned organisation. But to change organisational culture, we must first understand what culture is. Organisational culture consists of the core assumptions, values, beliefs, norms and ideologies shared by those in the organisation. It also consists of the cultural forms which express these values—for example, unique language codes used by those in the organisation; distinctive language content, such as corporate myths and stories; distinctive patterns of repetitive behaviour, such as rituals and ceremonies; and other symbols and artefacts which carry emotional meaning for organisational members.

Culture is concerned with meaning; it provides organisational members with the rationale for what they do; it enshrines the purposes of the activities pursued by members of the organisation. Culture therefore exercises strong control over the actions of those in the organisation by setting the boundaries of what is acceptable behaviour and defining ideal behaviour. It is not surprising, therefore, that change leaders attempt to remould organisational cultures. Transformational leaders attempt radical cultural change, directed at replacing existing core values with new values that often contrast with, or even contradict, the traditional ones. On the other hand, transactional leaders seek to modify the culture, either building on or reinterpreting traditional values, or introducing new cultural elements that must eventually be integrated into the existing culture.

As members of the organisation share experiences in the process of communicating and working with the change program, the existing corporate culture is changed. New values evolve out of debate and conflict, out of failures and successes, and out of interventions by powerful stakeholders and organisational elites. The new culture can reinforce the new behaviours needed to promote the vision for future corporate success.

Cultural renewal cannot be left to chance but neither can it be clearly designed in advance as an intellectual exercise; it is above all the cumulative actions of change leaders which create a symbolic discourse around important value issues and so shape the emerging organisational culture. It is not so much what leaders say that modifies culture but the impact of what they do as they interact with others in the process of unrolling the events of a change program. Former Lend Lease Chairman, Stuart Hornery, was well known for telling employees: 'Don't just listen to what I say, watch what I do.' Cultural change is more like an improvised and spontaneous dance drama than a well planned and extensively rehearsed performance of *Swan Lake*.

What kinds of interventions do change leaders use to create and direct cultural change? There are basically three potential levels of intervention:

- *Structural interventions* These include corporate restructuring, redesign of workplace or plant layouts, introduction of new technology, and replacement of leaders. Paul Anderson, CEO at BHP, has used these liberally in his change program. These are essentially interventions into the 'hard wiring' of the organisation that can impact on existing patterns of behaviour.

- *Process interventions* These include changing human resource policies or other existing systems, such as supplier relationships. For example, we will discuss below how Qantas management negotiated with the unions a new performance management system that shifted the core values of the culture from a traditional, paternalistic emphasis towards a more market oriented, bottom-line and accountability focus.

- *Symbolic interventions* These include the introduction of new statements of directions, charters and core values; public actions that have strong emotive and symbolic content; and other interventions that directly challenge prevailing values, beliefs and attitudes. Of the three types of intervention, symbolic interventions are potentially more powerful because they directly address the issue of changing prevailing mindsets. However, because of this, they are also more likely to generate significant resistance to change.

Culture is one of the more significant elements of the change process: handle the cultural issues well and change is likely to be more effective. However, cultural management will be ineffective if the organisation's strategy is flawed, or its balance sheet unsound.

Change takes time

Now we return to Qantas and illustrate some of the points we have been making with the example of another change leader working closer to the organisation's grassroots.

Change takes time, persistence and personal courage on the part of those who lead it. We opened this chapter by citing what several CEOs from the Pricewaterhouse Coopers study regarded as Transformational leadership. But no CEO of a large complex organisation can single-handedly carry through corporate change. There need to be leaders at all levels who share the CEO's vision and who work to make it happen.

There is no such thing as good luck in business. If you are in the business of continuous change you must have a process, applied in a very disciplined way, that tells you where you are heading. You need to understand what you are heading. You need to understand what you are trying to achieve and make sure that when you do it, you do it right.

DON ARGUS, FORMER CEO, NATIONAL AUSTRALIA BANK[4]

One such leader at Qantas is Shane Garland, General Manager, Sydney Airport. From the mid-1990s Garland has played a key role in the implementation of the Qantas change program in this location. Garland was appointed to Sydney from his previous position of General Manager at Perth Airport. When appointed, he was the seventeenth Sydney Airport Manager in twenty-five years—an indication of the previously volatile nature of that worksite.

In the first six months he commenced his diagnosis of the terminal's needs for change by walking about the terminal, watching on-going operations and listening to the employees. He also organised information gathering and diagnostic sessions by setting up offsite discussions overnight in a Sydney hotel to discuss current workplace problems with groups of employees. The neutral location removed workplace barriers, and created an open environment for the exchange of information and ideas. He made particular efforts to form good personal relationships with union organisers. In particular, the strong personal relationship he formed with TWU delegate, Ross Lewis, was critical to the initial success of the project. Once on side, Ross was a significant force for change.

In this initial six months Garland also instituted employee workshops to improve work practice efficiency, and conducted a personal review of airline operations in the United States as a benchmarking study.

Garland soon realised that a directive, non-participative management style had been the dominant pattern at Sydney Airport. He determined to change this by maximising staff participation in the change process and in operational decision making. He saw that if this were to happen, there had to be a new level of trust between management and others, that there was a need to institute a team based culture and to entrust staff to make day-to-day operating decisions in the best interests of Qantas.

All this would not happen overnight. The Sydney terminal was heavily unionised. There was a history of ongoing confrontation and 'strong arm' tactics on both sides of the management/union divide, and there were a range of inefficient informal work practices that had grown up with management's tacit acceptance.

Garland determined to tackle the 'them versus us' culture. He did this by getting out of his office and continually walking the 'shop floor', engaging employees in conversation about their jobs, the change program and demonstrating a personal interest in their views and their lives. Some employees were sent to best practice terminals around the world to examine more efficient work practices. They returned with new insights into what was achievable.

At the end of six months, Garland had completed his diagnosis of the change needs at the Sydney terminal. He had formed an extensive network of informal relationships. He was fully briefed on the scope of the larger Qantas-wide change program and was confident that he had the support of the CEO, James Strong, and other key staff involved in introducing a wide range of change initiatives that would affect his specific change program at the terminal.

He set out his aim for his part of the ongoing change program:

1. *Increase flexibility* Passenger flows at the airport were subject to peaks and troughs yet all jobs at the airport were full-time and the unions had refused changes to these arrangements. To achieve flexibility, Garland planned to introduce significant numbers of part-time staff in customer service and on 'the ramp' (that is, the loading, unloading and cabin presentation of aircraft). This would lead to significant cost reductions if it could be achieved.
2. *Reduce costs* This was a critical issue for competitiveness. Staff reductions, particularly in the supervisory area, and productivity improvements would be vital.
3. *Change the culture* Prior to Garland's appointment, employees had regarded it as the manager's job, not theirs, to understand business issues. Garland decided to try to create a new awareness

throughout the terminal of how each person's work affected business results and an increased sense of ownership of business imperatives and key issues in customer satisfaction.

4. *Improve communication processes* Good communication systems would be critical to the development of a new culture and also to the increased interdependence between groups in the terminal that would be needed to make it work smoothly and effectively for Qantas customers.

Garland's vision is summarised, in few words, as: 'Turn airplanes around at the lowest cost and provide the world's best customer service.'

In mid-1996 Qantas Corporate initiated the third Enterprise Bargaining Agreement (EBA3). This included a request to undertake competitive tenders for the operation of the International Terminal in the areas of baggage handling and customer service.

Why competitive tendering? The Australian government decided to privatise Australian airports, creating a threat of outside contractors being brought in to provide ground-handling services for international airlines. Garland's investigations had shown that procedures were costly and inefficient, and credible international firms such as Jardines and Ogdens were showing interest in managing these operations. If Qantas were to retain control of the ramp function and Qantas employees (at least some of them) were to retain their jobs, a radical new initiative was needed. Competitive tendering was just such an initiative. After much negotiation, the two unions involved, the Transport Workers Union (TWU) and the Australian Services Union (ASU), signed the agreement.

In September/October 1996 Garland conducted a review of the terminal operations: over two months, work teams and all staff contributed to the review. A two day offsite conference was then held to put the cost reduction issue to a number of the staff. Garland indicated the scope of the issues arising out of the review, estimating that the staff would need to cut $5 million from operating costs at the international terminal.

All staff at the terminal were then briefed on the results of the offsite conference. Once the information had been gathered and the problems diagnosed, Garland then released a memo to his ninety managers, indicating the changes ahead. He also released a single page document, 'The future direction of Sydney International Terminal Customer Services', that provided the new supervisory job description. Seventy-five of the ninety managers accepted redundancy packages. Part-time staff also replaced many full-time staff in the terminal.

Meanwhile, the competitive tendering process had been initiated in the first set of airports to be sold off (Brisbane, Melbourne and Perth). Sydney was in the second set and so benefited from the prior experience of the others. In June 1997 a Competitive Tender Bid Team, comprised of employees from different tiers of the organisation, was established at the Sydney terminal. Outside consultants were chosen to develop the business knowledge of the team members, who had to move on to a steep learning curve. Some bid team members had never used a computer; most had never seen a spreadsheet of financial data. Members of the Bid Team faced severe criticism from some of their fellow workers who were cynical of management's motives and accused Bid Team members of 'selling out'.

External organisations also prepared bids. The internal team was successful in its bids, and was awarded the tender. Under the industrial agreement, signed subsequently, employees are responsible for reaching agreed levels of performance and driving a continuous improvement process. Competitive tendering has produced impressive results. These results include a $53 million decrease in labour costs per annum across the whole airline. Customer satisfaction has also risen, and continues to show significant improvement. But perhaps the most significant result has been the clear and decisive shift in the workforce culture. At least part of this change can be attributed to Garland's belief that employees should 'bring their brains to work and not leave them at the door', his willingness to question and challenge established procedures, his open information policy on everything, including financial information, and his willingness to risk his own personal career rather than compromise his deeply held belief that everyone should be involved in managing the change process.

This story[5] focuses on Garland's initiatives but, of course, just as James Strong could not transform Qantas single-handedly, neither could Shane Garland transform the workforce at Sydney Airport single-handedly. The real clue is to build effective change teams who increasingly also involve others in creating organisation–wide energy and momentum for change. At Qantas a network of other managers and staff specialists were taking supportive, complementary actions as they undertook their part of the overall organisational change program.

Four types of change leaders

In Chapter 4 we described four generic ways of managing organisational transitions. Each of these approaches demands a different style of change leadership, a different communication strategy and a distinctive approach to rebuilding corporate culture. In this chapter, we deal with these three central features of change—leadership, communication and cultural renewal—and illustrate how, in effective change programs, these three elements are closely co-ordinated but clearly differentiated according to the type of change program that is necessary for repositioning the organisation to take advantage of its shifting environment. We take up each of the differing change strategies in turn and systematically describe the characteristic leadership style, mode of communication, and approach to cultural regeneration used in each approach, illustrated with factual cases. Of course, no individual case conforms exactly to the model: real life is more varied than abstracted models, but the models are useful general guides to handling a range of related circumstances. In outlining each of the four strategies, we will also examine carefully the strengths of each approach and its vulnerabilities.

1. Coaches: Leading Developmental Transitions

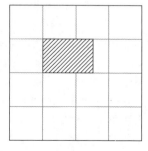

The characteristics of Developmental Transitions are outlined below. This kind of change strategy fits well with a skilled, informed and professional workforce which has the capacity to take and develop initiatives and a willingness to commit to new strategic directions and to change as a way of life.

This strategy also fits more readily with smaller organisations, where widespread consultation is less difficult to organise, is less time-consuming and where trust is more readily developed by face-to-face contacts.

Characteristics of Developmental Transitions

Developmental Transitions

Developmental Transition is the approach to change typically used when:

- the new strategy being adopted does not involve an immediate and radical departure from the current strategy being pursued in the organisation;
- changes can be implemented on a continuous, relentless basis over an extended time period;
- key groups favour change or can be persuaded to do so;
- the executive team favours change and team members are able to use a consultative approach to change.

The leadership of change in Developmental Transitions

Developmental Transitions are focused primarily on creating energy and momentum for change by developing voluntary commitment to change on the part of all key sectors of the workforce and empowering the workforce to translate a shared vision into action. The leadership of change therefore becomes analogous to coaching in that it is highly interactive and responsive, often depending equally on initiatives from the CEO and the top executive group and from various other organisational levels and workforce segments.

Effective leaders of Developmental Transitions are people centred, personable, inspirational and skilled at informal communication and negotiation. Coaches typically move freely around their organisation, emphasising relatively informal contact with employees at all levels. They exhibit interest in and curiosity about the views of organisational members, are skilled questioners and good listeners, and project a high degree of respect and trust in the capabilities of those around them. They set high performance standards for themselves and others but realistically resource those who assume responsibility, providing personal support and encouragement for them. They are seen to have personal integrity because they effectively model the new behaviour required in the organisation. They generate trust through rewarding those who take initiatives which contribute to the development of the shared vision. Shane Garland, discussed above, has all the characteristics of a typical Coach, although he can also draw on other styles when the situation warrants it.

The leadership style used by Coaches is typically the ideal style advocated as having universal applicability by the literature in the Organisational Development (OD) tradition. This school of thought evolved out of the Human Relations approach to change and was the dominant approach to organisational change in the United States and other English-speaking countries, such as Australia and New Zealand, throughout the late 1960s, 1970s and early 1980s.

In an environment of economic expansion, it was possible for leaders of this kind to downplay conflicts between interest groups in the workplace and develop an ideology that envisaged 'win–win' solutions for all those involved in the process of organisational change. The ideal change leader was seen as democratic and non-authoritarian, with an ability to manage an emerging consensus through the use of personal leadership skills.

Communication strategies in Developmental Transitions

The Coach's major goal in a Developmental Transition is to generate voluntary commitment to change. She or he may begin with a personal vision for organisational change but their emphasis is on the construction of a shared vision. Coaches believe, frequently correctly, that the most relevant information about the environment and its changed demands is already known to members of the organisation although it may not yet be systematically collected, analysed and disseminated throughout the organisation. Even if some critical environmental information is not currently known within the organisation, if it can be communicated to members of the organisation, the leader believes that members will be committed to making the necessary changes.

Consequently the first issue of the communication strategy in this approach to change is to involve significant numbers of people in the organisation, or a representative group, in a participative process of environmental scanning, and evaluation of the resulting data, which will create an agreement on a common vision to motivate commitment to the change process. The resulting vision will be evaluated on two criteria. First, will it result in the successful repositioning of the organisation to take advantage of the anticipated environmental changes? And, second, will it connect powerfully with the aspirations of organisational members, ensuring their commitment to the changes that need to be made? One danger of traditional approaches of this kind is that they have often involved only the employees of the organisation and have tended to neglect direct participation of other key stakeholder groups on whose support the future viability of the organisation depends. Consequently there has recently been an increasing tendency to widen the circle of participation to include other critical stakeholders such as clients, customers and suppliers.

The second issue in constructing a systematic strategy for change is to decide which parties are to be involved in the communication process and who are to be the key communicators representing them. As the primary aim is to increase commitment, Coaches try to progressively widen the range of key parties to the communication process as the change program proceeds. However, this choice opens up the risk of so diluting and extending the communication process that it is difficult to control, no one feels responsible for the outcomes, and the debate becomes superficial. The result can be lack of involvement, and cynicism, rather than increased commitment. To counter this threat, a major attempt is usually made to identify key opinion leaders in the informal network and to secure their active leadership of the communication process. Key executives develop an informal network of personal relationships with these leaders and work to create mutual trust.

The third issue in constructing a communication strategy is the choice of message content and coverage. As the major objective is to build commitment, the explicit content of communication is often of secondary importance to the symbolic communication. This is designed to arouse a positive emotional response to the communication initiative and to stimulate a reciprocal initiative that will build trust and encourage continuing meaningful communication between the parties involved.

The fourth issue in constructing a communication strategy involves the choice of channels through which communication will flow. In most organisations there is a wide variety of such channels to choose from, such as formal briefings cascaded throughout the organisation, use of the intranet, articles in internal magazines and the use of informal communication networks. Because the Coach's primary goal is to develop commitment to change, the channels preferred will be those that are more personal, encourage a ready response on the part of organisational members, and increase levels of participation and involvement. This generally means that the CEO and senior executives spend a good deal of time interacting at an informal grassroots level, eliciting the views of employees, maximising their own visibility, and developing an image of down-to-earth accessibility. It also means that there is a strong emphasis on participative workshops and focus groups where information is shared, options for change are considered, and outputs in the form of suggested options are cascaded up the hierarchy. The emphasis is on continuous, ongoing, two-way consultative communication designed to involve all or most of the organisational members in an ongoing debate about the change program.

Similarly, the choice of the direction of communication is one that emphasises multidirectional communication and is designed to stimulate openness, creative initiatives and continuing exchanges between the central parties. This demands considerable sensitivity to process on the part of change agents and a degree of opportunism combined with the flexible intervention skills needed to guide and shape the evolving process of developing a growing consensus. Similarly, political sensitivity and skill is needed to preserve the delicate balance of power between interest groups so that the leaders of all key groups perceive that there are rewards for their members in staying involved in the change program.

We have described the predominant leadership style and communication strategies used in Developmental Transitions. We move now to a description of how these in turn affect the approach to cultural renewal that is typically employed by Coaches.

Strategies for cultural renewal in Developmental Transitions

The approach to cultural change pursued by leaders of Developmental Transitions is what Chin and Benne have labelled 'normative–re-educative'.[6] In terms of the three kinds of cultural intervention strategies described earlier in this chapter, Coaches tend to favour process and symbolic interventions and place less importance on structural interventions. In seeking to modify the old culture, there is a strong reliance on interventions which promote value debate but with an emphasis primarily on building on, or reinterpreting, current values rather than challenging them at the core. Typical interventions consist of focus groups of employees who discuss key issues confronting the firm, or taskforces made up of representatives of key interest groups to consider new options for action on a key issue facing the organisation. These are often combined with training courses which are designed to raise the awareness of organisational members, to disseminate new information throughout the organisation, and to develop new attitudes to key change initiatives. Culture arises from the shared experiences of organisational members, so there may also be an emphasis on providing new shared experiences which generate high levels of commitment and new attitudes consistent with the direction of the change program.

Strengths and vulnerabilities of Developmental Transitions

The major strength of this approach to change is the level of involvement, commitment and ownership of the change program that it can generate in a wide range of organisational members. When the situation is appropriate and the leadership effective, the program can generate sustained energy and individual initiatives at the grassroots level. For most people in Western democracies, there is also a strong appeal in the humanistic values which dominate programs of this kind, for they are compatible with part of the core values of a democratic society.

> *I think what I value most in this job was that after two years I was sitting down having a chat to one of the union delegates and then something dawned on me. I said to him: we seem to be using a different language than we used to. We are all talking about partnerships; we are all talking about performance; we are all talking about saving money; we are talking about having a focus on the future, and that was impossible two years ago.*
>
> *So the language changed and it really stood out.*
>
> SHANE GARLAND, GENERAL MANAGER,
> SYDNEY AIRPORT, QANTAS, ON CULTURAL CHANGE [7]

However, there are vulnerabilities in this approach. For example, a particular area of difficulty for Coaches lies in the deliberate downplaying of authority, the cultivation of an ethos of egalitarianism, and the use of informal channels of communication. Coaches replace positional power with personal power and yet they wish to retain control over the general direction of the change program. The skill of remaining in charge while involving everyone and being 'one of the team' requires that the Coach maintain the respect and admiration of the members of the organisation. This is more readily achieved where the organisation is experiencing success under the Coach's leadership; it is much more difficult to achieve when there are extended periods of low performance.

Other risks that typically flow from the choices made in pursuing a strategy of Developmental Transition centre around threats to the central aim of this strategy—that is, the development of commitment throughout the workforce. In particular, the voluntary nature of the strategy renders it vulnerable to key interest groups who have a strong stake in the status quo, or in some other alternative unacceptable to management or to other key stakeholder groups. Such interest groups may choose not to co-operate, or to co-operate only on receipt of benefits which undermine the strategic goals of the change program. Similarly the dependence on trust makes the success of the program vulnerable to key players who are cynical, antagonistic, suspicious and manipulative. Trust takes time and patience to develop, especially in large organisations. However, it crumbles quickly when one key party is seen as betraying the trust that has developed.

Another threat to the success of developmental strategies arises from the time-consuming nature of consultative and participative processes. Developmental Transitions are successful when they create the high level of commitment to the continuous improvement which is often needed to maintain competitive advantage. However, unless the communication process is efficiently organised and is prevented from bogging down in fruitless debate, this momentum can be lost and the strategy rendered futile. This is compounded in most Western corporations by the unrelenting pressure from boards of management and shareholders for short-term results. Key stakeholders can become impatient with the time taken to produce bottom-line results, and intervene in ways which destroy the trust painstakingly established between senior managers and the workforce. To counter this threat, Coaches must put considerable effort into managing the change process upwards with boards of directors, and outwards with other external stakeholders. It is in some ways more difficult to do this than to build a committed workforce. Employees spend a large part of their life in the organisation while other stakeholders are often only very part-time participants with little or no direct involvement in the change process itself. Creating commitment in part-timers who are largely uninvolved demands an entirely different approach to the development of commitment within the workforce.

2. Captains: Leading Task-focused Transitions

The key characteristics of Task-focused Transitions are outlined below. This kind of approach to change fits well with organisations that are pursuing an Analyzer business strategy, particularly in low-growth, steady-state or recessionary markets. The directive nature of the change allows close

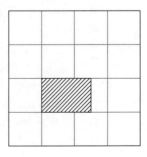

supervision of a range of task activities and the creation of a high degree of internal consistency in methods of operating.

The leadership of change in Task-focused Transitions

Task-focused Transitions are designed to produce compliance and conformity to strategies designed at senior levels, and are implemented with high levels of internal consistency throughout the organisation. We refer to the leaders of Task-focused Transitions as *Captains* because, like military commanders, they are directive, authoritative and focused on the task to be accomplished. Captains emphasise rationality and consistency rather than charisma; they use both the authority of position and the authority of expertise to legitimise change. Captains pursue incremental change in systematic ways, creating improvements through a process of systematic experimentation and testing of new initiatives, then diffusion of the new models of action throughout the organisation. Captains are instrumental and achievement oriented, eschew displays of emotion and irrationality, and favour rational planning. However, like military

Characteristics of Task-focused Transitions

Task-focused Transitions

The Task-focused Transition approach to change is typically used when:

- the new strategy being adopted does not involve an immediate and radical departure from the current strategy being pursued in the organisation;
- changes can be implemented on a continuous, relentless basis over an extended time period;
- key groups favour change or can be persuaded to do so;
- the executive group favour, and are able to effectively use, a directive approach to change;
- the dominant need is to redesign work teams, jobs and systems for successful change.

leaders, they can also display strategic opportunism when the action is running hot. They encourage and reward loyalty in others, set high standards for others and expect others to be responsible and reliable performers within the guidelines and procedures laid down from above. They are strong believers in the power of systems to direct behaviour, particularly when backed by appropriate rewards, so they devote a great deal of time and energy to creating formalised systems for task performance, including clear job specifications. When they use external or internal change agents, these change agents are primarily technical and procedural experts rather than people focused consultants with expertise in interpersonal and group processes.

The leadership style described here is one that is compatible with the norms of most managers trained in technical areas such as engineering, economics, commerce and law. These areas place emphasis on rational and pragmatic action directed at continuous improvement and inculcate positivistic beliefs in people's ability to control their environment. It is also compatible with traditional Australasian male beliefs about the desirability of limiting emotional expression and concentrating on practical action. At the executive level, Captains operate directively and often decisively. However, they encourage consultative leadership at the business unit level but contain consultative activity within a strong systems framework. Typically, Captains have a credible background in the industry, set clear priorities and targets for change, and delegate effectively.

Communication strategies in Task-focused Transitions

The Captain's major goal in communication is to focus attention on upgrading task performance and obtaining compliance with new work standards. Rather than emphasising the construction of an internalised shared vision by the majority of those in the organisation, the Captain aims to secure behavioural alignment with the vision and other key initiatives developed at the executive level of the organisation. The involvement of the workforce in putting new measures into place is encouraged as long as it does not introduce unwanted variation in workplace practices. Involvement is seen as an important way of generating commitment to change but the emphasis is on rational persuasion and negotiated agreement to change rather than on personal identification with inspirational leaders.

In communicating change, Captains prefer to use line authority and formal channels of communication rather than informal networks. As a major aim is to increase compliance, the communication strategies are chosen partly with the aim of strengthening line authority. In this way, communication tends to travel from the executive group down through successive levels of the organisation, reinforcing the authority of unit heads. Consequently, team briefings are often used sequentially down the organisation. Other key communicators chosen are technical experts whose expertise lies in efficiency, cost minimisation and quality enhancement.

Message content centres primarily around task relevant issues such as financial performance, productivity and quality enhancement. A great deal of attention is devoted to defining clear performance goals and negotiating agreement to them, and to achieving clear definition of evolving task roles through developing job descriptions, systems of performance measurement and structured reward systems. In these ways, Captains communicate a tough-minded commitment to improving standards of performance and meeting changing market demands. They pride themselves on a matter-of-fact, 'no nonsense' approach to change leadership which conveys a clear message of: 'We are creating an increasingly better designed performance management system in which everyone knows what changes are needed, what their new jobs involve, and where resources are available to support high performance. If you perform, you will be rewarded; if you fail to perform, you will be out of the organisation.' As new systems are put in place or progressively modified, the changes are documented in clear, operational terms as new procedures.

Captains try to maintain a balance of power that favours authoritative executive leadership. They foster leadership initiatives from below that support rather than challenge executive strategies; they are quick to recognise and reward new leadership talent and expertise and to deploy resources, including human resources, to areas where more resources are needed. They approach change rationally and plan carefully for continuous corporate development.

Strategies for cultural renewal in Task-focused Transitions

In managing cultural renewal, Captains favour empirical/rational strategies—that is, they assume that people are rational beings and will change their behaviour when information is made available to demonstrate that the changes are in their own interest. They are careful, however, to ensure that the information comes from an authoritative, credible source (hence the emphasis on the use of authority of position and expertise). External advisers are used at times as sources of authority or as change catalysts.

In addition to ensuring that people are informed, Captains focus on changing structures and systems as a means of encouraging behaviour modification. By reworking the organisation's task systems through progressive role redefinition and modification of reward structures, Captains are continually developing new behavioural patterns around key workplace tasks. By focusing on the changing demands of the organisation's central activities, legitimisation of change is relatively easy; change is seen to be necessary 'to get the job done more effectively'. Thus there is no need to challenge the central values of the organisational culture; rather, there is constant adjustment of values to meet the changing circumstances of the firm's environment. Ongoing value change is achieved primarily through progressive modification of behaviour. Behavioural research indicates that this is an effective approach to inducing behaviour change.[8]

Cultural change is maintained and reinforced through creating tightly focused task units at the Strategic Business Unit level and below. Structural redefinition plus work redesign are funnelled down to the basic organisational units; the parallel changes taking place simultaneously across multiple units performing similar functions can create a powerful resonance that reinforces the emerging cultural redirection. Under such conditions, lateral communication channels in the organisation can operate as self-reinforcing feedback for cultural change. To be effective, a major change program may require different leadership styles to be used for different components of the program.

Returning to our Qantas example, we will examine the role of Alison Berner, Manager of Product Delivery Airports Division

(PDA). The PDA was set up in March 1997 to implement organisation-wide Service Standards at all Qantas airport offices. The reason for establishing this new unit was to improve the quality and consistency of customer service. Service Standards were developed to express the forms of behaviour—including profess-ionalism, ownership, helpfulness, co-operativeness and possessing adequate skills, initiative, empathy and the ability to understand customer needs—desired in a Qantas employee. Key customer contact divisions of airports, cabin crew, telephone sales and the Qantas Club have also adopted these standards.

Introducing new standards

The Qantas front-line change program commenced with major top-down communications via worldwide summit meetings, regional meetings and regular meetings with airline staff. These were augmented by Berner interviewing staff at airports and setting up informal teams to brainstorm ideas. The aim of the program was to significantly improve Qantas's service levels and make it comparable with the world's best airlines. More specifically, performance targets covered a range of specific goals such as:

- ensuring an accessible and prompt telephone answering service;
- improving product knowledge to exceed the customers' expectations;
- prompt delivery of baggage and reducing the number of lost bags;
- better co-ordination of services between airport divisions;
- empowering frontline managers to solve customer problems.

The program was directed to all Qantas frontline staff located at over 100 airports in twenty-nine countries. The new business imperative was 'To become a world class airline offering pre-mium quality service in line with the industry's best practice'. This meant a shift from the cost-cutting approach of the previous period to a new 'accountability plus superior service' focus.

To implement the new standards across the organisation, a Service Standards Change Program was launched in October 1997. The program was initiated by senior management to overcome the slow 'buy-in' by employees and to improve the quality of customer service. Alison Berner was put in charge of this program.

Berner's change style was consistent with the top-down nature of this part of the change program. While she listened to and consulted staff, she adopted a primarily directive style. She has also acted as an informational expert, developing and sharing her knowledge on how to improve customer service, as a trainer and educator in assisting staff develop new skills, and as a monitor of progress.

The program resulted in a marked improvement in the key performance indicators measured in the Customer Service Monitor, indicating that a directive management style can, in the appropriate circumstances, improve performance. Alison was an effective Captain.[9]

Strengths and vulnerabilities of Task-focused Transitions

The central strengths of this approach are its strong focus on task related issues, the clarity of communication, the emphasis on creating clear role definition as the change proceeds and the ongoing, systematic approach to change. The availability of some time to make the changes means that people may have time to acquire and test the new behaviours.

There are, however, some potential problems associated with the change strategies used by Captains as leaders of Task-focused Transitions. The emphasis on compliance with top-down directives can limit commitment. This contrasts with the impact of Coaches, for example, who typically provide greater opportunity for wide-ranging initiatives and who are more responsive to initiatives, including those that challenge elements of the new directions and business imperatives. The top-down, authoritative and formalised approach can lead to a neglect of powerful informal communication networks, which may actually be used by others who are opposed to the changes that the executive group is planning to introduce. Similarly, the emphasis on rationality and expertise can prove ineffective in reaching groups in the workforce who have strong emotional feelings about the proposed changes, and can leave others feeling uninspired and uncommitted. These limitations can result in the change program tapering off into fine tuning change that is inadequate for effectively repositioning the organisation.

3. Charismatics: Leading Charismatic Transformations

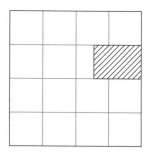

The characteristics of Charismatic Transformations are outlined below. This kind of strategy fits well with Prospector (Product/ Market Innovator) organisations radically redefining their business strategies to be industry leaders, or with start-up organisations. The key requirement is a workforce with a readiness to change, perhaps because they already realise that their interests are threatened by existing strategies which are becoming outmoded. While this strategy is almost universally advocated by US management writers, we have, in fact, identified only a relatively small proportion of large Australian organisations which have used this approach to organisational transformation. The clearest cases are Australian Airlines and Qantas under James Strong, Telstra under Frank Blount and Optus under Bob Mansfield. In all cases the transformational changes took place during the early period of their leadership. There are many more cases, however, among smaller organisations in the e-business and new economy sectors.

We believe that charismatic leadership is not as widely practised in large United States corporations as many US management writers indicate; there is a strong streak of romantic idealism in the US management literature which tends to overlook the strategic use of force by change leaders and to idealise their actions as more warmly charismatic than they are.

The leadership of change in Charismatic Transformations

Charismatic Transformations are similar to Developmental Transitions in that they are focused primarily on the development of commitment to new directions and a vision. In this case, however, the vision is much more radical and represents a fundamental challenge to the existing core cultural values of the organisation and to its traditional behavioural norms. The speed with which the organisational transformation needs to be accomplished also places substantial constraints on the degree of active participation in decision making possible for organisational members. Consequently, unlike Developmental Transitions, the vision is often largely developed by the executive team and delivered in a top-down fashion. However, there is an emphasis on symbolic interaction and vicarious participation so that organisational members develop a strong feeling of identification with the ensuing changes and a sense of ownership of them. This is more readily accomplished if the changes are exemplified in the actions of a 'heroic' figure. The leader personifies the desired changes and becomes the appealing key actor in an emerging dramatisation of the main features of the change process. This is large-scale change with a human face. We refer to the leaders of a charismatic change process of this kind as Charismatics because they use their personal image as the major lever for change.

Characteristics of Charismatic Transformations

Charismatic Transformations

The Charismatic Transformation approach to change is typically used when:

- the new strategy being adopted involves an immediate and radical change from the current strategy being pursued in the organisation;
- radical changes must be implemented quickly;
- key groups favour change or can be persuaded to do so;
- the executive team favour and are able to use a fast paced but consultative approach to change.

Charismatics usually create dramatic organisational change. They actively seek to become the central figure in an unfolding drama which they create in an entrepreneurial and opportunistic fashion.

The drama contains sequences of events which are designed to portray symbolically the major change issues confronting the organisation; it is vital that the change process has a sense of momentum, is high on energy, is emotionally compelling, and that change towards the goals expressed in the vision is seen to be taking place—in fact, is seemingly inevitable. Leaders of key interest groups also find themselves swept up in the drama and gain status and a sense of pride from their association with the central charismatic leader. Through their own behaviour and through the choice of other change leaders, Charismatics develop radical new role models which are internalised by others in the organisation.

Communication strategies in Charismatic Transformations

The major goal of the Charismatic leader is to gain emotional commitment to the new vision. Because the vision is at first unknown to most organisational members, it must be 'revealed' and this can only happen if the attention of organisational members is captured and their emotions are engaged. Speed is also vital. In large organisations multimedia communication channels lend themselves to rapid and dramatic presentation of the new vision. Charismatic leaders focus attention on their vision initially through attention-getting initiatives, and they use their personal qualities to draw attention to the new directions. Like Coaches, Charismatics may widen the circle of active participation in decision making but they retain key decision making in the hands of a trusted few. They do, however, attempt to create effective channels of upward feedback in order to monitor the level of commitment to change across the workforce and to alert themselves to potential sources of opposition.

The central content of the communication is the need for dramatic change and its inevitability. The charismatic leader creates a sense of excitement about change and presents involvement as an opportunity and a privilege—for example, John F. Kennedy: '...ask not what your country can do for you—ask what you can do for your country'. In choosing channels of communication, charismatic leaders tend to prefer mass meetings and live media presentations where they can project their personality to large numbers. The direction of communication is primarily one-way. However, they also use symbolic interactions where they are portrayed as having the humility to interact with the rank and file and to seek their contributions (but in fact they would not accomplish the needed changes in time if they did this often). They spend a good deal of time ensuring that the myth of their powerful change actions is cultivated and extended so that people will feel it is attractive to march under their banner. They arrange celebrations of achievements and create heroes who are visibly acclaimed for their successes. In maintaining a sense of momentum, they may in fact spend time negotiating change with leaders of interest groups and with opinion leaders to ensure that their commitment is maintained. This is, however, a less public part of the change program.

Strategies for cultural renewal in Charismatic Transformations

The approach to cultural change followed by Charismatics is similar to that used by re-educative Coaches—that is, what we have referred to as 'normative–re-educative'. Charismatics exercise power by reworking the symbolic environment in the organisation. They challenge the core meanings in the existing culture and attempt to produce what Argyris[10] has referred to as 'second-order learning'. Much of this second-order learning is created, not by direct participation in shared activities as in Developmental Transitions, but through vicarious experience in staged events which are designed to reconstitute key elements of the culture. These events challenge the adequacy of the traditional culture to deal with environmental change, but more importantly present an appealing positive alternative that promises a more adequate fulfilment of the aspirations of members of the organisation.

Strengths and vulnerabilities of Charismatic Transformations

The major strength of this approach to change is that, under the right circumstances, it can powerfully motivate many within the organisation to channel energy into a major transformational program. This can occur without large financial costs, as the main benefits to active participants in the change program are intangibles such as excitement, status and a sense of renewed purpose and meaning. At its best, this strategy can achieve rapid change in organisational direction, clear focus and continued commitment to maintain the momentum of change.

The right circumstances for successful change of this kind are relatively rare, however, except in the case of small start-up enterprises where the founder's driving energy buoys and motivates those within. There must be a widespread awareness of the need to change and a general willingness to make change in a majority of members of the workforce and key stakeholders. While willingness may not be fully present at the beginning of the change program, it must grow quite quickly for the program to get under way effectively. Even when these conditions are met, there must be an available leader or leaders with the personal characteristics to lead the change process.

The vulnerabilities of the approach are, however, also quite clear. There is always some confusion between developing commitment to the vision and commitment to the charismatic leader. This usually creates problems in succession as the loss of the leader can result in loss of commitment to the vision. Charismatic leaders are often motivated to begin Transformations, but they sometimes tend to lose interest as the change demands consistent attention to detail in the implementation phase. They are usually better innovators than sustainers and therefore frequently leave before the changes they have initiated are consolidated. They genuinely believe that the changes they have launched are more firmly in place than they are in fact, and they tend to overlook the degree to which their personal presence is maintaining commitment.

4. Commanders: Leading Organisational Turnarounds

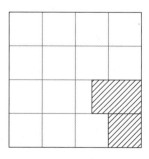

The characteristics of Turnarounds are outlined below. This kind of strategy is typically undertaken in cases where performance has dropped off or lagged behind that of competitors, where divestment of non-core business areas is essential for regaining performance, and where environmental change has made current business strategies non-viable. These conditions can occur as a result of environmental circumstances such as changed government policies, new technologies and gyrating global markets. In such circumstances strategies for repositioning the organisation are highly likely to cut across the interests of some organisational members and, in some cases, external stakeholders. For example, a proportion of the workforce may be made redundant, operations may be sold off or closed down and resources redeployed from one part of the organisation to another. In such circumstances strong resistance to change can be expected and 'win–win' solutions are difficult or impossible to organise.

Characteristics of Turnarounds

Turnarounds

The Turnaround approach to change is typically used when:

- the new strategy being adopted involves an immediate and radical departure from the current strategy being pursued in the organisation;
- changes must be rapidly initiated;
- key groups oppose change;
- the executive team favours a directive or coercive approach to change and can take power effectively.

The leadership of change in Turnarounds

How are Turnarounds led? Turnarounds are focused primarily on overcoming resistance and opposition to change and ensuring compliance to the unpopular measures needed to transform the organisation by refocusing the core business and divesting non-core business areas. Effective leaders of Turnarounds are tough-minded, directive and prepared to take forceful measures if necessary to counter resistance to the new vision they impose on the organisation. They frequently anticipate where opposition is likely to arise and may take pre-emptive action to remove or neutralise those who are likely to initiate such action. They attempt to progressively consolidate their power base in the organisation so that they can ensure that the changes they are seeking are carried out. To this end, Commanders try to ensure that they have full legal authority to undertake the planned changes. They are often brought in from outside the organisation, and they often recruit outsiders to key positions so that they receive the undivided loyalty they need from those playing key roles in the change program. They use strong sanctions to discourage active resisters.

The actions of Commanders are unilateral, directive or coercive, and top-down. They do not hesitate to divest unprofitable businesses or operations that lie outside the new strategic direction of the enterprise. They work to create a cohesive top team with a clear sense of purpose and full commitment to the new vision, and may act consultatively with this group. However, below this group, their leadership style is more directive.

When Commanders encounter powerful resistance from particular power elites which they cannot overcome, they engage in tough bargaining behaviour to negotiate a compromise as close to their desired program of change as possible. However, making change in this way can be a high-risk strategy, particularly if they are successfully opposed by one or more powerful key interest groups. The positional and personal authority of the leader is therefore paramount to the success of this strategy.

We have witnessed many examples of Commanders in Australian organisations in recent years. As organisations have moved into crisis, boards often seek to appoint tough-minded CEOs to turn the situation around. But toughness in itself is no guarantee of success. For example, in September 1998, the CEO of Seven Network, Gary Rice, resigned. The Network was ranked as number 2 but it reported a 77.1% slump in annual net profit. Rice was appointed as CEO three years earlier because of his reputation for taking tough measures. The Network had already lost millions in revenue, leading to the departure of the previous Chairman and the Managing Director. Despite a series of major initiatives, Rice failed to turn Channel 7 around in his three year tenure. In commenting on his resignation in the Business Section of the *Sydney Morning Herald*, Sue Lecky and Anne Hyland noted that he had 'now had a stint running all three major networks' and added: 'By resigning yesterday he has avoided the distinction of also being axed by all three.'[11]

On the other hand, other executives have run successful careers specialising in Commander-type roles. One spectacular example is Lebanese-born but Australian raised, Jacques Nasser. Nasser has had an impressive career in the Ford Motor Company. He began as a cadet in Melbourne, became a financial analyst within the Australian company, and in 1973 moved to the United States and operated around the globe. He eventually became and is currently CEO of Ford worldwide. Along the way, he acquired the nickname of 'Jac the Knife', as *Fortune Magazine* described him, for 'kicking butt'. *Herald* writer Phil Scott described Nasser as 'less a trimmer of fat than a one-man guillotine'. Under his leadership, workforce numbers in Ford worldwide have been slashed, profits boosted and the value of Ford shares increased by more than 200%.[12]

Commissioner as Commander

Perhaps the toughest organisational change program in Australia in recent years has been the restructure of the NSW Police Force. The person leading that restructure and playing a classic Commander role is Police Commissioner Peter Ryan. Ryan was appointed from the United Kingdom to stamp out corruption in the Force and modernise it. In his own words, he initially adopted a management style that was 'firm, hard and autocratic, and it had to be that because that is what the organisation understood'. Ryan has made a major impact on the Force but admits that he and his team still have a long way to go to create the highly skilled, community focused organisation he believes it should be.[13]

Communication strategies in Turnarounds

The major goal of the Commander is to overcome resistance and to create compliance with the radical new vision for the future of the organisation. Consequently the communication strategy centres around transmitting clearly the nature of the planned changes, the costs of non-compliance and the advantages of compliance. Because of the urgency of the situation, communication is put on a wartime

Shortly after taking over as CEO of Philips, the Dutch electronics company, Jan Timmer invited the company's top 100 managers to an offsite retreat at the Philips training centre in De Ruwenberg, Holland. He handed out a mock press release stating that Philips was bankrupt. Its survival was at stake. It was up to the managers in the room to bring it back. Operation Centurion, the process Timmer would use to turn Philips around, had begun. He offered his managers new compacts, which were like the assignments given to officers by their superiors in the Roman Army:

> Centurion was the rank given to an officer in the Roman Army, who received his assignment in the form of a personal contract. Philips managers, too, will have to handle their personal assignments, that is their budget, as a personal contract. It will mean keeping your word by following through on your promises.

Timmer's terms for change were tough and unambiguous; those present had no choice but to accept the new compact framework, or prepare their exit...

If Turnaround is to succeed in the long run, commanders have to avoid the pitfall of excessive hubris. Success in managing crisis often creates boundless self-confidence. Commanders begin to trust their intuition and judgment more and more exclusively, feel more and more infallible in their approach to change, and step out beyond their abilities.

Timmer's attempts to find a blockbuster new product reflect this classic pitfall, which often arises after the Turnaround has been accomplished. Timmer repeatedly pushed hard for large new product introductions. They were disasters: DCC, a digital tape cassette system flopped, while interactive CD-ROMs and SRAM memory chips each cost US$1 billion before the plug was pulled. These disasters eventually accumulated into a loss of US$313 million in 1996, and Timmer resigned in favour of Cor Boonstra. After the weak product lines had been cleared out, however, Philips returned in 1997 to record profits.[14]

footing. It is planned like a military campaign; it is frequent, concise and forceful. A central focus of the communication content is the existence of a state of organisational crisis which provides the rationale for change. Communication is top-down. Consequently the chief executive chooses to be highly visible in the organisation and ensures that he or she is seen as the originator of the demand for change.

Below the CEO, communication operates through selected change leaders who are regarded as loyal and who act as the architects of change. An attempt is made to capture all communication channels and to prevent dissenters gaining access to them. In this way the propaganda for change is delivered in a consistent and total way: all channels tell the same story. Formal channels are preferred, as these reinforce the authority of the line to carry out the desired changes. However, mass meetings addressed by the CEO and other senior executives may be used to speed up message transmission and to ensure that the message is not watered down by dissenters or resisters in line positions. Similarly memos, in the form of directives, are also frequently used, mostly in the name of the CEO.

Strategies for cultural renewal in Turnarounds

The approach to cultural change pursued by Commanders is what Chin and Benne[15] have labelled 'power-coercive'—that is, the leader uses all available forms of power to impact on and transform existing cultural values and norms. The survival of the organisation is usually at stake. One way in which coercives achieve an impact is to remove, if possible, the traditional carriers of the culture and to replace them with others from outside the organisation who personify the new values that are to be substituted for the old. In addition to changing key people, coercives use an iconoclastic approach to cultural symbols: wherever possible they destroy symbols of the old culture, choosing particularly some of those symbols which embody values central to the old order.

Commanders often substantially restructure the organisation, partly to reorient it to the new external realities, but also to break up old coalitions and power bases. Finally they bring in new systems, particularly human resource management systems, which change goals and reward structures. An important aspect of operating an effective coercive strategy is to create confusion among the traditional supporters of the old regime and, before the resisters can regroup, to act decisively and powerfully in creating new leaders, new structures and a new ethos.

> *Leadership is about 'bringing everyone along' in a balanced way, not just in their minds so they understand it, but emotionally as well, in their hearts, so they are really energised and identify with it, and they themselves take part in the leadership.*
>
> FRANK BLOUNT, FORMER CEO TELSTRA[16]

However, Commanders also create clear positive models of key elements of the new culture they are attempting to create. The nihilism of their early actions has to be offset by demonstrating that the new culture is a more viable alternative.

Strengths and vulnerabilities of Turnarounds

The major advantage of a Turnaround strategy is that it creates a crisis situation which catalyses action and focuses organisational energy. If well planned, it also provides clear direction and leadership, redistribution of resources to the new strategic initiatives, and rapid repositioning of the organisation. While the moves made may not be popular, the sense of purpose and renewed energy may be reassuring. In the words of one person from an organisation undergoing massive change under directive leadership: 'While many people do not like the changes that have taken place, as well as the continual change and the concomitant uncertainty, there is, nevertheless, a sense of satisfaction in having a clear direction.'

Strategic Turnarounds, however, can be high-risk strategies. If the strategy chosen is not viable, there is little chance to discern this before disaster intervenes. The speed of the change and the discouragement of upward feedback from within the organisation place full responsibility for getting the strategic positioning right with the top executive group. In addition, even if the chosen business strategy is viable, major resistance and conflict can develop within the organisation and this can dissipate energy in futile infighting, and fear, anger and guilt can destroy morale and motivation. The first stage of strategic Turnarounds tends to destroy fairly quickly the existing patterns of loyalty and commitment in the organisation; the creation of a new system of commitment proceeds slowly and depends on the ability of the senior executive group to provide rewards for new behaviour and to achieve organisational success soon enough to restore hope and build commitment. If the Turnaround is delayed, the resulting confusion can undermine the probability of it taking place at all. Our research indicates that a period of two years may be the maximum an organisation can remain in a Turnaround mode without putting anything in the place of a shattered culture. After that the executive must concentrate on strategies for rebuilding, such as those used in Task-focused Transitions.

Beyond 'strategic dithering'

There is no more critical issue in today's corporation than that the leadership of change for corporate survival and growth depend on continued adaptation. Charles Fombrun summarises a study of fifty-seven large-scale corporate bankruptcies in the United States and notes:[17]

> . . . few failures were sudden. Most experienced a prolonged 10-year decline in accounting performance, suggesting that, as managers, we are typically much slower to change than the environments our firms inhabit. Ultimately, these companies' trajectories came to represent a downward spiral. A period of marginal existence and strategic dithering was followed by one in which managers used up their firm's accumulated slack. The decaying trajectory built up to a fatal death struggle as stress precipitated more wavering in their final two years of existence.

This quote from Fombrun vividly describes the fate of firms that lacked effective change leadership. In this chapter we have described four alternatives to this kind of 'strategic dithering'. Table 5.2 shows the links between the various approaches to change and suitable

Table 5.2 Key characteristics associated with change leaders

Change type	Developmental Transitions	Task-Focused Transitions
Change leader type	*Coaches*	*Captains*
Goal of change	Voluntary commitment to a shared vision of continual improvement	Compliance to an internally consistent progressive redefinition of task performance systems
Leadership behaviour	Highly interactive Responsive to lower level initiatives Vision is an emerging phenomenon Use of personal power and expertise Extensive use of role modelling	Directed interaction around key system changes Strategic initiatives come from the executive, technical initiatives are delegated Vision is planned and systematically orchestrated Use of positional power and technical/task expertise
Communication strategies	Aim is to gain voluntary commitment, broaden involvement, develop trust Widespread involvement in the communication process Multidirectional initiatives Use of task teams/focus groups to process change issues Emphasis on face-to-face communication	Aim is to gain behavioural alignment with the vision and key executive initiatives Use of line relationships for communication Primarily top-down communication with built-in feedback Use of technical expertise to advise teams Emphasis on formal communication (e.g. instructions, memos, email)
Cultural renewal	Normative–re-educative in strategy Creating shared experiences around development of new norms Appeal to shared values Use of intrinsic rewards, sense of achievement	Empirical/rational strategy Competence enhancement through retraining Focus on changing systems as a means of encouraging behaviour modification Constant adjustment of norms to match changing strategies Use of intrinsic and extrinsic rewards related to the task

Change type	Charismatic Transformations	Turnarounds
Change leader type	*Charismatics*	*Commanders*
Goal of change	Voluntary commitment to a radical new vision requiring significant reinterpretation or revision of core values	Compliance to radically redefined behavioural goals, norms and performance standards
Leadership behaviour	Symbolically interactive Major strategic initiatives from top teams Vision is entrepreneurial and opportunistic Use of personal charisma Development of radical new role models	Unilateral directive action Strategic and structural initiatives Radical new vision imposed or negotiated Use of positional power and sanctions Reference to and infusion of new role models
Communication strategies	Aim is to gain emotional commitment to the vision, re-examination and revision of core values and beliefs Use of multimedia communication channels but personalised Top-down communication with built-in feedback and symbolic two-way communication Use of strategic task forces Personalised corporate communication	Aim is to communicate a sense of organisational crisis, rationale for change and cost of non-compliance Communication is put on a 'wartime' footing; frequent, total and forceful Top-down communication Use of selected change leaders as key communicators Emphasis on formal, authoritative communication
Cultural renewal	Paradigm-shifting strategy Creating vicarious participation and identification with new role models Radical challenge to existing values Infusion of a new core business culture Use of intrinsic rewards and identification with charismatic leader	Power-coercive strategy Emphasis on remoulding behaviour as an approach to value change Radical challenge to existing values Recasting and re-forming of core culture Use of extrinsic rewards and coercive sanctions

Note: The strengths and vulnerabilities of these four overall approaches are covered in Appendix 8A.

leadership styles. All four approaches are viable strategies in appropriate circumstances; all require insight, skill and courage on the part of those who lead the change. Each represents an internally consistent approach to the task of developing a vision for the corporate future, communicating that vision effectively to others and renewing the organisational culture so that it eventually supports the new order that is being introduced.

We have primarily focused here on executive leadership. But executive leadership is not sufficient for introducing change effectively. In the next chapter we deal with change in the organisation's core workflows and we stress the kind of grassroots leadership that is vital if the strategic change program is to be realised in the actions of those who carry out the essential day-to-day processes of making products and delivering services. Effective organisations have networks of leaders at all levels who actively combine the day-to-day management of ongoing operations with the changes required for strategically repositioning the organisation for future success.

References

1. J. Cavanagh, 'Australia's most admired', *Business Review Weekly*, 15 October 1999, pp. 68–75.
2. See, for example, A. Pettigrew & R. Whipp, *Managing Change for Competitive Success*, ESRC, Blackwell, Cambridge, 1991, Chapter 4: 'Leading change', pp. 138–67; D. C. Dunphy & D. A. Stace, *Under New Management: Australian Organisations in Transition*, McGraw-Hill, Sydney, 1990, Chapter 6: 'Leading the transition', pp. 145–77; J. G. Hunt (ed.), *Emerging Leadership Vistas*, Heath, Lexington, Massachusetts, 1987; P. M. Senge, *The Fifth Discipline: The Art and Practice of the Learning Organisation*, Chapter 18: 'The leader's new work', pp. 339–60.
3. J. Kotter, *A Force for Change*, Free Press, London, 1990, p. 6.
4. J. Cavanagh, op. cit., p. 72.
5. We are indebted to former AGSM 1998 MBA students Robert Hemphill, Ronald Sodoma, Glenn Cordingly, Denise North and Gerard Moody for much of the detail of this account, in addition to Dexter Dunphy's extensive discussions with Shane Garland and others through the period of major change.
6. R. Chin & K. D. Benne, 1973, quoted in D. S. Lewis, 'Culture Change—Communication, Management and Effects: An Empirical Study of Change in an Australian Tertiary Institution', PhD dissertation submitted to Division of Commerce and Administration, Griffith University, February 1991, p. 58.

7. From an interview conducted by Denise North in 1998.

8. See A. Bandura, *Social Foundations of Thought and Action: A Social Cognitive Theory*, Prentice-Hall, New Jersey, 1986; R. Waldersee & F. Luthans, 'Social learning analysis of organisational management', in C. Johnson, W. Redman & T. Mawhinney (eds), *Handbook of Performance Management*, Pergamon Press, 1994.

9. We are indebted to former AGSM 1998 MBA students Gautam Chari, Wee Lyn Chen, Albert Tan and Julia Yan for material used in this account.

10. C. Argyris, *On Organisational Learning*, Blackwell, London, 1992.

11. S. Lecky & A. Hyland, 'No answers to tough questions', *Sydney Morning Herald*, 9 September 1998, pp. 29–36.

12. P. Scott, 'Our poor migrant kid kicks butt in Detroit', *Sydney Morning Herald*, 15 September 1998, pp. 3–4.

13. H. Baker, 'A lesson in transformational leadership', *Management*, Australian Institute of Management Journal, May 1997, pp. 5–7.

14. Extract from P. Strebel, *The Change Pact: Building Commitment to Ongoing Change*, Financial Times Professional, London, 1998, pp. 93, 100.

15. Chin & Benne, op. cit.

16. F. Blount, 'Changing places: Blount and Joss', *Human Resources Monthly*, December 1999, pp. 10–14.

17. C. Fombrun, *Turning Points: Creating Strategic Change in Corporations*, McGraw-Hill, New York, 1992, pp. 22–3.

Chapter 6

The new flexible work order:

Managing change where it matters most

The workplace: Focus of change

When we evaluate comprehensive organisational change programs, the workplace is where the rubber hits the road. Strategic re-alignments, mergers, acquisitions, downsizing, Re-engineering, Total Quality Management...all in the end must be evaluated in terms of whether they contribute to the day-to-day work of creating the products and services needed by customers and clients. If change programs do not impact positively on the workplace by resulting in innovative new products and services, or by making it possible to improve the efficiency, quality or flexibility of delivery of existing products and services, they have failed. Too often workplaces are simply thrown into increasing disorder by change interventions, work processes are made more confusing, and staff become demoralised and defeated.

Effective change programs may create some initial disorder but they then move quickly to create new motivating high performance workplaces where people are challenged but excited, quality and effectiveness are enhanced, desirable customers are attracted and retained, and there is the buzz of disciplined, ordered work processes. This chapter deals with how to effect change of this kind where it matters most—in the workplace.

Despite forty years of experimentation in work design in Australia and overseas, many Australian and overseas workplaces are still organised along very traditional lines. Much of our discussion in this chapter deals with the challenge of transforming these workplaces to bring them into line with contemporary needs. This is a necessary first step, but only the first step in a longer journey. In the latter part of the chapter, we extend our analysis of the emerging forces of a new virtual work order that will revolutionise our central notions of how work should be organised, changing our understanding of careers, work groups and managerial roles.

The modern workplace is being dramatically transformed and, as we will discuss below, even the notion that work occurs in a *place* is being challenged. But to understand the transformation of work we must first return to the origins of the system which we inherited as a basic model for work organisation—the traditional mass production system.

The traditional mass production system

The traditional mass production system grew out of the factories of the early Industrial Revolution where unskilled and often illiterate agrarian workers (often women and children) operated the new machines that progressively displaced the traditional skilled craftspersons.

Two figures were the key architects of its evolving design: Frederick Taylor and Henry Ford. Taylor's impact on the formation of industrial culture was made in the latter part of the nineteenth century. His 'Scientific Management' approach systematised workflows and introduced major economies based on work specialisation.

At his vehicle assembly factory in Detroit in 1913, Henry Ford added automation and the assembly line to the Tayloristic principles of work simplification. The industrial system inherited from Ford and Taylor is today commonly referred to as Taylorism or Fordism in recognition of their distinctive contributions. The system they devised was responsible for enormous productivity increases which testified to the power of the underlying principle that the more specialised labour could be made, the greater would be the corresponding gains in productivity. Nevertheless it became clear throughout the 1970s and 1980s that the system was failing to cope with the increased demand for innovation and flexibility. To understand why, we must look first at the key features of traditional mass production systems which produce standardised goods and services. These are outlined in the box below.

Characteristics of traditional mass production systems

Mass production systems

- Vertical work organisation, subdivided into functional groupings (functional silos)
- Narrowly specialised repetitive jobs with low skill levels (deskilled work)
- Many highly differentiated job classifications (task specialisation)
- Individualised work and low interdependence between workers (minimal social interaction)
- Strict segregation of managerial from non-managerial responsibilities: close supervision and low levels of discretion in decision making; in some cases a machine controlled workplace (external control)
- Separation of intellectual work from manual work (white-collar/blue-collar distinction)
- Few career advancement opportunities for blue-collar workers ('dead end' jobs)
- Payment by seniority or piece rates (reward for loyalty and experience, or for achievement of externally set performance standards)

These features, when introduced, initially created a 'virtuous cycle'—that is, an increasing flow of relatively cheap goods and services which an increasingly highly paid workforce, with more leisure time available for consumption, were able to purchase. Mass production came to dominate and outperform all other production systems throughout the major part of the twentieth century, and its principles were extended to organisations far removed from factories. For example, banking, insurance and many government bureaucracies were systematically reorganised on assembly line principles. The system was, however, dependent on specific social and economic conditions: in particular, on largely oligopolistic national economic systems and on a social contract whereby the workforce in bureaucracies and factories exchanged their labour for increasing purchasing power, a higher standard of living and more leisure. This type of social contract has all but disappeared in most modern economies.

Pressures for change at work

Over the past quarter century, advanced economies in particular have experienced powerful pressures for change in the traditional work order. Many of these pressures were more fully explored in Chapter 2, but can be summarised as changes which have taken the following forms:

- *Pervasive technologies* The pace of technological innovation and adoption is so fast that to remain competitive organisations can no longer lag in technological uptake. Organisations need to develop a skilled workforce that quickly and competently adopts and adapts the latest technological advances to meet or anticipate changing consumer needs.
- *More sophisticated customers* In this period, there has been a significant increase in the level of sophistication of consumers. The globalisation of business, the ubiquity of information and the ease of international travel have raised the consciousness of consumers who are now highly mobile, and information rich. Organisations must meet this rising level of consumer expectation or go out of business.
- *Increased productivity* The globalisation of business has led to higher levels of competition and the only way firms can survive is to make dramatic increases in their international competitiveness and productivity. The challenge is to translate increased capital investment allocations into correspondingly increased productivity.

- *Increased quality* An abundance of goods and a growing consumer awareness has led to consumers demanding substantially higher quality in products and services; however, traditional mass production methods often failed to produce products of a consistently high quality because of low skill utilisation, high job dissatisfaction, lowered morale and organisational commitment.[1]
- *Increased responsiveness* Increasingly, the profitability of firms is directly related to their ability to determine or predict changing consumer demand and to respond to the changing tastes and interests of the marketplace. The massive capital investment required by traditional mass production systems has inhibited this kind of flexible response. Newer technologies are making such responsiveness possible.
- *Increased product differentiation (customisation)* Success, particularly in mature markets, is increasingly associated with an ability to distinguish categories of consumers with distinctive needs and to differentiate products so that they appeal to these distinct groups, or to customise to individuals.
- *Greater speed of response* Not only is it necessary to identify and respond to changing consumer demand, but increasingly the rewards for doing so go to those firms that respond fastest to meet the emerging need. Traditional manufacturing methods demand time-consuming retooling and set-up delays which inhibit a speedy response.
- *Continuous innovation* Keeping up with competition and with changing consumer demand requires continuous innovation, not only in the production of new or differentiated products and services, but also in the production process itself. Traditional work organisation was designed to foster standardisation and actively discouraged innovation.
- *Demands for higher quality of worklife* In the 1960s and 1970s, a major social movement, centring on the humanisation of work and the quality of worklife, emerged in the Western democracies.[2] It reflected the demand of a more educated workforce for a safer, more satisfying worklife designed to fulfil human needs and led to a variety of initiatives intended to redesign workplaces to adapt them to the needs of people rather than of machines. While the recessionary period of the early 1990s, with its high

unemployment levels, dampened the power of this emerging demand, the subsequent economic expansion and shortage of skilled employees is now changing this.

All the above pressures combined represent a powerful force for developing increased flexibility in the work order—that is, the capability to adapt procedures and products swiftly and effectively in order to retain and extend the firm's customer base and to build a highly skilled and committed workforce. This flexibility is lacking in the traditional mass production systems that set the basic model for work organisation in the past, and this lack has represented a process of workplace deconstruction of major proportions.

Transforming the old work order

Old-style work environments are now being swept away in the new revolution that is transforming the workplace, the nature of work itself and the distribution of authority and power in organisations. The revolution is being signalled by the increasing use of terms like 'devolution', 'empowerment', 'self-managed work teams', 'flexible work practices', 'multiskilling', 'Re-engineering' and 'core process redesign'. Behind the words there is emerging a new managerial philosophy that represents a sharp break from the received wisdom of at least 100 years of an evolving industrial system.

For those firms that have successfully revised their major strategies and restructured the organisation accordingly, the focus of the strategic thrust has moved to the grassroots activity of developing, producing and providing goods and services for customers and clients. This is what Elliott Jaques has referred to as the 'operating spine'[3] of the organisation, and what Ostroff and Smith refer to as the 'core processes'[4] of the organisation. By 'core processes', Ostroff and Smith mean the flows of information, decision making and material that deliver against key performance objectives.

We prefer the term 'core workflow' to either of these terms, and we use it to describe the organised flow of activity through which resources are gathered up, assembled and modified to add value, turned into a new product or service, and delivered to the consumer. Throughout much of the literature to date, the revolution taking place in the production activities of the firm has been referred to as 'workplace reform'. The term 'workplace' is misleading, for this flow of activity is often not limited to one place of work but occurs across several. In fact, the most revolutionary aspect of the new work design is that it breaks down traditional workplace boundaries in establishing lateral links that emphasise horizontal workflows across traditional functions such as Research and Development, Production and Sales, and now extends beyond organisational boundaries to include relationships with suppliers and customers.

In addition, the proliferation of new integrated information technologies such as intranets, the Internet and mobile phones has seen the evaporation of the work*place* in many cases. The globalisation of business has also contributed to this trend. So the workflow may happen in a virtual reality rather than a workplace. For example, software architecture may be designed in Silicon Valley, the actual programming then performed in India and the final product delivered to a client in Saudi Arabia.

Given the extension of work beyond the workplace to a global stage, it is no wonder that a report commissioned by the American Management Association found that 63.7% of executives rated team building as 'very important', but then rated the success of their firm in doing it at 24.7%. The message is clear: 'Teambuilding is vital but it's tough to implement it.'[5]

Jaques's analogy to the spine is an apt one in that the spine carries key information in both directions and links thought to action, and vice versa. Another analogy that we find useful is the process of transpiration and capillary action in plants, whereby water is drawn up through a plant's roots, stem, branches and leaves. The function of the plant cells in providing a continuous channel linking one end of the system with the other is analogous to the work processes of the new team based horizontal organisation responding to the pull of market demand. Organisation of this kind is being developed in many modern enterprises.

For leading-edge organisations, the challenge of effective change management has moved beyond devising the new strategic direction, restructuring the firm and developing new human resource strategies. The challenge is to do all that and then to ensure that the unfolding strategies are effectively translated into changed behaviour directed at maximising added value in this chain of day-to-day activities leading to the consumer. In this sense, the frontier of strategic change is increasingly moving to the level of the core workflow in the organisation. At this level, two key issues emerge:

- how to ensure that the strategy, devised at the nerve centre of the organisation, is effectively translated by the members of the workforce responsible for the core workflow in their day-to-day actions; and
- how to capture the experience of this key section of the workforce as they grapple with the production process and relate to customers, so that their experience increasingly informs and redirects strategy.

A changed work order

We now summarise the emerging features of the work order in many leading enterprises. These features are far from uniform, but they are distinct enough to represent a trend.

Radical delegation

In organisations that have been hierarchical, there is now increasing and radical delegation to the team level, there are fewer levels of management between the team and business unit management, and members have a high level of discretion in taking decisions relevant to the activities of their work unit—that is, they are largely self-supervised or self-managed. There are strong support functions which provide the information, tools and other resources that the group needs to perform to a high level. Group activities are interdependent and co-ordinated, and interaction between team members is encouraged because it is essential for achieving effective co-ordination and agreed performance levels. Existing team members are involved in the selection of new team members.

Freedom and responsibility

The group members have a clear understanding of the business strategy being pursued by their strategic business unit and the role of their particular work unit in achieving that strategy. There are few rules imposed from above; instead the group has freedom to work within negotiated parameters. Integration occurs mainly through shared goals and values. The group schedules its tasks and allocates them to members. Overall, these kinds of changes are referred to in the literature as 'empowerment'.

Broad skills and learning individuals

Team members are multiskilled both in terms of technical tasks to be performed and in terms of supervisory functions; work is designed to emphasise whole tasks and integrates thought and action. Technical specialists are integrated into the teams, either as full or part-time team members. Work is varied. There are few job classifications and there is a structured and uninterrupted career progression based on the systematic acquisition of higher level skills. There is on-the-job cross-training and an emphasis on continual learning; both technical and experientially based knowledge are valued; there is also training provided which is directed at enhancing members' interpersonal and group skills ('teambuilding').

Relentless improvement

There are programs of relentless productivity improvement for which the teams are responsible and within which they are encouraged to take significant initiatives. Productivity improvement is focused on strategic business unit or company-wide processes that ultimately link to customer needs. Productivity is measured in ways that give the team members feedback on performance and encourage them to take action to improve performance in areas over which they have control. There is a strong emphasis on achieving optimum equipment utilisation and the reduction of inventories. Information technologies are used to provide timely, relevant information and co-ordinate the total workflow. Total factor productivity replaces labour productivity as the major criterion for productivity measurement. Speed and flexibility of response to changing consumer demand are regarded as critical.

Reward for skill and performance

Renumeration systems are linked to skills, and to group performance; some form of gain sharing is practised to ensure that the work group is rewarded for increased productivity.

People as the core of the business

The workplace is anthropocentric in that the health, safety and social rights of the workforce are protected, and opportunities for personal and professional development are provided. Employees, particularly those using sophisticated technical equipment and interfacing with customers, are highly skilled. Commitment to strategic goals, and high skill levels, are regarded as central to achieving competitive advantage. Initiative, ingenuity and judgment are encouraged. Work design is undertaken jointly by team members and external technical experts to ensure the optimisation of members' needs for work satisfaction and the demands of technical efficiency.

New leadership roles at the workface

The reconstruction of the core workflow is having a major impact on the traditional supervisory and managerial roles.

Old style supervisors are eliminated or, if retained as team leaders, no longer 'supervise' because teams are largely self-supervising. 'Team leaders' or 'team co-ordinators' become managers of mini-businesses and now concentrate primarily on co-ordination with other units, particularly those contiguous in the core workflow, and on process and product improvement. Consequently, they need to develop the ability to think strategically and to have the level of financial management and business communication skills needed to operate their unit effectively. They must also develop a sound understanding of the external market in which their small business is operating and the internal 'customers' they are serving if they are not directly interfacing with the market. They need a high level of self-management, interpersonal, leadership and team-building skills to influence and respond to those in their work group and those in other interdependent work groups. They need these skills because they primarily co-ordinate and coach rather than control, using communication and consultation rather than the authority of position and authoritative orders. They need sufficient understanding of the technology employed in their unit to be able to work effectively with technical experts on design and system changes.

Changes of these kinds were widely instituted for the first time in Australia in the late 1980s. A 1990 Andersen Consulting survey of supervisors working in new focused subplants in production organisations showed how dramatic the shift in the supervisory role was in some new workplaces. For any single team leader, the average number of employees rose by 76% when the shift to the new system took place. At the same time, the hours spent on traditional supervisory activities and training dropped by 73% per employee. Team leaders were therefore able to devote the time gained through these changes to process and product improvement.[6] One of the central problems of reorganising into semiautonomous teams is the difficulty experienced by traditional supervisors, trained in Fordist work organisation, in adapting to the radical role shift from supervisor to team leader. Typically only about one-third of supervisors can make the transition. For example, in the reorganisation of the Steam and Power Plant at the ICI Botany site, 'eventually out of the six supervisors one took a middle management position in a training role, one left the company, two took voluntary redundancy and two elected to stay'.[7]

Middle managers have become planners of change across teams, propelling their units into the next phase of upgrading and productivity improvement. Increasingly, many of their management functions are being delegated to team members. More radically, the old supervisory functions are distributed among team members who operate as a self-managing group. We will now describe how this can be achieved.

Introducing self-managing teams

Our research has revealed a number of key principles about how to introduce and support the development of a horizontal form of work organisation which is increasingly self-managed rather than directed in detail by a hierarchical managerial structure. To draw out the lessons for the progressive implementation of these semiautonomous or self-regulating teams, we outline below a process for phasing in a system of this kind. Figure 6.1 illustrates the basic dimensions of the changes to be introduced and we discuss each phase of the process in more detail below.

Our discussion assumes that there has, however, been a thorough review of business strategies, organisational structures, workforce numbers and technology to ensure that they are appropriate. In moving to a group based structure, these supporting features need to be in place, otherwise their subsequent change can cause serious disruption to organisational performance and to the process of group formation.

Phased implementation of self-managing teams

We outline below the key steps needed for progressively implementing self-managing teams. The reader should keep in mind that it is, however, not necessarily appropriate for all organisations to create self-managing teams, or, if they do, to proceed through all the stages outlined.

Phase 1: Basic technical skilling

First, identify the main technical functions (jobs) which need to be performed by team members and train each group member to perform the technical skills necessary for carrying out one such job—that is, ensure that within each team there is at least one person who is fully competent to perform each technical role. This may involve significant expenditures on technical training. This initial step simply brings the group to the point where it has within the group all the skills necessary for it to operate as an effective traditional work group under the direction of a supervisor.

Level of skilling

Skills	Single skill	Multiskilled
Technical skills Goal: achieving flexible group technical competence	*1. Basic technical skilling* Group members each achieve excellence in one technical function: formerly separate technical support functions, such as maintenance, are built into the group	*2. Technical multiskilling (the semiautonomous team)* Group members each achieve excellence in several technical functions: technical specialists are fully integrated into the group
Supervisory skills Goal: achieving flexible self-supervision	*3. Basic self-supervision* Group members each achieve excellence in one supervisory function: formerly separate HR functions, such as selection of new group members, are built into the group	*4. Supervisory skilling (the self-managed team)* Group members each achieve excellence in several supervisory functions
Managerial skills Goal: achieving flexible self-management (full empowerment)	*5. Basic managerial skilling* Group members each achieve excellence in one managerial function	*6. Managerial multiskilling (the self-led team)* Group members each achieve excellence in several managerial functions

Figure 6.1 Six stages in the introduction of team self-management

Phase 2: Technical multiskilling

Next, negotiate multiskilling and 'available as needed' flexibility through an enterprise agreement. Include, if possible, pay for productivity. It is not unusual for this step to take eighteen months to two years to complete. In the reorganisation of the ICI Botany plant, for example, this step alone took eighteen months.[8] However, technical multiskilling must be accompanied by the elimination of inflexibilities associated with traditional union demarcation barriers and multiple award systems. In one of the reorganisations of the NSW State Rail Authority, for example, eight federal and eight state awards were replaced with one common award, and 3300 salary points were reduced to 200.

Systematically introduce off-the-job training and on-the-job training to widen the range of skills so that each member of the group learns as many of the skills as he or she is capable of performing. Where possible, the group members who were skilled in Phase 1 act as instructors and role models for those who do not yet possess that skill. This lays the basis for the later move to distribute traditional supervisory skills to group members and for creating a positive attitude towards continual learning. The achievement of technical multiskilling creates a 'semiautonomous team'—that is, the team is now fully empowered to take charge of technical tasks; however, it is still led and controlled by a full-time 'team leader' or 'co-ordinator' to facilitate the introduction of Phase 3.

Phase 3: Basic self-supervision

Delegate the main internal functions of the existing supervisory/ team leader role to group members—that is, each group member learns one such function (for example, chairing group meetings, ensuring that safety rules are observed, scheduling maintenance of equipment). Provide coaching and training in these roles, particularly emphasising the development of interpersonal skills such as communication, assertion and conflict resolution. Ensure that each group member achieves excellence in one of these roles.

Phase 4: Supervisory multiskilling

Progressively rotate group members through these supervisory functions, having each of them understudy and 'stand in for' another function before they occupy the role. One way to achieve this is to rotate group members through the different areas of responsibility at, say, three monthly intervals.

Provide team-building activities to build group and organisational commitment. Ensure that the group understands and accepts production targets and quality goals, and involve the group in Benchmarking against best international practice on comparable tasks.

Phase 5: Basic managerial skilling

Delegate the main external or 'representative' roles of the team leader so that each group member progressively adopts one of the key external leadership and co-ordination roles (for example, ordering supplies, liaising with other work groups). If the supervisory role has not already been eliminated, this should happen now so that the group becomes effectively 'self-managed'.

Phase 6: Managerial multiskilling

Rotate group members through the acquired external team leader functions. Then progressively delegate further managerial functions from middle management—such as goal setting, performance improvement and client liaison—so that the group is increasingly empowered to direct its own activities within negotiated parameters. Provide relevant training in goal setting, decision making, basic accounting, and so on. Ensure that the group is increasingly oriented to the clients' key product/service requirements and actively involved in continuous improvement activities with other groups in the core workflow.

In attempting to introduce multiskilled teams, most organisations grossly underestimate the complexity of the task, the resources needed to support the process, and the time needed to develop self-management at the work group level, particularly while trying to maintain high production levels.

Additional points

We suggest that substantial resources are needed at each phase of the introduction of team self-management. These are managerial time, staff time, particularly in training, and team members' time which must be diverted from tasks that are immediately productive. Even with the addition of extra resources, there is normally an initial decrease in group performance at each phase. It is better to reduce the extent of these performance deficits at any one time by sequencing the changes described above rather than 'bunching' them, or the group commitment to change may be weakened and management may question whether the system is workable. As group members acquire the next level of skills and achieve mastery of the situation, performance is normally regained and then progressively exceeded.

Adopting a sequenced approach also allows clearer assessment of how far and how fast group members can progress. The current skills levels and potential of the workforce to learn new skills will vary widely and affect the speed with which each phase can be completed. In most cases, spoken language and literacy skills are necessary to attempt Phase 1. If members lack English language skills, group interaction may be severely limited and there may be no basis for increasing the technical skills of individuals. Similarly, attitudes of dependency on authority, often inculcated in members of the workforce over years of traditional supervision, may place severe limitations on their ability to take over supervisory functions.

Basically each phase is aimed at 'ramping up' the performance of the group by increasing skill levels, mobilising latent energy, and developing motivation and commitment by increasing group members' control over their position in the workflow. In addition, their control over their work environment is further increased by extending their ability to co-ordinate the activities of their own group with the activities of other 'cells' in the horizontal workflow.

This final phase of the group development creates the necessary foundation for moving to a learning organisation. We conclude by stressing that introducing this modern type of work organisation takes substantial time. The time involved will be less in the case of a workforce which is already highly skilled and includes a substantial proportion of trained people. However, introducing such a system into a production unit with outdated equipment and a workforce which is mainly semiliterate is a much more prolonged and complex process. Nevertheless, the cultural change represents an opportunity to transform attitudes in the workplace from destructive bloody-mindedness to active co-operation, commitment and innovation.

Is this fantasyland?

No doubt there will be readers who will regard the model outlined above as a pleasant fantasy, far removed from the realities of worklife in some plants and offices in Australia, and globally. Many of the changes currently taking place in the conditions of the workforce do in fact militate against the introduction of the kinds of measures we have been advocating. For example, many call centres are simply a new form of Tayloristic workplace with even more sophisticated forms of behavioural controls than even Taylor envisaged.

The use of downsizing by global and local companies as their dominant approach to change management over the last one to two decades demonstrates that many companies have primarily pursued a cost competition strategy. The result has often been a 'dumbing down' of the workforce with a consequent loss of innovation, quality and flexibility. Workforce commitment has also declined. There is increasing evidence that downsizing has not produced the results that were intended. In fact, used as a stand alone change strategy, it has destructive results.[9]

On the other hand, the evidence is now convincing that good people management, investment in workforce skill formation, new forms of work organisation, investment in research and development and higher employee participation result in superior performance.[10] As Jeffrey Pfeffer notes: 'Organizing people into self-managed teams is a critical component of virtually all high-performance management systems.'[11] The challenge for managers is to move to Ostroff's 'horizontal organization', referred to in Chapter 3.[12] Ostroff outlines the value of a team-based organisation in combining cross-functional core process redesign, with bottom-up performance improvement and problem solving and top-down direction setting—all in the interests of increasing the effectiveness with which value is added for the customer.

Beyond the single organisation: The importance of supplier networks

We have emphasised that the term 'workplace' is misleading and should be abandoned in favour of the term 'core work process'. One of the reasons for this is that, in production organisations in particular, there has been a tendency to focus on the plant (usually a workplace) when seeking efficiencies and to neglect the efficiencies that can be made elsewhere in the workflow. In automobile manufacture, for example, 65% of the value-added typically comes from work performed by suppliers rather than work done on the plant assembly lines, and 60–70% of the costs of manufactured goods flow from materials and purchased components. Consequently time and effort invested in reorganising supplier relationships and processes may yield greater returns than time and effort spent increasing efficiencies in the plant. As Harmon has concluded: 'The "pipeline" of supply, from the lowest level in the chain to end customer, is the arena where most work needs to be done; it is also the area that holds the greatest potential for improving the cost of manufactured products.'[13]

Networking is the contemporary method for reaping gains from specialisation and co-ordination. Where once companies pursued policies of vertical integration through takeover, today these same companies are divesting themselves of these acquisitions and converting them into networks of negotiated relationships, which also achieve control over supply lines but introduce far more flexibility and efficiency. The management of change in the future will centre increasingly around stabilising networks of subcontractors and joint ventures and ensuring that they are moving in a co-ordinated way to establish advanced work forms. A large part of the success of Japanese auto manufacturers in the 1980s came from just such a policy; while this was occurring, all Western eyes were focused on the Japanese factory organisation where the prior generation of reforms had taken place. The significance of what Japanese firms were doing in terms of reorganising their supplier relationships was overlooked, until it became glaringly obvious in terms of a massive increase in efficiencies and improved product quality. When Western corporations realised what had happened in Japan, they speedily adopted the new practices.

The costs of thoroughly reorganising core work processes and introducing modern work methods is initially higher than simply introducing some flexibility into a traditional Fordist-type organisation. However, the benefits are potentially greater, although they are usually only attained in the medium to long term. The benefits include:

- dramatic reduction in overheads due to reduction in middle management and supervisory personnel and in co-ordination costs;
- continuing improvements in performance levels, sometimes of dramatic proportions;
- increased responsiveness to changing customer demands;
- flexibility and speed in redesigning products, services and production flows to meet those demands;
- increased quality and speed of delivery; and
- substantial increases in the motivation and commitment of the workforce associated with decreases in industrial strife, shirking and passive resistance.

These changes represent nothing short of a cultural transformation. Perhaps this is best summarised by quoting a typical response from a team member after the successful transformation of their workplace:[14]

> It's the best place I have ever worked; it's not perfect; our expectations have been raised; there are still some gaps; we are taking more initiatives. It has allowed me to develop personally and professionally. The people I work with are the most competent I've ever worked with; I have to watch them and stop them working at times so they don't burn themselves out; they are committed to the organisation and care how things happen.

The new virtual work order

What we have discussed in this chapter so far are simply the steps required for more traditional organisations to modernise in order to meet current market demands for cost control, added value and innovation. But it is becoming clear that we face further challenges that will effect fundamental changes in the way we conceive of and organise for work. In the blunt words of Capelli: 'The old employment system of secure, lifetime jobs with predictable advancement and stable pay is dead.'[15]

The most powerful force impacting on the traditional workplace production unit is modern technology—both production technology and information technology. Production technology, such as robots and a variety of computer based systems, are now well advanced along the road to replacing human physical labour in the movement and processing of material goods, and are also replacing much of the decision making once carried out by middle managers and supervisors. The sophistication of modern manufacturing is eliminating mass production and facilitating the break-up and redistribution of centralised production facilities. (For example, large centralised steelworks are being replaced by more localised, distributed mini-mills.) Consequently, a major proportion of the workforce in developed countries has moved out of manufacturing into services.

But an even more significant impact on work organisation has been made by new information and communication technologies. Many professionals and tradespeople no longer have an office that has a particular location. Their laptop and mobile phone are their 'office' and with these they can traverse a city, a country or the world, carrying their intellectual capital with them and remaining in touch with clients and the organisation they work for, if they are not self-employed.

Virtual teams

We are seeing the emergence of more and more virtual teams whose members co-ordinate their interdependent activities using mobile phone, email, voicemail and videoconferencing. One of the challenges is to understand the different kinds of skills needed to work effectively in, and to lead, such virtual teams.

An OECD report notes: 'Virtual organizations will emerge without fixed locations and with flexible, demand-oriented, production networks.'[16] Mobile professionals are increasingly working in such virtual groups and organisations. While some professionals do have an office which is a 'home base', they simply use whatever desk is vacant and book in to other office facilities, such as meeting rooms, when they need them. For those who work in teams rather than alone, the team may seldom or never meet in the one place on a face-to-face basis.

The concept of a team implies a clearly defined membership boundary—you are in or out—and that all members have a relationship with each other. But more working relationships are moving from team relationships to network relationships. A network has a much less distinct boundary than a group, and while some members may interact frequently with each other, others may interact infrequently and with a selected subset of members only. Once again, the skills of operating effectively in and providing leadership in a network, particularly the leadership of change, have not been clearly identified.[17] As far as we can foresee the future, there will be a continuing need for both real and virtual workgroups in most organisations. But networks will become increasingly important in organising work.

Communities of practice

Another 'virtual' work form that is increasingly common among professionals is the 'community of practice'. This may exist within the one organisation as, for instance, an accountancy community of practice in a broad based consultancy firm. Or it can transcend organisational boundaries as, for example, in the case of a special interest group in a professional association (for example, trainers in a human resource association who have a common interest in developing experiential training methods). The community of practice is a voluntary association of professionals who are interested in maintaining and developing their knowledge and skills; increasingly those are 'on line' networks which may, from time to time, organise face-to-face meetings.

These kinds of developments are seeing a steep increase in the number of self-starting professionals who operate their own small businesses, either working solo, or in small groups or networking with others. This development is being driven in part by increased educational levels and the development of lifelong learning. They often belong to one or more communities of practice as a means of continuing their professional skill development. They are no longer permanently employed by a larger organisation and so carry the business risks themselves, often creating their own business opportunities entrepreneurially. Their work is undertaken on a project basis where they are accountable for results. This, of course, emphasises the need for the continual upgrading of skill levels.

Project work and a 24 hour economy

Project work of this kind usually demands that the project organisation be instantaneously or rapidly assembled, a finite task undertaken and then the organisation dismantled. Project work requires very different working skills, particularly an ability to build effective working relationships fast, to establish trust, pool resources and move into a productive phase of operation in minimum time. It telescopes the group formation process. Other boundaries are dissolving also. We have seen supermarkets move to open on a 24 hour basis most days. This symbolises the onset of the '24 hour economy'.[18] Similarly, some law firms, having invested in expensive information technology, are maximising their return on that investment by offering services 24 hours a day. They are finding that many clients prefer the convenience of accessing their services at night.

In the 24 hour economy, service work in particular will see an expansion of flexible working hours and part-time work. Hunter's research shows that service establishments adopt somewhat different innovative work practices from manufacturing establishments.[19] In particular, they readily adopt flexitime and job sharing.

So what we face is a world of work which is going beyond the traditional boundaries. We have been used to thinking in terms of 'jobs'—that is, defined repetitive sets of prescribed activities with a clear place in a workflow and an identifiable status and salary, located in a physical setting owned and controlled by a particular organisation.

As we move into the much more fluid work of the future, there will be a core of longer term employees in most organisations, but employers will increasingly also have to negotiate with independent professionals, contracts which specify time spent on organisational tasks, processes to be adopted, outputs to be generated, fees and working conditions.[20] The work will frequently be conducted off the premises (where these exist); communication will take place through a variety of channels; structures of relationships will emerge, be modified, cease; work activity may take place on a 24 hour basis rather than from the once standard 9 to 5, and in many cases, at different places on the globe.

Managing a virtual career

This future has powerful implications for careers. One metaphor for the traditional career is the ladder, set vertically. In this world, one started at the lowest rung and, if successful, progressed up the hierarchy to the top by the end of one's working life. Massive social change of the kind we have described has swept away this type of career. An appropriate new metaphor for the career of the future is the climbing frame one sees in children's playgrounds. This is more horizontal and multidirectional. You move up, across, down, around. How do you 'progress' in this new climbing frame world of work? The individual moves through a series of work experiences, developing and enlarging their knowledge base and repertoire of skills in the process, essentially building up a knowledge/skill portfolio. The emphasis is on developing competencies that maximise career opportunities and can be deployed flexibly.

To achieve this the individual seeks work experiences which will maximise future earning potential by upgrading skill sets rather than letting them deteriorate or atrophy. (On leaving one work experience, the individual wants to have enhanced knowledge and skills that create more choice for future employment.) Vital also is work satisfaction and quality of work and private life. As we move into the knowledge economy, knowledge workers will be in high demand, well paid and concerned to create a satisfying lifestyle.

Globalisation will reinforce this, forcing countries like Australia and New Zealand out of the economic 'low road' activities associated with high-volume, low-cost business strategies and into the economic 'high road' of customised service delivery. The high road demands 'high involvement' work practices to be effective so reinforcing the trend to workforce upskilling.

What is managerial work in this developing world of work? Kotter's distinction between management and leadership, discussed in Chapter 5, becomes even more important. The managerial tasks of planning, budgeting, organising and staffing, controlling and problem solving will still have a place in formal organisations. However, the leadership tasks of establishing direction, aligning people to the direction, and motivating and inspiring in order to produce change will become even more important.[21]

These activities will, however, be more complex. It is a truism of organisational change that effective change depends on the support of the CEO and the senior executive team. However, in a world of fluid organisational boundaries, alliances, networks and subcontractors, the process of leading change will depend far more on influence than authority, on relationship management than edicts, on human than technical expertise. The architecture of work organisation will be more like the Internet than a traditional organisation chart. The greatest influence will be exercised by those who contribute to network design followed by those who, through their vision and lateral organisational skills, create expanding spheres of influence directed at creating goods and services that satisfy the needs of a global community.

Conclusion

The creation of a dynamic learning organisation is a continuous journey in which achievements are celebrated, expectations are raised and new goals are set as the vision and mission of the organisation shift to reflect changing market and social needs. In the future, however, it may be more relevant to think in terms of organising—that is, leading a dynamic, extensive process—than of an organisation which implies managing a fairly static, bounded entity. Developing the new forms and processes required for highly productive future work is a central challenge for all change agents. If we devoted the attention to this issue that it deserves, Australia and New Zealand could move to the forefront of the world's most productive societies while providing the meaningful and satisfying work that is an important prerequisite for living a high-quality life.

References

1. P. Capelli, *The New Deal at Work: Managing the Market-Driven Workforce*, Harvard Business School Press, Boston, MA, 1999, pp. 128–36.
2. A fuller treatment of this movement can be found in D. Dunphy & A. Griffiths, *The Sustainable Corporation*, Allen & Unwin, Sydney, 1998.
3. Elliott Jaques, *A General Theory of Bureaucracy*, Heinemann, London, 1976.

4. F. Ostroff & D. Smith, 'Redesigning the corporation', *The McKinsey Quarterly*, No. 1, 1992, pp. 148–67.

5. American Management Association, 'Change Management: A Survey of Major U.S. Corporations', Research Report prepared by Deloitte and Touche LLP for AMA, AMA, NY, USA, 1995, p. 6.

6. Quoted in R. L. Harmon, *Reinventing the Factory II: Managing the World Class Factory*, Free Press, New York, 1992, p. 65.

7. T. Mealor, 'ICI Australia: The Botany experience', *UNSW Studies in Organisational Analysis and Innovation No. 8*, Industrial Relations Research Centre, University of New South Wales, October 1992, p. 45.

8. ibid.

9. See discussions in: D. Dunphy & A. Griffiths (op. cit.), Chapter 6, pp. 140–70; R. Curtain, 'The workplace of the future: Insights from futures scenarios and today's high performance workplaces', *Australian Bulletin of Labour*, Vol. 24, No. 4, December 1998, pp. 279–94; P. Gollan, 'Human resources, capabilities and sustainability', in D. Dunphy, J. Benveniste, A. Griffiths & P. Sutton, *Sustainability: The Corporate Challenge of the Twenty-first Century*, Allen & Unwin, Sydney, 2000.

10. See R. Curtain (op. cit.), D. Dunphy & A. Griffiths (op. cit.), P. Golan (op. cit.) and L. Gratton, *Living Strategy: Putting People at the Heart of Corporate Strategy*, Prentice-Hall, London, 2000, for summaries of these studies.

11. J. Pfeffer, 'Seven practices of successful organizations', *California Management Review*, Vol. 40, No. 2, Winter, 1998, pp. 96–124. This quote can be found on p. 104.

12. F. Ostroff, *The Horizontal Organization: What the Organization of the Future Looks Like and How It Delivers Value to Customers*, Oxford University Press, NY, 1999.

13. R. L. Harmon, op. cit., p. 106.

14. D. A. Stace & D. C. Dunphy, 'Beyond acquisition to access', *Centre for Corporate Change Working Paper No. 005*, Australian Graduate School of Management, University of New South Wales, 1991, p. 16.

15. P. Capelli, op. cit., p. 17.

16. Organisation for Economic Cooperation and Development, *The OECD Observer*, Paris, Summer 1999, Vol. 14, No. 11, p. 1.

17. R. Curtain, op. cit.

18. H. B. Presser, 'Toward a 24 hour economy: The US experience and implications for the family', Chapter 4 in D. Vannoy & A. J. Dubeck (eds), *Challenges for Work and Family in the Twenty-First Century*, Aldine de Gryter, New York, 1998.

19. L. W. Hunter, 'The adoption of innovative work practices in service establishments', *International Journal of Human Resource Management*, Vol. 11, No. 3, June 2000, pp. 477–96.

20. R. Batt, 'Strategic segmentation in front-line services: Matching customers, employees and human resource systems', *International Journal of Human Resource Management*, Vol. 11, No. 3, 2000, pp. 540–61; R. D. Lansbury & J. Kitay, 'Towards new employment relations: Continuity, change and diversity', in J. Kitay & R. D. Lansbury, *Changing Employment Relations in Australia*, Oxford University Press, Melbourne, 1997, pp. 218–46.

21. A. Dart & D. Stace, 'Roles in the knowledge economy', *Monash Mt. Eliza Business Review*, July 1999, pp. 52–7.

Chapter 7

Choosing change intervention tools

Strategies or fads?

For over a decade, well known American management writer and speaker, Tom Peters, encouraged his audiences to adopt zany strategies for zany times: let go, destructure or destruct your corporation before the competitor does; once an organisation reaches the size of sixty to eighty people, it should be split and two companies created, said Peters.[1] For Peters, the sole emphasis seemed to be on reducing the size and complexity of organisations as a means of spawning creativity, innovation and overall economic growth. Many authors in the 1990s espoused the need for relentless focus on customer service as the critical determinant of organisational success. More recently interventions and techniques such as the Balanced Scorecard[2] and Economic Value Analysis[3] have been productively introduced by some organisations, and seized on almost in desperation by others. Others argued that Total Quality Management (TQM) was the answer; the emphasis on TQM, by a plethora of writers, appeared like a tidal wave of compelling thought to leaders and managers in the 1990s who were in the midst of making choices about which waves of change to ride. At the turn of the century, e-commerce and e-business appeared like a giant 'tsunami' wave of change for incumbent and start-up organisations alike.

Are you willing to be sponged out, erased, cancelled,
made nothing?
Are you willing to be made nothing?
Dipped into oblivion!
If not, you will never really change.
The phoenix renews her youth
Only when she is burnt, burnt alive,
Burnt down to hot and flocculent ash.
Then the small stirring of a new bub in the nest
With strands of down like floating ash
Shows that she is renewing her youth like the eagle
Immortal bird.

FROM 'PHOENIX' BY D. H. LAWRENCE

Yet, is change primarily about riding the new waves? It certainly is about taking risks and, for that reason, many of the new swells in the management ocean tempt the innovatory, risk-taking spirit of successful leaders. Leadership, after all, is not about timidity, nor is it about irresponsible risk taking or change for change's sake. Effective leaders avoid change fads, but learn to lever change interventions into the broader directions of the organisation in order to increase the momentum and effectiveness of change.

Our research observations lead us to suggest that, far from being faddish, successful change interventions have several major features. Successful change interventions:

- are linked to, and promote, the vision and emergent strategy of the organisation;
- are focused at an appropriate level of intervention (does the whole system need change, or only particular elements of it?); and
- have longer life and greater effect if they have 'depth' rather than mere surface appeal, and are clustered into groupings to form a blend of related practices or methods: they have an intellectual coherence.

The first of these we covered in Chapter 4 where we discussed the linkage of change strategies to business strategies. The other features we cover in the following sections.

Levels and depth of change intervention

The appropriate levels of change intervention

The choice of an initial level or breadth of intervention is crucial, particularly at a time when so much help or advice is available in the form of packaged solutions from outside advisers, consultants, academics and networkers. It is easy for managers to be attracted to solutions rather than first to analyse at what level, or what breadth of, change is needed. Figure 7.1 (section 1) shows four levels of change intervention.

We suggest that the change entry point or level is crucial. For instance, intergroup conflict resolution interventions may achieve some results, but will be ineffective if the real need is to build completely new business units, and a totally new business ethos and culture. Care is also needed to ensure that the level or breadth of required intervention is matched by the intending change agents' skills, and even their ideology of how to effect change.

For example, many systems of public health have been in turmoil for substantial periods during the last two decades. They have been faced with continuous, radical, macro-change (almost constant ministerial reshuffles), with rolling strategic and structural changes at the highest levels of the system, and with flow-on consequences to area boards, hospitals and private providers. But what has changed? It could well be argued that these constant macro-interventions were largely unproductive in delivering better health care. An appropriate level of change intervention, after one or two major system-wide changes, may have been better focused at the business unit (hospital, health care unit) or personal levels. Imposed change at the macro level may be necessary, but is not effective if used as a constant change strategy. The better hospital boards and health service professionals now realise that change inspired at lower levels

1. Levels (or breadth) of change
- Whole organisation or system (macro-intervention)
- Division or business unit (major intervention)
- Intergroup or workgroup (team intervention)
- Personal (individual change)

2. Type (or depth) of change intervention
'Hard' interventions
- Mergers/acquisitions
- Strategic repositioning/restructure
- Technical + systems change

'Soft' interventions
- Work design
- Human system design
- Cultural change

Figure 7.1 Breadth and depth of change intervention

can be far more productive than constant macro-interventions. This links to our second point.

The depth of change interventions

While change can be effected at various levels, not all types of intervention guarantee the longevity of change for the organisation. Figure 7.1 (section 2) also shows the depth of change interventions, from the relatively 'harder' interventions of mergers/acquisitions, strategic repositioning/restructuring and technical/systems change, to the relatively 'softer' interventions of work design, human system design and cultural change. Harrison,[4] an earlier writer in the field of organisational change, maintained that while many macro and 'hard' interventions can, on the surface, radically reshape an organisation, only 'deep' behavioural change can achieve long-lasting results. In our view, however, it is not only depth which is important, but also the blending of depth with breadth. The desired blending of depth and breadth for one organisation may be different for another. The problem with many 'change programs' or interventions is that too frequently they focus only on achieving breadth without consideration of the depth and interrelationships in change.

For instance, much systemic change, particularly that inspired by large corporate consulting groups, has been concerned primarily with changing the strategy, structure or systems of organisations with little or no attention to the behavioural aspects—the group dynamics and personal attitudes associated with the recommended changes. Large consulting groups often exit from organisations, laden with financial rewards for their recommendations but, in reality, they may leave an impoverished organisation because the behavioural aspects, the people factors, have not been considered. Conversely, many 'deep' change interventions—involving Organisational Development-type, people oriented and team-building change processes—have raised hopes and created temporary new attitudes, only to have them dashed against the rocks of archaic or misguided strategy, structures and systems. While behavioural interventions may go deeper, their effectiveness depends on finding the appropriate blend of changes in the system which facilitate and nurture desired changes overall.

In Figure 7.2, we illustrate the intersection which is essential between the depth and breadth of change interventions. The start point for change may vary—for instance, at whole organisation, or work group levels—just as the type of intervention will vary—for instance, a strategic repositioning or a cultural change intervention. The object of change interventions, however, must be to ensure that change effectiveness is sustained. At the end of it all, this involves leadership by individuals who collectively come to embody the culture of the organisation.

A production oriented company in our research provides an excellent example of such blended change. Through the decade of the 1990s its process of business analysis was relentless: analysis of domestic and overseas markets, analyses of customer needs and requirements, and analysis of the firm's positioning against world best practice. This was linked to incisive and, at times, painful work on redirecting strategy: closure of non-viable production units, and the installation of new processes, technologies and systems. In the main, this was very hard-nosed 'systemic' change. Yet this was blended with a range of powerful 'behavioural' interventions: a

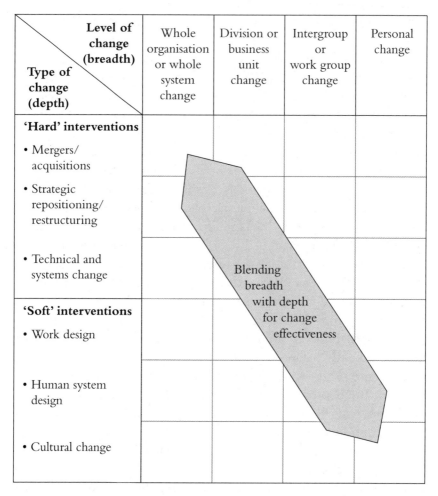

Level of change (breadth) / Type of change (depth)	Whole organisation or whole system change	Division or business unit change	Intergroup or work group change	Personal change
'Hard' interventions				
• Mergers/ acquisitions				
• Strategic repositioning/ restructuring				
• Technical and systems change		Blending breadth with depth for change effectiveness		
'Soft' interventions				
• Work design				
• Human system design				
• Cultural change				

Figure 7.2 Change Intervention Analysis

relentless focus on training; constant communication of company and production units' directions; disbanding hierarchical staff/wages distinctions and separate staff and wage employees' meal rooms and canteens; and work area improvements to create safer and cleaner working conditions. One of the key elements in achieving such a blend was the introduction across the company of the Quality Management (QM) approach: in this case, QM was not a panacea, or change bandaid, but a way of thinking and managing throughout the company. Systemic and behavioural change were blended in the Quality Management System.

Many 'new economy' companies are less likely to think of change in such structured terms, particularly if they are owner managed firms such as Look Smart, or Silicon Valley start-up ventures. They look more like Peters's fluid organisation, following an almost zany approach to change. However, with growth, or after acquisition of smaller companies by larger ones, a more systematic approach and an overall architecture of change will be essential if the organisation is not to be buffeted around from one change fad to another. A good example of this has been Lend Lease and MLC, quoted at the end of Chapter 4. Lend Lease has traditionally prided itself on its innovatory approach to work structuring, and its 'can do' operational culture. Internally it is called 'a three phone call culture—and it's done'. However, on acquiring MLC, a much more systematic approach to change—restructuring, downsizing, systems change, workforce redesign and service excellence—was required. More than three phone calls are required to succeed in this type of transformation. This brought MLC to the point in the latter 1990s where the culture had become more innovatory, so that it began to look more like the original Lend Lease than Lend Lease itself, particularly in the development of the innovative Campus MLC concept. Campus MLC involved substantial change 'architecture' on the part of MLC's Rosemary Kirkby. Then with Lend Lease's massive acquisition of international businesses in 1999, and its subsequent sale of MLC to the National Bank, Lend Lease itself called in a leading adviser to recommend on the cultural aspects of its changing global business. The company mixed the 'hard' interventions of mergers/acquisitions/divestments with the 'softer' intervention of cultural change. Lend Lease, which has historically prided itself on having no human resource managers, has now appointed an executive member to be responsible globally for its new process of cultural change.

Another example is the recruitment and human resource service firm, Morgan & Banks. It is now the stuff of entrepreneurial history that the company was established as a new venture by two former recruitment industry competitors, Geoff Morgan and Andrew Banks in 1984; acquired by the UK recruitment company, Select, in 1988 for A$41.0 million; and then reacquired by the Morgan & Banks's partners from the bankrupted Select in 1990 for A$2.5 million. In 1995 the company was floated on the Australian Stock Exchange for

A\$84 million and in 1998 acquired by the global US firm, TMP, for A\$400 million. Fast and profitable evolution indeed![5] However, concentration on the undoubted success involved underplays the considerable insight within the fledgling Morgan & Banks company about a sea change beginning to take place in human resource and recruitment practices across the Australian and international business landscapes. In this emerging environment Morgan & Banks has consistently worked to the strategic adage—'creating the dust, not eating it'. This was achieved for many years by an almost opportunistic approach to strategy and change. Said one of our interviewees: 'To understand the strategy of this place you just keep following the managing director as he goes up the hallway.'

However, after listing, and with increasing size and complexity, Morgan & Banks found that a more effective change 'architecture' was required. Anne Whyte, an Australian, was brought in from the World Bank to head up Morgan & Banks's Learning Team to provide more linkage between the harder business and the softer human systems aspects of the burgeoning business. Morgan & Banks's acquisition in 1998 by TMP has seen a further systematisation of change processes.

We are not advocating here that organisations need to create internal human resource or 'learning' departments to be successful. Many do, and find them enormously helpful, while others have found that human resource departments become entrenched in an ideological cul-de-sac which limits the value they add to the business. What we do advocate is blended change interventions, and the development, either formally or informally, of an overall schema or architecture of change which provides a context for change and management initiatives.

Overall, we also advocate thoughtful selection of change agents who may assist in facilitating processes of change. Figure 7.3 provides an illustration of the positioning of some of the consultancies typically used in change processes. While the larger consultancy groups have greater market power and presence, it will be immediately obvious from this illustration that they more typically concentrate on 'hard' change interventions: on the surface they also potentially offer integration, but one could argue that it is management's job to integrate. Someone internally must still do the blending—which is why these

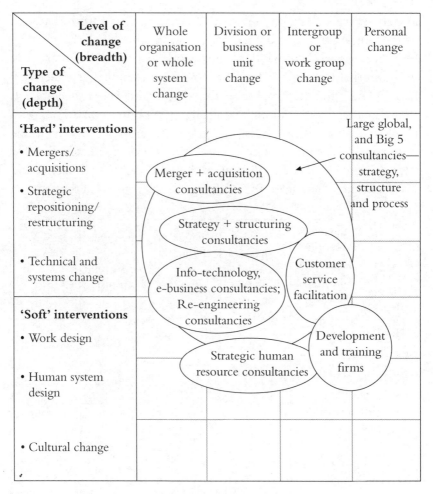

Level of change (breadth) / Type of change (depth)	Whole organisation or whole system change	Division or business unit change	Intergroup or work group change	Personal change
'Hard' interventions				Large global, and Big 5 consultancies—strategy, structure and process
• Mergers/ acquisitions	Merger + acquisition consultancies			
• Strategic repositioning/ restructuring	Strategy + structuring consultancies			
• Technical and systems change	Info-technology, e-business consultancies; Re-engineering consultancies	Customer service facilitation		
'Soft' interventions				
• Work design	Strategic human resource consultancies	Development and training firms		
• Human system design				
• Cultural change				

Figure 7.3 Typical positioning of consultancies

large-scale interventions sometimes yield so little in terms of permanent change if the change is not effectively led internally. Equally, smaller consultancies, whether involved in hard or soft interventions, may provide valuable specialist assistance, but the leadership task, the task of blending, still remains a core internal responsibility. Abrogating the task of leadership of change to outsiders is not an option.

It is equally important to ensure that an organisation has complementary leadership skills. Figure 7.4 illustrates how our categories of change leaders—Charismatics, Commanders, Coaches and Captains—fit on to the change intervention matrix. Charismatic leaders typically have the greatest capacity to move from 'hard' to 'soft' interventions, and vice versa across the levels of change. However, good Commanders often work in a complementary way with internal Captains or Coaches to ensure that change effectively has 'breadth' and 'depth'. Ineffective Commanders see their style as the one-style-fits all, dominant approach to be used on an ongoing basis. They brook no rivals, and often develop a cadre of mini-commanders around them, when they should be aiming for complementarity. The challenge on the other hand for Coaches and Captains, if they are leading the change, is to ensure that they source

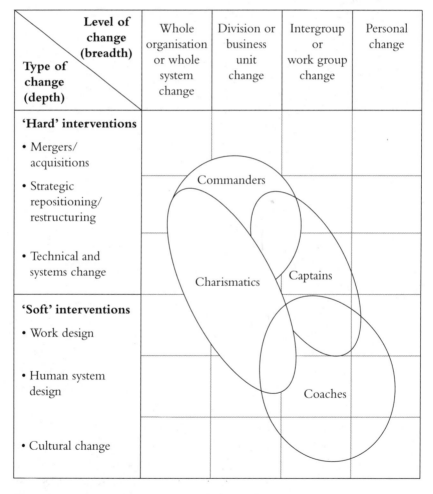

Type of change (depth) \ Level of change (breadth)	Whole organisation or whole system change	Division or business unit change	Intergroup or work group change	Personal change
'Hard' interventions • Mergers/ acquisitions • Strategic repositioning/ restructuring • Technical and systems change				
'Soft' interventions • Work design • Human system design • Cultural change				

Figure 7.4 Typical positioning of change leaders

appropriate assistance, internally or externally, to provide either the necessary harder or softer edge to their styles.

If Figures 7.3 and 7.4 were to be overlaid, they would demonstrate that most consultancies do not effectively deal with cultural change: it is the task of leaders to do so. However, cultural change on its own is not an independent variable: it arises from the effective blending of breadth and depth of change.

The message is clear: one-stop change interventions, panaceas, the latest 'buzzologies', and change bandaids, are rarely successful. Change agents need to aim for change interventions which are targeted and focused on critical variables, but which are comprehensive enough in their scope and depth to achieve results. Change agents must build confidence that change, however painful it might be, is an ongoing journey rather than a one-intervention event, and involves changes in strategies, systems and structures as well as behaviours. Leaders must be cognisant of the need for a change architecture which, while from time to time emphasising one approach, needs counterbalance to achieve lasting change.

Some current change intervention tools

Over the past decade there have been several meta, or larger-than-life, forms of change intervention employed by organisations seeking to raise or keep their performance at world-class levels. A book such as this would be incomplete without any analysis of some of these dominant change intervention tools. The intervention tools and systems of thinking we refer to are:

- the Balanced Scorecard;
- Total Quality Management and Benchmarking;
- Re-engineering of Work Processes; and
- e-Change.

These have been, and are, some of the most quoted programs or systems of change intervention within organisations. Associated with them are a plethora of useful change methodologies and exhortations by internal and external change agents. In an earlier period—for example, the 1970s–80s—similar programs or systems of thinking would have been Team Building, Industrial Democracy, Participative Management and even 'Japanese' Management. In an earlier period still—say, the 1950s–60s—Operations Management and Management-by-Objectives would have been equivalent major methods used for change intervention in organisations.

This raises such questions as: Are these 'meta' interventions fads or useful interventions? Do they have universal applicability to all organisations? Are they essential for high performance? Are they suitable as generic interventions or is a high degree of customisation necessary? Are they merely panaceas offering ephemeral benefits? These are the questions organisations face as, searching for business success, they consider seeking consulting assistance in these areas.

In each of the four major change intervention areas above, our view is that each constitutes a key form of intervention which can often assist in organisational survival and vitality. However, there are a number of caveats we attach to such a view:

- The intervention must help deliver the business strategy of the organisation, rather than the intervention being the strategy per se (beware of means–ends inversion). The intervention must be sponsored by the chief executive and executive group, and be symbolised by their behaviour (executives must 'walk the talk').
- Change agents associated with the intervention should report directly to a key member of the executive to give the intervention the necessary leverage and credibility.
- The intervention must be customised and internalised by the organisation (beware of generic-style interventions in which little effort is made to use organisational terminology and images).
- The intervention must be specific to the organisation's change needs (a service quality program introduced during a massive downsizing will rarely be effective).

We now provide an introductory commentary on each approach.

The Balanced Scorecard

The Balanced Scorecard has been developed from work undertaken by authors Kaplan and Norton in their seminal article 'The Balanced

Scorecard—Measures that drive performance'[6] and their later more detailed book.[7] These authors and others have since leveraged their concepts into commercially available strategy and change packages which have widespread use globally. Starting from the premise that managers rely too heavily on traditional financial accounting measures to assess business success, the authors set out to devise a balanced scorecard of measures to provide a fast but comprehensive view of the business. These measures include four perspectives and goal areas:

- Financial Perspective (How do we look to shareholders?)
- Customer Perspective (How do customers see us?)
- Internal Business Perspective (What must we excel at?)
- Innovation and Learning Perspective (Can we continue to improve and create value?)

Typical intervention practices
- Strategic planning processes
- Alignment of strategic planning, resource allocation and budgeting
- Linkage of strategic-planning and performance-planning processes

Levels of intervention
- Corporation-wide
- Divisions and business units
- Across larger systems (national and state)

Typical gains
- Focus on a few, visually represented effectiveness areas
- Focus of goals beyond financial factors
- Clear line of sight between corporate and business unit goals

Risks
- Inadequate measures are developed for other than financial goals
- The goal areas do not translate into behaviours
- Imposed behaviours and top-down goals may stifle bottom-up innovation

Figure 7.5 The Balanced Scorecard   KEY WRITERS: ROBERT KAPLAN AND DAVID NORTON

The Scorecard approach retains financial measures such as return-on-capital employed and economic value added, and supplements these with measures on value creation for customers through enhancement of internal processes and innovation, and the creation of capabilities in employees and systems.

The important issues for Kaplan and Norton were to achieve alignment between strategy and implementaion by focusing on external as well as internal aspects of change. Conceptually, at least, the set of techniques associated with these concepts appeared as a blended approach to change, mixing as they did the hard and soft measures of performance. Their use of a clock dial, plan-on-a-page approach has been appealing to many organisations wishing to develop a graphic, simple set of measures for all to see. Some use the clock dial approach, but substitute their own broad measures and goals, regardless of the structured methodology provided by Kaplan and Norton. Our major critique of the approach is that it is really a sophisticated version of management-by-objectives or, alternatively, a top-down goal-setting system which generates too much detail. Used thus, this intervention can be imposed on the organisation as a 'hard' strategic intervention. While it espouses the internal and human perspective, the behavioural perspective is often not actually operationalised. Our experience of this methodology is that where it is used almost as a stand-alone panacea, its effect is negligible; where it is used actively as part of a total management and leadership process, the results can be extremely effective.

Total Quality Management and Benchmarking

When Western industrial and resource based economies demonstrably lost their position of economic leadership to Japan during the 1980s, their major corporations launched into a frenetic search for some of the key factors of Japan's success and identified Total Quality Management as a critical variable in the then high-performing Japanese economy. The Japanese had a quality tradition in their superb working skills in their ancient crafts. However, similar quality standards were not achieved in Japanese business until after World War II, particularly in the late 1960s and 1970s. The emphasis on quality was introduced by US management experts, Dr W. E. Deming and Dr J. M. Juran, and was augmented by the work of Dr K. Ishikawa, and soon became a widespread movement in Japanese industry.

TQM then evolved worldwide as one of the most widely used change interventions involving workforce participation in work process redesign, system changes and work team goals, all key components of business performance improvement. TQM is not participatory for the sake of participation per se: it uses participation in a process of continuous business improvement. By the 1990s most large to medium-sized organisations had adopted some form of TQM. This was particularly true of manufacturing or repetitive process service industries. It is a method of bottom-up involvement, of devolving accountability to work teams, and of encouraging employee commitment to problem solving.

Even though it was used by many leading organisations, there remained a significant risk that process improvements might dominate the thinking of work teams in place of more strategic thinking about the positioning of the business. Worse still, a preoccupation with process improvements often gave the comforting delusion of progress in situations where the process of improvement was focused on the business variables irrelevant to business success. Like other interventions, TQM must therefore be heavily integrated with the processes of strategy and corporate directions to ensure that the right business questions are being addressed in the first place. (An example of this in practice is given in Appendix 4C.)

TQM practised within this type of framework can augment the process of business improvement. It is easy, however, to become lost in 'process myopia'. Paul O'Neill, former Chairman of Alcoa,

> *Continuous improvement is exactly the right idea if you are the world leader in everything you do. It is a terrible idea if you are lagging the world leadership benchmark. It is probably a disastrous idea if you are far behind the world standard—in which case you may need rapid quantum-leap improvement.*
>
> PAUL O'NEILL, CHAIRMAN OF ALCOA[8]

235

summarised the dilemma of continuous operational improvement for its own sake (see box).

Unfortunately, many of the early followers of TQM fell into this trap, believing that relentless operational improvement would preclude the need for decisive strategic actions. There is also evidence that approximately only 20% of TQM programs fully achieved their goals—not because of inadequacies in their overall conceptualisation, but in the daily detailed implementation of the concept.[9] An international 'Quality of the Year' award-winning firm was close to bankruptcy five years later because it failed to examine key strategic questions. Integrated with strategy, however, TQM can provide a very powerful intervention leading to performance improvement.

Benchmarking, a key subset of Total Quality Management, involves the search for industry best practices that lead to superior performance. Benchmarking involves intracompany and inter-company, national and international performance comparisons of process efficiencies, work methodologies and systems, and key organisational performance output measures—identifying performance gaps and then striving to be the best of the best.

There are essentially two levels of Benchmarking. Strategic Benchmarking relates to inter-organisation business comparisons in areas such as pricing policy, percentage of funds expended on research and development, financial performance ratios, organisational structuring, measured levels of customer satisfaction, and total factor productivity measures. Many companies obtain early impetus in the process of change from such comparisons.

Process Benchmarking, on the other hand, relates more to the operational processes employed in producing products and services. Here, the comparisons are of product and service features, system flows, tactical targets and planning processes. Process Benchmarking necessarily involves employees working close to the process to undertake the Benchmarking.

Companies active in Benchmarking estimate that approximately 10% of performance improvement comes from Strategic Benchmarking, while 90% comes from process improvements. World-class organisations thrive on such comparisons with other international competitors.

Typical intervention practices
- Company-wide TQM systems
- Quality Circle teams (QC), quality assurance and statistical process control
- Just-in-Time inventory systems (JIT)
- Benchmarking training for executives, managers and team leaders

Levels of intervention
- Strategic TQM and Benchmarking—corporate level (e.g. customer service, processes and measures; development processes; pricing policies; organisation levels; financial performance ratios) compared against best-in-class organisations
- Process TQM and Benchmarking—unit level (e.g. product features; system flows; tactical targets; work processes) compared against best-in-class organisations

Typical gains
- Company survival in a globally competitive environment
- Company regarded as a 'world best practice' organisation within its industry
- Setting realistic, yet challenging targets
- Radical reductions in waste, work and product errors/returns, materials and product levels; achieving breakthroughs in thinking
- Employee ownership of problem solving, work unit outputs and company results; reducing the learning curve (so as not to reinvent the wheel)
- Better employee relations, higher productivity, greater customer satisfaction, increased market share, improved profitability

Risks
- TQM introduced as a bandaid or panacea
- Relentless focus on process improvements when a new business strategy, not improvement of present business processes, is required
- TQM introduced by the training department, rather than by the executive and/or managers
- Benchmarking the wrong performance variables
- The time taken for the process
- Death by acronym and management glossary (e.g. JIT, PDCA, CIP, Pareto, Fishbone Chart, Cross-functional Team)

Figure 7.6 Total Quality Management + Benchmarking   KEY
WRITERS: W. E. DEMING, J. M. JURAN, K. ISHIKAWA, ROBERT CAMP

Re-engineering of Work Processes

One of the most common forms of change intervention over recent years has been the Re-engineering of Work Processes.

The need for Western economies to be cost competitive with low cost producers, particularly in the Asian economies, provided the initial impetus for this trend. This has now been compounded by the rapid rate of technology uptake in organisations. Re-engineering initially connoted a productive process of structural and process review. The reality is somewhat different in that it is not uncommon for organisations to have shed or 'downsized' up to 30% or more of employees in the last decade using Re-engineering techniques. Yet downsizing for its own sake often achieved little other than reduced costs and demoralised organisations. Downsizing often reduces the employee head count but fails to reconfigure, redistribute or reduce the workload. On the positive side, Re-engineering of Work Processes usually involves dramatic reductions in the levels of organisational hierarchy, followed by refocusing on core business, outsourcing secondary work, eliminating non-value-added activities (such as unnecessary levels of approval, reports and reviews), refocusing on work that adds value to the customer, devolving authority to the lowest possible level, and concentrating on workflows that cross traditional functional boundaries. It has the potential to provide empowerment.

A critical question in Re-engineering is whether the dramatic changes needed in work organisation can be achieved incrementally, or whether more radical change strategies are required. Two of our earlier research organisations provided interesting comparisons. The first is Comalco Rolled Products (CRP) Division, Yennora, Sydney—an aluminium products manufacturer. In the early 1990s, CRP's business was trading unprofitably, with the possibility that the plant could be closed by the parent company, CRA. The Plant General Manager, Terry Palmer, introduced a major downsizing program in association with Coopers and Lybrand, using the Coopers and Lybrand BPR (Business Process Re-engineering) methodology; the latter aimed at ensuring that all work processes were challenged, thoroughly examined, recast or abolished. CRP was initially traumatised by such a radical approach to change, but came out of the process more financially sound and viable in the competitive world of aluminium processing.

Typical intervention practices
- Analysis of core and secondary business(es)
- Downsizing to reduce absolute staff numbers, followed by rightsizing to reconfigure organisational structures and processes
- Value Analysis—examination of levels of approval, reporting methods, work processes and systems

Levels of intervention
- Re-engineering typically commences with the announcement of major new strategic initiatives or a process of radical business refocus
- The intervention cascades from the corporate to the business and work unit levels in the form of breakthrough task teams, autonomous work groups

Typical gains
- Company survival
- The creation of a market/customer/product oriented company, less concerned with structure and hierarchy than performance
- Business strategies supported by process capability
- Elimination of unnecessary work

Risks
- Re-engineering may in fact be simply work process reform under a different label—the title may create too great an expectation
- A radical approach, not properly formulated, may bust the company, not just the work paradigm
- Work process re-engineering driven or sponsored from too low a level in the organisation
- The process founders on endless consultation

Figure 7.7 Re-engineering of Work Processes   KEY WRITERS: W. R. WEISBORD, R. B. KAPLAN

Contrast this with our second case of the State Library of NSW in the early 1990s: no downsizing, minimal trauma, but a major challenge to the workforce to enact a new vision of a qualitatively different library of world-class standard. Here, work redesign was driven in part by the progressive introduction of new technologies, and in part by the creation of semiautonomous and multiskilled work teams whose task it was to change their own work processes and routines. In this process, unlike in CRP, there was minimal use of consulting interventions. In CRP's case its survival was at stake. In the case of the State Library, the issue was not survival but an opportunity to invent a new future based on creating value for State Library clients. Both are valid approaches to Re-engineering.

The mistake in Re-engineering is to assume that the task is ever completed. The business environment is unforgiving, and is particularly tough on those organisations that do not ensure that their work organisation is constantly reviewed, sometimes radically, in the light of emerging business strategies and technology capability. A second major problem may arise from the 'drift of consolidation'— that is, assuming that consolidation rather than constant change is the norm, and so allowing the work culture to drift back into bureaucratic work processes.

e-Change

The capacity and reach of information technologies has become so pervasive in organisations, large and small, that we believe technology systems uptake has become a change intervention itself.

The frenetic trade in dot.com stocks at the turn of the twentieth and twenty-first centuries, and the rise, fall and gyrations of the Nasdaq stock index have been indicative of an unfolding business revolution. With business revolution comes change, and the challenge of how to manage the change is that the organisation is sustained by change rather than destroyed by it. Organisational longevity is a rarer commodity than most believe: in the early decades of the twentieth century there were over 700 car manufacturers. By the turn of the twenty-first century there were five major global car makers and a handful of boutique manufacturers.

Typical intervention practices
- Installation of Internet platforms and interactive Web pages
- Development of a Web market, or an industry portal (the new integrators)
- Establishment of virtual networks

Levels of intervention
- Industry-wide systems
- Global corporations
- Corporate, divisional and business unit
- Individuals (operating as virtual networkers to corporates and markets)

Typical gains
- Transition from old to new economy wealth creation
- Reduced communication hierarchies
- Creation of information ubiquity and transparency (outside and inside the organisation)

Risks
- e-Change introduced solely as technical systems change without strategic purpose or behavioural buy-in
- Overestimating the effect of e-Change on the business
- Overpromising on what e-Change will deliver

Figure 7.8 e-Change   KEY WRITERS: SEE *HARVARD BUSINESS REVIEW*, MAY–JUNE 2000, 'THE E-BUSINESS FRONTIER'

Older companies like IBM, and newer ones like the ubiquitous dot.coms and associated consultancies, are active in providing advice and solutions to mainstream companies on the integration of a change into their businesses. This takes the form of both business-to-business (B2B) and business-to-consumer (B2C) solutions and systems. e-Change appears at first as a systems intervention, in the middle area of our depth of change intervention scale in Figure 7.2—somewhere between the hard and soft types of intervention. Yet e-business and e-commerce have the capacity to alter the fundamental strategy of many corporations and the work patterns of whole groups of employees.

Recruitment consultants Morgan & Banks provide an illustration of these principles. The company was formed in the mid-1980s as a classic face-to-face style skills matching and recruitment service. Its mode of operating was for consultants to take briefs from businesses to conduct a search or advertising process, then conduct interviews with selected applicants. 'Hi-touch' all the way. By the latter 1990s Morgan & Banks had introduced an Australian orien-ted Internet based search system called Jobhound in which consultants played a minimal role in matching applicants with companies. Evidence soon started to emerge that appointments made from matches originally introduced via Jobhound lasted longer within positions than those matches introduced through the consultancy process. 'Hi-tech' human services were starting to emerge. The Morgan & Banks merger with TMP has now provided it with access to a global Internet search methodology, Monster-board. Hundreds of consultants are still engaged in the Morgan & Banks business, but simultaneously it is taking on some of the characteristics of a dot.com business. In this transition from a face-to-face human services consultancy to a dual human services/dot.com company, huge strategic, technical systems and human systems change has been involved.

Morgan & Banks's e-Change was successful because it saw the strategic, technical and human significance of the changes necessary for creating a twenty-first century business. The initially risky-looking strategic decisions to go global, and to seek partnership with a global firm with a strong technology platform, were blended with assiduous work on the part of the company's learning team to develop staff capabilities for the change. This, together with the young age profile of staff and the high turnover of employees in the industry, has assisted the company in recruiting new staff for whom e-Change is almost a way of life.

The risk in e-Change is in not achieving the necessary strategic, technical and human system integration—or, simply put, introducing e-Change as the latest fad or panacea.

We return now to our original model of change, and its relationship to the range of change intervention tools covered in this chapter so far.

Integrating change strategies and change intervention tools

In Chapter 4 we introduced the characteristics of four different change strategies:

- Developmental Transitions (constant change);
- Task-focused Transitions (constant change);
- Charismatic Transformations (inspirational change); and
- Turnarounds (frame-breaking change).

In the following figures, we illustrate how different types of change intervention tools cluster against each of the major four overall change strategy types.

A detailed review of these analyses will show that systemic change interventions (major changes in strategy, structure and systems) are most often effected by either Charismatic Transformation or Turnaround change intervention strategies, whereas deeper behavioural-type interventions (intergroup and personal interventions) are most often effected by Developmental or Task-focused Transitions.

Charismatic Transformational and Turnaround change intervention strategies are not necessarily 'deep' and must be linked in the longer run with interventions that have greater 'depth' in interpersonal and personal terms. Transformational and Turnaround change intervention strategies have an effective shelf life of up to two years before the need for greater depth becomes crucial.

Developmental and Task-focused Transitions overall represent the more normal state of change for a healthy organisation. Developmental Transition is deeper in the personal sense, but can become so person focused that critical task issues are ignored, or tough business decisions that are likely to cause pain to individuals or groups are not taken. This can have the effect of slowing the response to dramatic and ongoing change in the organisation's environment. Developmental change may therefore need to be linked with aspects of Task-focused change if the process of adjustment becomes too slow. We see this in the case of MLC, where former CEO Peter Scott, using the Campus MLC concept,

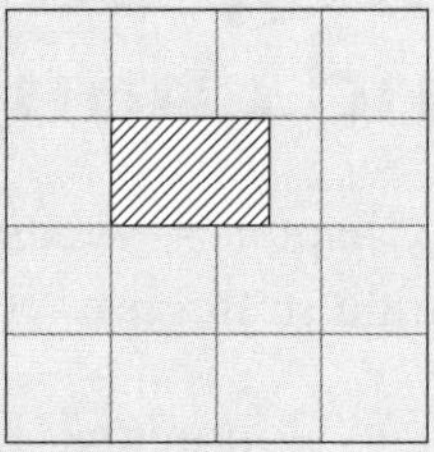

Change 'type' characteristics
- Constant incremental change (normative–re-educative)
- High commitment/involvement
- Value based change

Change intervention tools typically used
- Vision/mission development (consultative)
- Culture enhancement programs
- Team building (self-managed work teams)
- Management and team leadership development programs
- Service quality programs
- Personal and professional development/skills formation
- TQM, Process Benchmarking
- Building corporate competencies
- Radical delegation/empowerment
- Developing horizontal organisation structures

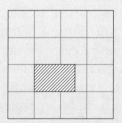

Figure 7.9 Developmental Transitions

Change 'type' characteristics
- Constant incremental change (strongly directed)
- Clear strategic intent (determined by executive)
- Change through systems, work structures and personal performance accountability mechanisms

Change intervention tools typically used
- Systems redesign
- Negotiated skills-base changes
- Job redesign/business process redesign/engineering
- Productivity measurement and improvement
- Strategic and Process Benchmarking
- Objective setting/management-by-objectives/performance contracts/appraisal
- Strong technical skills training
- Management and team leadership development
- TQM, continuous improvement

Figure 7.10 Task-focused Transitions

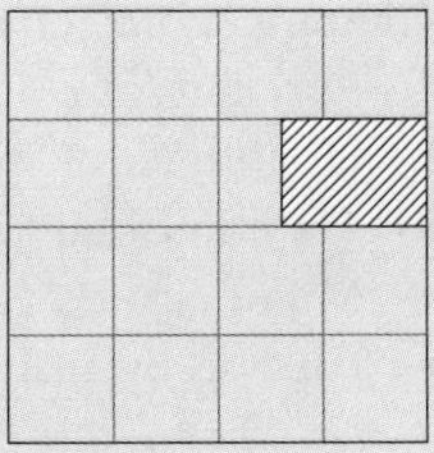

Change 'type' characteristics
- Radical redefinition of business strategies
- Building of widespread workforce commitment
- Cultural renewal
- Anticipatory change
- Voluntary commitment to a compelling vision

Change intervention tools typically used
- New vision/'strategic intent', Balanced Scorecard
- Radical organic restructuring, voluntary redundancy schemes
- New executive recruits, often from outside
- Strategic alliances to infuse new concepts, introduce 'new' economy and e-Change techniques
- Top team-building programs
- Cross-functional task teams
- Service improvement programs
- Symbolic communication (change of corporate name, logo and wardrobe; employee excellence awards)

Figure 7.11 Charismatic Transformations

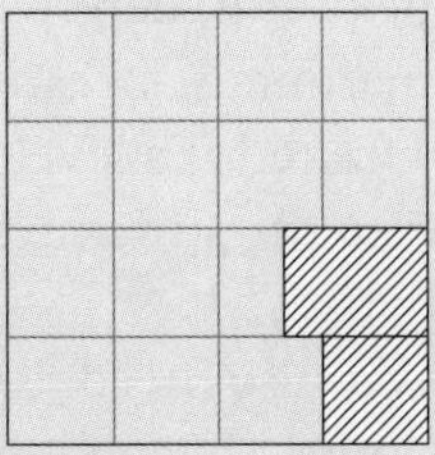

Change 'type' characteristics
- Rapid radical redefinition of the core business
- Market redefinition and segmentation
- Business and cultural re-formation

Change intervention tools typically used
- Strategy and market segmentation analysis
- Merger/acquisition/divestment of non-core businesses
- Restructurings/downsizing/rightsizing/forced retrenchments
- Reconstruction and development of the top team
- Cultural and industrial confrontation strategies
- Radical changes in business processes and systems
- Radical human resource strategy redesign

Figure 7.12 Turnarounds

Change 'type' characteristics 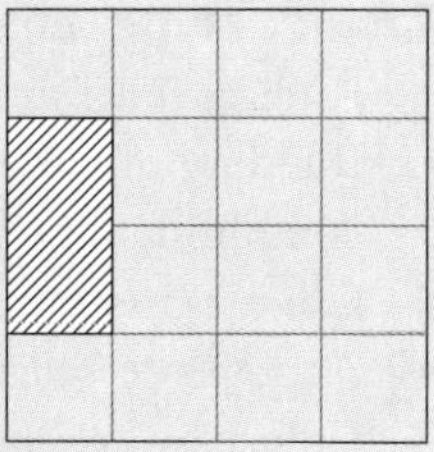
- Avoiding variation and change
- Uniformity of approach
- Traditional bureaucratic organisation
- Minor change
- Paralysis by analysis (risk-averse)

Change intervention tools typically used
- Organisation and methods studies
- Structural fine tuning (without reducing levels of structure, or creating greater flexibility)
- Industrial awards set the management–workforce agenda
- Operational, procedural and 'supervisory' training
- Interpersonal survey feedback and team building, unrelated to corporate purpose
- Exclusive emphasis on an 'internal' labour market

Figure 7.13 Taylorism

drove a dominantly Developmental change strategy, but from time to time used stronger, less consultative change interventions to obtain results quickly.

Task-focused Transitions, while system oriented, have greater longer-term depth than radical Charismatic Transformations or Turnarounds, because the system and work process interventions are enacted at a level closer to the individual, in ways which directly change the structures and systems within which people work on a daily basis.

We also need to examine a fifth type of change strategy—Taylorism. In contrast to Charismatic Transformations, Turnarounds, Developmental or Task-focused Transitions, Taylorism (see Figure 7.13) represents the most superficial approach to change. Our research shows that its continued use in a radically changing business environment is associated with low performance or is used only in very limited mass production situations where the organisation has an absolute monopoly on stable markets/products/services.

Tayloristic change strategies are used as devices for 'control' and uniformity of procedures and operations, often for their own sake.

Taylorism emphasises formal and rigid job descriptions, and formalistic and often adversarial employer–employee industrial relationships, and industrial 'awards' set the human resource management agenda. Unlike the focused approach of the new 'Prudent Mechanistic' organisations discussed in Chapter 3, a Tayloristic approach to change emphasises consolidation around the work practices of previous eras. It is an inappropriate change strategy in a competitive world as we move our organisations beyond the old boundaries.

The dynamics of change interventions

In Appendix 8 of Chapter 8 we draw together all the elements and characteristics of change associated with our four major change strategy types—Developmental Transitions, Task-focused Transitions, Charismatic Transformations and Turnarounds. It will be clear from this that each of the major change strategies and the business, change and human resource practices associated with them have an 'intellectual coherence'. They are not, however, iron-clad categories or sets of rules to be followed. We are seeking to provide guidance for leaders, managers and change agents to ensure that their approach to change is informed, rather than driven by the fads of the moment. Yet there is an element of opportunism and change which must be captured. Many of our case study organisations illustrate this.

As internal and external conditions change, organisations typically need to modify their change intervention strategies. In our research, we have been able to chart the way in which many organisations have modified their change strategies over periods of several years. Figure 7.14 shows some of the typical 'paths of change' taken by organisations we have researched.

Figure 7.14 shows that:

- Tayloristic-type change in an organisation that has maintained the status quo or slowed down typically needs the inspiration of Transformation or the shock of a painful Turnaround to re-energise the organisation. The 1990s in particular saw some key

Scale of change

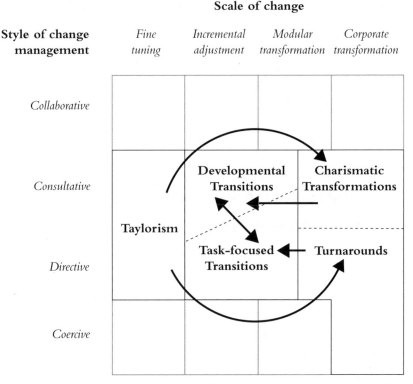

Style of change management	Fine tuning	Incremental adjustment	Modular transformation	Corporate transformation

Collaborative

Consultative — **Developmental Transitions**   **Charismatic Transformations**

Taylorism

Directive — **Task-focused Transitions**   **Turnarounds**

Coercive

Note: While the patterns of change are the dominant ones from our research, they are not only the ones. Other patterns are possible.

Figure 7.14 Some common dynamics in corporate change, over time

examples of such radical change: by Transformation—Qantas, Telstra and the State Library of NSW; by Turnaround—the Victorian public sector in the 1990s, Pacific Power, MLC Insurance, BHP under CEO Paul Anderson, and global players such as Philips and IBM.

- Turnarounds, if successful, typically take two or so years of initial shock therapy, but are rarely successful in the longer term if the approach does not then modify to a Task-focused Transition, which translates the corporate level changes to the business unit and work unit levels.

- Transformations, depending as they do on the energy and personal qualities of the Charismatic leader, often suffer from a wish by participants to keep the charisma and hype going over the longer term, in which case the intervention only has a 'surface' effect. To reap the benefits of fast-moving Charismatic Transformations, it is necessary to go 'deeper', most commonly by moving to those change interventions characteristic of Developmental Transitions.

• Developmental and Task-focused Transitions involve constant change, and represent the more normal state of change for higher performing organisations. However, they are not mutually exclusive categories. Mixed with the interventions of a Developmental Transition will often be some of the interventions (for example, job redesign, work restructuring) of a Task-focused Transition, and vice versa. However, if Developmental and Task-focused interventions are unsuccessful in delivering or assisting the vision, strategic intent and business imperatives of the organisation, the organisation may quickly revert to a painful Turnaround strategy.

In Chapter 1 we looked at the change dilemma facing one of Australasia's leading corporations, Westpac, in the 1990s. Westpac illustrates the use of different change strategies at different business stages. In the 1980s the Bank underwent a major and successful (Charismatic) Transformation under the inspirational leadership of Bob White. By the latter 1980s this had modified to a successful Developmental Transition, during which time the Bank developed a very strong corporate culture and a reputation as a leading bank. However, business conditions changed rapidly in the period immediately following the 1987 stockmarket crash. After a lengthy and damaging leadership succession process within the Bank, the newly appointed Chief Executive, Stuart Fowler, introduced a directive, harder nosed approach to leadership, characterised by our Task-focused change strategy. However, the consultative and innovative culture of the Bank was so strong and the independence of some key business units so entrenched, that it was difficult, if not impossible, to achieve the amount of business repositioning required quickly in radically different business conditions. This continued during 1991–92 under the leadership of Frank Conroy: extremely useful changes were made, but seemingly insufficient to meet key shareholder demands, resulting in the boardroom dramas recounted in our first chapter.

Which approach to change? To satisfy shareholders, there was no alternative for Westpac's newly appointed Chief Executive in 1993, Robert Joss, but to move swiftly, incisively and in a way which challenged the power structure and culture of the Bank. In effect he operationalised much of the change strategy which had been crafted but not fully implemented by Conroy. The effect internally was traumatic, but during subsequent years the Bank's performance improved dramatically. Now under the leadership of David Morgan, Westpac's approach to change is a mix of a Task-focused and a Developmental approach which we believe will last for several years. The Bank is now operationalising a more stable approach to its change processes, avoiding the hype of its mid-1980s period. Westpac is a key example of the successful situational use of change strategies, except in the latter 1980s when a more radical approach should have been used to quickly, and successfully, reposition the business.

An Australasian model of change?

Even though many change strategies generalise across industrialised economies, it is important to examine whether cultural characteristics modify their 'generalisability'. In the past, Australian and New Zealand change agents and leaders have been heavily influenced by two major traditions of change which, by the 1980s, had almost become ideologies:

- the European Sociotechnical approach (emphasis on work and job design; technology and work; industrial democracy). Focus: the sociology of work.
- the North American Human Processual approach (emphasis on individual needs; team processes; managerial style; individual motivation). Focus: the psychology of the individual worker.

To a large degree many change interventions still split around this ideological divide: do you change the system, or change the person? In the 1980s other models emerged as almost complete models within themselves:

- the Swedish model of work organisation (emphasis on a combined sociotechnical and human processual approach within the context of a benevolent social welfare state). Focus: create a model workplace.
- the Japanese collectivist model (emphasis on lifelong employment; quality management; extensive worker participation in workplace change and process redesign). Focus: the collective good.

Advocates of these approaches were very persuasive and many managers slavishly adopted one model or tradition to the exclusion of others.

What works in North America, Western Europe and Japan often also works in Australia and New Zealand, but not always or in full. We suggest that managers should be sensitive to the possible cultural specificity of intended change interventions. For example, North American voluntarism may work well with a sales force, but not necessarily with call centre operators. Similarly, the Japanese tradition of collectivism in change may work better among manufacturing workers than with foreign exchange dealers or the dot.com innovators. The North American tradition of individual voluntarism has been a dominant ideology in the mainstream change management literature and among change agents, consultants and trainers. Yet in applying this ideology to change programs, often little allowance has been made for the more egalitarian and collectivist nature of the Australian workforce. In our terms, this ideology has frequently led to an inappropriate emphasis on Developmental Transitions or Charismatic Transformations, when a fuller range of potential change strategies should have been explored. Overall, the challenge is to be eclectic in melding together our own model of change rather than slavishly adopting whole models—for example, the Organisational Development model, the 'Japanese Way' or the 'Volvo Way'.

Australia faces a unique set of challenges in change. Our country is strategically positioned in relation to the Asian economies, yet culturally and ideologically our modern historical roots are in the Northern Hemisphere. To lean too heavily on our historical origins for change models will distance us from our economic future. Yet our Asian partners and competitors operate from a powerful collectivist cultural model of their own. To prosper in this environment will require Australasian solutions, an eclectic approach, and a belief that Australasia can be a key bridging point between Asia and the northern industrialised economies.

The purpose of this book has been to provide maps of the territory of change, rather than instant recipes or solutions. Our change strategies and interventions need to reflect a sense of urgency in building world-class enterprises in Australasia. Our sporting teams and heroes are world-class. Our organisations can be too.

References

1. This is a theme of T. Peters's book, *Liberation Management: Necessary Disorganization for the Nanosecond Nineties*, Macmillan, London, 1992.
2. R. S. Kaplan & D. P. Norton, *The Balanced Scorecard: Translating Strategy into Action*, Harvard Business School Press, Boston, MA, 1996.
3. L. M. Sjoblom, 'Shareholder value creation—Old wine in a new bottle?', *Perspectives for Managers*, Vol. 53, Issue 12, IMD, Lausanne, 1998, pp. 1–4.
4. R. Harrison, 'Choosing the depth of organisational intervention', *Journal of Applied Behavioural Science*, 1965, Vol. 6, No. 2, pp. 181–202.
5. See D. Stace, 'Fast evolution at Morgan and Banks: Going global in services', *Centre for Corporate Change Working Paper No. 095*, AGSM, University of New South Wales, 1998.
6. R. S. Kaplan & D. P. Norton, 'The Balanced Scorecard: Measures that drive performance', *Harvard Business Review*, January–February, 1992, pp. 72–9.
7. R. S. Kaplan & D. P. Norton, 1996, op. cit.
8. P. O'Neill, Chairman, Alcoa, in a worldwide letter to Alcoa staff, November 1991.
9. *Catalyst*, Newsletter of the Centre for Corporate Change, Issue 8, August 1993, p. 1, quoted research by R. Waldersee & G. Eagleson.

Chapter 8
Beyond the boundaries

Adventuring across boundaries

In the late fifteenth century, in an endeavour to open up a sea route to India and the Orient, a number of Portuguese navigators sailed beyond the boundaries of the then known world. They pushed further and further down the west coast of Africa until they rounded the Cape of Good Hope. It was not long after their earliest voyages that a Genoese navigator, Christopher Columbus, backed by the Spanish king, defied commonsense to sail due west in an endeavour to reach the same destination. The expedition reached the Americas instead. As further expeditions sailed around Africa and the Americas, these great continental barriers were bypassed and an immense new area of the world became accessible for European exploration, trade and conquest. It seemed as though all known boundaries were gone; huge trackless areas of the world opened up before the intrepid adventurers; unimagined and limitless resources were there for the taking; the opportunities seemed endless.

In the early twenty-first century an analogous exploration is being undertaken. The boundaries we face are not geographic, as in the fifteenth century, but economic, social and technological. We are in a period of transformative social change as old industrialised economies switch to knowledge based economies, or blended industrial/knowledge based economies, and from narrowly focused domestic economies to globally competitive economies. The powerful undergirding force is the new technology which makes it possible. In Australia's case the benefits of a period of significant change have been profound, resulting in:

- a more dynamic economy;
- a broadening economy, now significantly less reliant on resources and manufacturing;
- high GDP growth relative to the rest of the world;
- higher productivity growth than the entire OECD group of nations;
- income from company investments abroad, and from service exports, rising by a factor of 10 in the decade of the 1990s.

Yet, as in many advanced economies, this type of growth contains paradoxes. Despite impressive productivity and employment growth, the nation still has chronic underemployment. People have work but for how many is it meaningful? Are many just automatons in a huge global labour pool? Despite a booming economy, there are significant poverty traps in both cities and regions. Despite the strength inherent in Australia's cultural diversity, there is still significant bridging to be achieved across the span of our cultures, including the nation's indigenous peoples, the Aboriginals. These and other paradoxes are at the base of skittish public, electoral and organisational moods.[1]

Economic journalist Paul Maidment makes a cogent case that the economic, social and technological changes sweeping the globe are similar in scope to the period of the Industrial Revolution. 'This (the Industrial Revolution) was a painful time for many people who must have yearned for a more Elysian past, and thought their lives ruined by the economic forces transforming the country.'[2] Yet the Industrial Revolution, much like the current 'Information Revolution', led to the forging of new forms of work and productivity. 'Some sectors of society enjoyed unparalleled prosperity because of the industrial revolution. The sheer productivity of the age laid the basis for a burst of unprecedented wealth. Lives were wrenched by the change, but we now look back on it as capitalism's golden age. Today, the same process may be unfolding in a new form.'[3]

Author Thomas Friedman uses the metaphor of the high-tech Lexus car and the olive tree to traverse the paradox of the current age. The Lexus is symbolic of the pervasive turbo-charged, globalising, Internet-linked new economy, while the olive tree symbolises the older economy, a more Elysian past, and more communal values. The challenge, according to Friedman, is for societies to find a balance between these two forces and worlds.[4]

There are undoubtedly great opportunities in the current transitional period. However, we must also be aware of the risks in some of the complex issues we face as modern day navigators between these two worlds. The issues of change—at global, national, organisational and personal levels—are profound. We have already addressed some in this book. However, there are several other complex global issues which we believe will become increasingly significant for national and corporate strategists alike. They are not issues which we have carefully researched or for which we have definitive answers. Rather the issues are so large as to convince us that in the early decades of the twenty-first century, leaders in government and enterprises will be managing change on an even greater scale than over the two decades just past. We briefly introduce four such issues which constitute major leadership issues for the twenty-first century.

Leadership issues for the twenty-first century

Globalisation without soul

Globalisation could be loosely defined as the system of worldwide integration by which goods, capital and labour are free to move across national borders. At the centre of it all are three complementary global institutions: the World Trade Organization (WTO), the International Monetary Fund (IMF) and the World Bank. During the decades of the 1980s and 1990s the conceptual underpinnings of globalisation and 'economic rationalism' became the almost accepted intellectual orthodoxy among governments, policy makers and elites in most advanced and emerging economies.

Yet, as we noted in Chapter 2, by the turn of the century the orthodoxy was under challenge from a variety of sources. The challenges came in the form of well organised protests from interest groups which had not been winners from years of economic reform and free market policies. Symbolically these forces found their focus at a series of high profile WTO, World Bank and IMF meetings in Seattle, Davos, London, Washington, Melbourne and Prague in late 1999 and 2000. At issue, among many other things, were:

- *Distributive imbalances between nations* The theory and reality of open markets have not, for many countries, coincided. While many smaller countries, including Australia and New Zealand, have opened their economies to international competition, larger players, notably the United States and Japan, have not been so consistent in their actions. Size and global dominance do not sit easily with a level global playing field in which the benefits flow uniformly to all players. For instance, the fall of the Berlin Wall and the Iron Curtain was supposed to usher in a period of gathering prosperity across Europe as market economies were created in Eastern Europe. A decade or so later the income disparities across countries provide cause for concern, per capita incomes differing by factors of 50–60 between rich Northern and Western Europe and many of the former Eastern bloc countries. As we enter the twenty-first century, 60% of the world's population have still never used a telephone, let alone sent an email message. The rich, and the richer economies, are becoming smarter while the poor are being left behind. At issue are not only the failure of free-market policies to distribute benefits more evenly: cultural and historical factors also play a significant role. Nevertheless, as an issue of change, continuing distributive imbalances between societies will present significant strategic challenges to governments and corporations alike. The assumption that world markets are there for the taking may not be practically, commercially or socially sustainable. Unless the benefits of globalisation are perceived as being more evenly shared, re-regulation of many markets is a distinct possibility.

- *Distributive imbalances are also increasingly occurring within our societies*
The paradox of advanced societies is that global competition and the application of burgeoning new technologies are having the effect of rapidly increasing overall productivity. Higher productivity can be associated with a pattern of increasing wealth and employment opportunities for everyone. However, in this revolution, despite the higher productivity, our societies are facing persistent underemployment, radically different career paths and uneven distribution of wealth and work in our advanced societies.

The corporation has a role in the reinvention and sensible distribution of work, as do governments and individuals. The classical model of a 35–44 hour per week, full-time employment and predictable lifetime career is largely redundant. In its place, corporations are experimenting with flexible contracts and part-time work. Governments are experimenting with job-start and training programs, radically different industrial and labour market laws and redesigned 'mutual obligation' welfare programs. Many individuals are experimenting, often for the first time, with being entrepreneurs. We suspect that the reinvention of work has only just begun. Corporations have an obligation to be active in reinventing the work relationships which will sustain, rather than divide, our societies. At a societal level the challenge is to ensure that the middle class—usually an 'aspirational' class—is not gutted, as the society divides into a rich entrepreneurial and corporate sector class, and a piece-worker class. At the corporate level the challenge is to ensure that the egalitarian spirit, which has been a pervasive, distinctive and unifying feature of Australian work culture, is not replaced with a Dickensian elitist/working-class divide within corporations. At issue here is the growing, and unsustainable, disparity between rewards for executives and the general workforce. Also at issue is the growing imbalance in the system of capitalism: in the past, an internal focus persisted—staff and unions had significant power. Now an almost totally external focus pervades: institutional shareholders are virtually the masters of the corporation. A more sustainable balance must be achieved.

World population pressures

The current expansion in world population stands as a potential barrier to the achievement of an ordered and prosperous global society. There are about six billion people in the world today. The most widely accepted population projections put forward three scenarios based on different assumptions about fertility rates. If we take the medium projection based on an assumed average of two children per woman, it is clear that we will have a significant problem over the next fifty years. World population would reach 8.9 billion by 2050,[5] with much of the growth occurring in less advanced economies.

However, the exponential population explosion which has taken place since the Industrial Revolution is slowing and may actually reverse in the more distant future.[6] An assumption of lower fertility replacement may be a more accurate representation of future trends. Already 44% of the world's population lives in countries—such as Europe, China and Japan—where the birth rates are stable or actually do not achieve replacement levels.[7] Some other countries are moving toward stabilisation at least—for instance, for most of last century Australia has had one of the highest rates of population growth in the world (births plus migration). But on current trends, Australia's population, currently 19 million, may also stabilise at about 23 million people in fifty years.[8]

A stabilised world population would eventually ease the enormous pressure of human demands on the biosphere. But in the next fifty years, the pressure will continue to increase, whatever the fertility rate, and so we must use resources more efficiently, maintaining and renewing rather than exploiting and downgrading them. We must also deal with the complex social and economic issues involved in having an ageing population, particularly in the more advanced economies.

The problem of how to resource the world's growing population is exacerbated by the vast difference in birthrates between the developed and undeveloped regions of the world. Most of the population growth will occur in the less developed economies like Africa, some parts of Asia and the Indian subcontinent. While population increases may provide global trade opportunities, they do so only where people have the economic resources to purchase goods and services. We need a global commitment to raise standards of living in these areas. However, we must not replicate the existing unsustainable production and consumption practices of the developed countries, rather we should try to ensure that more sustainable practices are instituted in all countries.

In Australia, as in other developed economies, the issue of how to treat illegal immigrants, usually from the poorer countries, is a very contentious political issue. It is clear, however, that in a world which is increasingly interdependent, countries like Australia and New Zealand cannot remain as islands of privilege without intensifying this problem. World population pressures will bring into sharp relief the economic, social and labour market policies of our governments and the human resource practices of enterprises as we try to achieve the global and local integration needed for an ordered and productive world society.

Global warming

The unique atmosphere that surrounds the earth is vital to all life on the planet. The mixture of gases which make up the atmosphere act like the glass panels of a greenhouse, retaining some of the sun's heat instead of letting it radiate out again, as on the moon. It is this greenhouse effect that determines the earth's climate. In the last 100 years, human activity has begun to have an extraordinary effect on the atmosphere.

Since the beginning of the Industrial Revolution, atmospheric concentrations of specific gases have increased significantly. Carbon dioxide (CO_2), for example, has increased by nearly 30%, methane by over 100%. (Currently concentrations of CO_2 rise by 0.5% per year.) These gases trap more heat and, as a result, the earth's climate is changing. It will change even more dramatically unless we modify the way we produce goods, heat houses, travel, cultivate crops and harvest trees.[9]

Why is global warming important? Global warming makes the weather more volatile, increasing the number of natural disasters such as tornadoes, floods and droughts. Convection patterns distribute the heat unevenly, melting icecaps and changing sea currents, raising sea levels and eroding coastlines, threatening low-lying islands, significantly influencing rainfall patterns and so disrupting agriculture. The impact on nations will vary considerably: average temperatures in the United States, for example, 'will probably rise 5 to 10% Fahrenheit—nearly twice the projected warming for the planet as a whole' and the 'snowpack will diminish 50% on average'.[10]

> *The greatest challenge of the new century is global warming.*
>
> PRESIDENT CLINTON, STATE OF THE UNION ADDRESS, 2000

That is the bad news. Fortunately there is also good news. One aspect of the good news is that, over time, collective action can stabilise and then reverse these trends, and the costs of doing this may be outweighed by the productive efficiencies achieved. Hawkin, Lovins and Lovins, in their book *Natural Capitalism*, outline numerous cases where the attempts to reduce emissions have resulted in stunning new energy efficiencies, previously unrealised. At Dow Chemical, for example, over about ten years to 1993, a suite of such projects were initiated and carried through which by 1993 were returning shareholders an extra US$110 million a year.[11]

Other companies are moving into establishing themselves as leaders in using renewable resources which will be the energy industries of the future; a local example is Pacific Power. The means for stabilising and restoring climate is available to us now and its adoption actually offers us economic as well as environmental benefits. We need the imagination to think beyond the formulae of the past to new solutions, and the will to put the solutions into practice.

And this is beginning to happen. The scientific evidence for global warming is now so convincing that an increasing number of governments and corporations are initiating actions which are already contributing to an eventual solution. This must not engender complacency because these are only the beginning steps in an enormous process of change that we must commit to. An example of a private sector initiative is the Pew Center on Global Climate

Change in Washington DC—a 'club' of global companies committed to supporting research and action in the area. Such initiatives, which are now many, signal a new level of environmental concern and a growing sense of responsibility. At the governmental level, the Kyoto Convention has already stimulated many national initiatives to reduce emissions, although at the time of writing the Protocol is still to be officially ratified by many countries, including the United States. What is envisaged in the agreements arising out of the Kyoto Convention amounts to a massive series of governmental, community and corporate change programs.

Ecological sustainability

The way of life we have created, particularly in the industrialised nations, is not sustainable in the long term unless we significantly change the impact we make on the planet as we go about our business. It is difficult to envisage the rate at which we are wasting resources which are vital to the continuing existence on the planet: we are living as if there is no tomorrow.

The statues on Easter Island stand as a lonely reminder that we must live within the limits of the resources available to us and live with an eye to the future. The original handful of people in the canoe that discovered and settled Easter Island found a fertile land, covered with forest. Eventually the population increased so much that they outran their resource base. In particular, the sculpting, moving and erection of more and more giant statues for the spirits of the ancestors took so much timber that the island was deforested. The population imploded in internal warfare that left only a remnant living in a debased ecosystem.

Since 1970, across the world, rainforest equivalent to half the area of Australia has been destroyed. Like the Easter Islanders, we too are deforesting our world with the consequence that vital topsoil that took thousands of years to create is being blown away, deserts are extending and species becoming extinct daily. Pollution is degrading water supplies and affecting the quality of the air we breathe; the sea is also being polluted on a massive scale and its marine resources are becoming seriously depleted.

> *The sustainability agenda is developing faster than any other part of the business agenda and...the relevant understanding and skills are likely to be the necessary conditions of success in the twenty-first century business world.*
>
> LIVIO DESIMORE, CHAIRMAN OF 3M

Private sector organisations must operate profitably and make returns to their shareholders. It is not sustainable any longer for corporations to plunder and pollute the planet or to exploit and degrade the workforce and society. Corporations have been a large part of the problem; they must now become part of the solution. This means developing positive policies that help enhance the planet's ability to maintain and renew a viable biosphere which maintains all living species. In addition they have a responsibility to enhance society's ability to maintain itself by solving its major problems and increasing the competency levels of the world's human inhabitants. We are moving into the age of resource renewal and enhancement—whether those resources be human or non-human. All the earth's human inhabitants deserve a decent standard of living and a sustainable healthy lifestyle. Corporations make themselves viable by establishing viable, profitable businesses that contribute to the wellbeing of all stakeholders, including present and future generations, and the planet that is our home.[12]

Thurow writes:[13]

Today's institutions need to be built to deal with global environmental problems. These institutions have to be linked with those promoting economic growth, since pollution and species preservation are inextricably linked with economic development. They are linked because markets misprice the cost of pollution and place no value on the elimination of species.

So, as we move into the twenty-first century, we face more change rather than less, and the pace of change will quicken for both governments and enterprises alike. In particular, we face the challenge of transforming organisations, traditional production and consumption patterns and our personal lifestyles to reflect the fact that we are an integral part of a global human community and an ecology vital to our welfare and survival. We must all become change agents now.

Leading and recreating our enterprises

Global issues such as those we have discussed make it imperative that we learn to live with change, and to make change a productive, energising, transforming force within our enterprises and nations. For those who lead and manage enterprises, it will be essential to adventure across numerous boundaries to explore new ways for our enterprises to create wealth and quality of life for all people. In making these challenging, often boundary-challenging journeys, maps are often non-existent, have to be drawn on the way, or are handed on only in sketchy form by former adventurers. This book has been written to provide partial maps and frameworks for the corporate journeys on which we have embarked. However, we offer these frameworks for guidance rather than as definitive prescriptions. We offer frameworks for thinking, not recipes.

In Chapter 1 we commenced by examining some of the major dilemmas in managing change. In exploring these dilemmas, what are the important messages? There are many, but we perceive the major themes to be as follows:

- *Renaissance in the midst of deconstruction* Conditions in the global business environment are as fluid as anything experienced since the Industrial Revolution. Nevertheless, we are optimistic that, if managed well, the competing pressures will lead to the creation of new forms of productive enterprise. The force of economic and technological change in advanced societies is meeting with the powerful social force of people seeking emancipation from institutional control in performing their work. The pressure to create internationally competitive organisations is being matched by technological capability to allow people to perform work within networks, alliances, partnerships and self-managed teams rather than in large rigid hierarchies. What is for some a period of painful deconstruction has the potential to become an enlightened period of organisational renaissance.

- *Living with the tension of change* Change is frequently non-linear, messy and full of contradictory messages and messengers. Successful change leaders manage the interpersonal and political tensions created because of seemingly irreconcilable polarities, becoming skilled in managing adaptive and rational strategy, cultural and structural change, constant improvement and radical transformation, empowering and commanding. They also successfully reconcile a strong social/human agenda with an equally strong economic/financial agenda. In effect they are able to manage the overall tension between the soft and hard approaches to change.

- *Situational and countercyclical change strategies* Our research indicates that successful enterprises use different change strategies to good effect, even at similar periods of the business cycle. No single strategy, structure or form of leadership is universally right. At times the use of countercyclical change strategies may give a corporation a competitive advantage if there is consistency and intellectual coherence within the strategy. In Appendix 8A we summarise the main features of the four different types of change strategy covered in this book, all of which have been used to good effect by Australasian corporations. Some strategies are 'hard', some are 'softer', some are a combination of the two. However, each of the strategies has an 'intellectual coherence', and it is important that a correct choice of overall strategy is made. These change types should be regarded as frameworks rather than as iron-clad sets of rules.

- *Permanent change is deep change* To be effective, change must go to the core of the organisation, to positively affect the behaviours and attitudes of its people. This calls for skilled management across the 'hard'/'soft' divide rather than a singular focus on either strategic or behavioural change. This presents one of the more complex dilemmas—how to challenge the system, developing new strategies, restructuring and re-engineering the corporation while at the same time communicating direction and gaining the commitment of staff. If the latter is neglected, a negative feedback loop is created, leading to cynicism about new strategic directions, and resistance to their implementation.

Intelligent learning, not fads. A plethora of change intervention tools and packages is available for the intending change leader—programs and processes such as the Balanced Scorecard, Quality Management, e-Change, strategic alliances, Process Re-engineering, Values-Based Leadership—which have worked well for many organisations. Will they work well for all organisations? Not necessarily. They work least well when chosen for their fad appeal, the imperative of doing it 'because others are doing it'. Intervention techniques often seem to work best when used by organisations well before their fad status arrives; some of the early adopting organisations which struggle with new process methodologies, with all their imperfections, seem to learn more than those which buy the refined package. The gain is often in the learning, not necessarily in the particular technique involved.

Change is the steady state

We are seeing the end of universalistic models for national economic development and of universalistic models of corporate development. Just like Columbus in the fifteenth century, the real breakthrough may be made by those who are bold enough to adopt the radically new directions that demand rethinking of widely held assumptions, ideologies and preferred means of change.

The phenomenon of 'new adventurers'—organisations and people bold enough to chart new territory, to transform current industries or create new industries—is the striking feature of the twenty-first century business environment. These organisations and individuals create or ride the waves of change rather than become engulfed by them. Change for all of us is the only steady state possible; the issue is how we learn and grow from it—nationally, corporately and individually.

'Consolidation', or the desire to 'let it all pass and return to the status quo', is not an option. The challenge is to lead and recreate our corporations as change-seeking, productive enterprises fully participating, but also contributing to social wellbeing, as well as economic wealth, in the twenty-first century.

References

1. For further discussion of these issues see H. Mackay, *Turning Points: Australians Choosing their Future*, Macmillan, Sydney, 1999.
2. P. Maidment, 'We have been here before', *Newsweek*, 1993, p. 65.
3. ibid.
4. T. Friedman, *The Lexus and the Olive Tree*, HarperCollins, London, 1999, p. 474.
5. Estimate from Population Division of the United Nations Secretariat, 1999, 'Long Range World Population Projections', ESA/PWP, p. 153.
6. L. Brown, M. Renner & B. Halweil, *The Environmental Trends Shaping Our Future*, Earthscan Publications, London, 1999, p. 98.
7. Population Division of the United Nations Secretariat, op. cit.
8. Australian Federal Department of Immigration, 'Population Issues: Impact of 2000–2001 Immigration Intake', 3 April 2000.
9. Environmental Protection Agency, 'Global Warming' at http://www.epa.gov/globalwarming/climate/; Pacific Institute for Studies in Development, Environment and Security, 'Global Climate Change: Selective List of Online Resources' at http://www.pacinst.org/ccresource.html; United States Department of Agriculture (USDA), USDA Fact Sheet 'Soil Carbon Sequestration: Frequently Asked Questions' at http://www.usda.gov/oce/gcpo/sequeste.htm; United Nations Environment Program, Information Unit for Conventions (IUC), 'Sea Levels, Oceans and Coastal Areas' at http://www.unep.ch/iuc/submenu/infokit/fact11.htm; United States Global Change Research Program Report, 'Climate Change Impacts on the United States' at http://www.usgcrp.gov.
10. United States Global Climate Change Research Program Report, 'Climate Change Impacts on the United States' at http://www.usgcrp.gov. Some of these effects are reversible only in the long term—for example, 'sea levels are expected to continue rising for hundreds of years after atmospheric temperatures stabilize'.
11. P. Hawkin, A. Lovins & L. Hunter Lovins, *Natural Capitalism: Creating the Next Industrial Revolution*, Little, Brown and Co, Boston, 1999, Chapter 12: 'Climate: Making sense and making money', pp. 233–59.
12. D. Dunphy & R. Griffiths, *Organisational Renewal in Australia*, Allen & Unwin, Sydney, 1998.
13. L. Thurow, *Head to Head: The Coming Economic Battle Among Japan, Europe and America*, Allen & Unwin, New York, 1992, pp. 219–20.

Appendix 8

Four approaches to change: An overview

Appendix 8A
Developmental Transitions

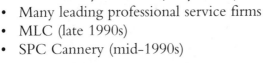

Case examples
- Macquarie Bank (continuing)
- State Library of NSW (early 1990s)
- Many leading professional service firms
- MLC (late 1990s)
- SPC Cannery (mid-1990s)

Conditions for use
Use when markets are growing and product/market innovation is desired. Organisational change strategies must create cross-organisational change synergy, and a 'market leader' culture. Strong emphasis on individual development, corporate culture management, developing a strong internal labour market and team skills.

Goal of change
- Voluntary commitment to a shared vision of continual improvement

Business strategy
- Dominantly product/market innovator (Prospector), *or*
- Successful low-cost producer of high-quality products (Defender)

Business planning
- Primarily 'bottom-up' planning, within corporate parameters—business units strongly influence corporate directions

Change strategy characteristics
- Constant relentless mid-range change (change as a way of life)
- Executive leadership which operates on a collegial, consultative basis
- Team leadership which is sometimes directive, to balance the consultative executive style
- An emphasis on changing dominant values and mindsets in order to change the organisation

Change leader type
- Coach

Leadership behaviour
- Highly interactive
- Responsive to lower level initiatives
- Vision is an emerging phenomenon
- Use of personal power and expertise
- Extensive use of role modelling

Change intervention tools typically used
- Vision/mission development (consultative)
- Culture enhancement programs
- Team building (self-managed work teams)
- Management and team leadership development programs
- Service quality programs
- Personal and professional development/skills formation
- TQM, Process Benchmarking programs
- Building corporate competencies
- Radical delegation/empowerment of staff
- Developing horizontal organisation structures

Communication strategies
- Widespread involvement in the communication process to develop trust
- Multidirectional initiatives
- Use of task teams/focus groups to process change issues
- Emphasis on face-to-face communication

Cultural renewal
- Normative–educative strategy
- Creating shared experiences around development of new organisational norms
- Appeal to shared values
- Use of intrinsic rewards, sense of achievement

Strengths of this approach
- Involvement, commitment, sense of ownership, sustained energy, individual initiatives

Vulnerabilities of this approach
- Potential loss of control and direction; vulnerability to diversion and dissolving of climate of trust; time-consuming nature of participative processes; competitors move more quickly

Appendix 8B
Task-focused Transitions

Case examples

- MLC (early 1990s)
- Lend Lease (ongoing—re project management business)
- Many public sector enterprises, after a process of Turnaround
- Rio Tinto, and many large product manufacturers
- Electricity industry

Conditions for use

Use when markets/products/services are undergoing change and 'niche' exploratory strategies are prevalent. Organisational change strategies must deliver the capacity for rapid structural, systems, skill and cultural changes. Strong emphasis on business unit autonomy, maximum devolution, outsourcing, workforce redesign.

Goal of change

- Compliance to an internally consistent progressive redefinition of task performance systems

Business strategy

- A focused strategy. Cost containment in some business areas, product/market innovation in others (Analyzer), *or*
- Successful low-cost producer of high-quality products (Defender)

Business planning

- Clear statement of corporate 'strategic intent'—implementation cascading down to business units
- Mixture of 'top-down' and 'bottom-up' business planning

Change strategy characteristics

- Constant improvement and relentless mid-range change
- Executive leadership which operates on a decisive/strongly directional basis
- Business unit leadership is mostly consultative, but within a strong framework of well organised systems
- Focus on improving structures and systems

Change leader type

- Captain

Leadership behaviour
- Directed interaction around key system changes
- Strategic initiatives come from the executive; technical initiatives are delegated
- Vision is planned and systematically orchestrated
- Use of positional power and technical/task expertise

Change intervention tools typically used
- Systems redesign
- Workforce planning/rightsizing
- Job redesign/business process redesign/Re-engineering
- Productivity measurement and improvement
- Strategic and Process Benchmarking
- Objective setting/management-by-objectives/performance contracts/appraisal
- Strong technical skills training
- Management and team leadership development
- TQM, continuous improvement

Communication strategies
- Aim is to gain behavioural alignment with the vision and key executive initiatives
- Use of line relationships for communication
- Primarily top-down communication with built-in feedback
- Use of technical expertise to advise teams
- Emphasis on formal communication (e.g. instructions, memos, email)

Cultural renewal
- Empirical/rational strategy
- Competence enhancement through retraining
- Focus on changing systems as a means of encouraging behaviour modification
- Constant adjustment of norms to match changing strategies
- Use of intrinsic and extrinsic rewards related to the task

Strengths of this approach
- Clear focus on task related issues, clarity of communication, clear role definition; steady, relentless approach to change

Vulnerabilities of this approach
- Limitations of rational means of persuasion in emotive circumstances; reduced commitment from lack of participation and involvement; possibility of change tapering off to fine tuning

Appendix 8C
Charismatic Transformations

Case examples
- State Library of NSW (late 1980s)
- Qantas (mid-1990s)
- Optus (early 1990s)
- Telstra (mid-1990s)
- Start-up organisations (ongoing)

Conditions for use
Use when the business environment changes dramatically, or when a radical repositioning of the organisation is necessary for meeting future business challenges. Organisational change strategies must help to create a new vision and organisational mindset, where changes to a new business culture are welcomed by the majority of participants.

Goal of change
- Voluntary commitment to a radical new vision requiring significant reinterpretation or revision of core values

Business strategy
- Product/market innovator (Prospector)

Business planning
- Entrepreneurial, not systematised
- Strong emphasis on intuitive thinking and calculated risk taking

Change strategy characteristics
- Rapid, radical redefinition of the business, or creation of the new business domain
- Reshaping of corporate strategies and competitive executive leadership which provides an inspiring vision, and generates the respect and support of staff

Change leader type
- Charismatic

Leadership behaviour
- Symbolically interactive
- Major strategic initiatives from top teams

- Vision is entrepreneurial and opportunistic
- Use of personal charisma
- Development of radical new role models

Change intervention tools typically used
- New vision/mission
- Radical organic restructuring, voluntary redundancies
- New executive recruits, often from outside
- Top team-building programs
- Cross-functional task teams
- Service excellence programs
- Symbolic communication (change of corporate name, logo and wardrobe; excellence awards)

Communication strategies
- Aim is to gain emotional commitment to the vision, re-examination and revision of core values and beliefs
- Use of multimedia communication channels, but personalised
- Top-down communication with built-in feedback and symbolic two-way communication
- Use of strategic task forces
- Personalised corporate communication

Cultural renewal
- Paradigm-shifting strategy
- Creating vicarious participation and identification with new role models
- Radical challenge to existing values
- Infusion of a new core business culture
- Use of intrinsic rewards and identification with charismatic leader

Strengths of this approach
- Strong motivation to change rapidly; high energy for change effort; maintained momentum

Vulnerabilities of this approach
- Rarety of situation where all major stakeholders support radical change; scarcity of suitable leaders with the personal characteristics needed; problem of maintaining commitment when the charismatic leader leaves

Appendix 8D
Turnarounds

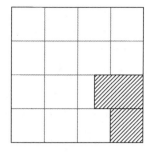

Case examples
- Patrick Stevedores (latter 1990s)
- CSR (latter 1990s)
- Victorian public sector (most of the 1990s)
- BHP (late 1980s and again in late 1990s)
- Fairfax (late 1990s)

Conditions for use
Use when the business environment changes dramatically and when the organisation is not aligned with its environment. Organisational change strategies must break redundant and ineffective frameworks of thinking, refocus the organisation on fundamentally new strategies and seek a new fit for the organisation in a changing business environment.

Goal of change
- Compliance to radically redefined behavioural goals, norms and performance standards

Business strategy
- Dynamic refocus on the core business and selected business areas, adoption of a focused, niche strategy (Analyzer) having previously been either low performers (Reactors) or medium performers and losing 'alignment' with the business environment

Business planning
- Top team holds frequent retreats to consider strategy
- Major focus on creating a new corporate plan and negotiating this with external stakeholders
- Business unit planning strongly influenced by the corporate plan

Change strategy characteristics
- Rapid, radical redefinition of the core business
- Divestment of non-core business areas
- Successive corporate and workplace restructures, downsizing and retrenchments
- Restructuring/abolishing traditional systems
- Chief executive welds together a strong top team
- Decision making is recentralised

Change leader type
- Commander

Leadership behaviour
- Unilateral directive action
- Strategic and structural initiatives
- Radical new vision imposed or negotiated
- Use of positional power and sanctions
- Reference to and infusion of new role models

Change intervention tools typically used
- Strategy and market segmentation analysis
- Merger/acquisition/divestment of non-core businesses
- Restructuring/downsizing/rightsizing/forced retrenchments
- Reconstruction and development of the top team
- Cultural and industrial confrontation strategies
- Radical business process redesign
- Human resource strategy redesign

Communication strategies
- Aim is to communicate a sense of organisational crisis, rationale for change and cost of non-compliance
- Communication put on a 'wartime' footing: frequent, total and forceful
- Top-down communication
- Use of selected change leaders as key communicators
- Emphasis on formal, authoritative communication

Cultural renewal
- Power-coercive strategy
- Emphasis on remoulding behaviour as approach to value changes
- Radical challenge to existing values
- Recasting and reforming of core culture
- Use of extrinsic rewards and coercive sanctions

Strengths of this approach
- Clear direction and leadership; significant redistribution of resources; rapidity of change

Vulnerabilities of this approach
- Vulnerability to leader's vision (may not be viable); can induce significant opposition from key interest groups; high risk if used as a preferred rather than a strategic approach to change; negative performance results if carried on for too long

Index